"Cockerill . . . presents the fruit of his work in a book that is accessible to every student of the Bible. What we find here are the reflections of a scholar who has marinated in Hebrews for years. The structure of the letter, the meaning of the text, its theological significance, and the pastoral application are unpacked clearly and profoundly. Pastors, students, and all who want to understand Hebrews will want to read this book."

—Thomas R. Schreiner, The Southern Baptist Theological Seminary

"Cockerill brings to fresh life the often-neglected book of Hebrews. Cockerill guides the reader through a magnificent seven-week journey through the glorious heights and peaks of this cherished landscape of biblical revelation. In the process, he reveals to us anew how Christ fulfills all of the great themes of the Old Testament, such as law, sacrifice, and priesthood. I encourage Christians to engage in this amazing journey and recapture anew the glorious identity of Jesus Christ for all time."

—Timothy C. Tennent, Asbury Theological Seminary

"*Yesterday, Today, and Forever* is such a treasure! Cockerill's many years of in-depth study and eager willingness to be mentored by the 'pastor' of Hebrews richly infuses this present volume. . . . Cockerill's own pastoral heart makes this seven-week study winsome, compelling, and accessible. This book opens the door to one of the most powerful, beautiful, and persuasive sermons ever written! Those who enter this door will be richly blessed."

—Dana M. Harris, Trinity Evangelical Divinity School

"The grandeur and beauty of the book of Hebrews are only matched by its avoidance and near ignorance in the church. . . . In *Yesterday, Today, and Forever*, Cockerill puts his lifetime of studying and living Hebrews on the table in front of us and in a plate served just to us. This beautiful, timely book is what the church needs!"

—Scot McKnight, Northern Seminary

"For some, the book of Hebrews is 'too difficult'. But unless they engage with it, they are likely to remain spiritual infants. In this superb seven-week guide, a leading Hebrews scholar takes us step by step through the book. Through its pastoral teaching, we can be shaped and formed into adult Christians. Highly recommended!"

—Thomas A. Noble, Nazarene Theological Seminary

"In this reading guide, Cockerill has masterfully and passionately show-cased the crown jewels discovered during his lifetime of exploration in the book of Hebrews. These rich meditations . . . provide a clear and concise guide for a life-changing seven-week journey. Listen afresh to the inspired sermon/letter of 'the pastor.' This is a journey not to be missed, and never to be forgotten!"

—Richard M. Davidson, Andrews University

"In a day when Hebrews is often overlooked, *Yesterday, Today, and Forever* is very much needed. Not only is it grounded in Gareth Cockerill's lifetime of scholarship, it's also an accessible guide for the faith and practice of the broader church. Readers will find their knowledge and experience of God in Christ strengthened and deepened."

—Matt O'Reilly, Wesley Biblical Seminary

"*Yesterday, Today and Forever* takes Dr. Cockerill's mind as a Hebrews scholar and combines it beautifully with his pastor's heart to give a study that is as spiritually formative as it is intellectually. . . . Whether used in personal devotions, textbook for a class, or study in the local church, the Holy Spirit will use it to form believers into greater likeness to God through our 'all-sufficient High Priest who remains forever.'"

—Christopher T. Bounds, Indiana Wesleyan University

Yesterday, Today, and Forever

Yesterday, Today, and Forever

Listening to Hebrews in the Twenty-First Century

Gareth Lee Cockerill

FOREWORD BY
Craig G. Bartholomew

CASCADE *Books* · Eugene, Oregon

YESTERDAY, TODAY, AND FOREVER
Listening to Hebrews in the Twenty-First Century

Cascade Books
An Imprint of Wipf and Stock Publishers
199 W. 8th Ave., Suite 3
Eugene, OR 97401

www.wipfandstock.com

PAPERBACK ISBN: 978-1-7252-9272-7
HARDCOVER ISBN: 978-1-7252-9273-4
EBOOK ISBN: 978-1-7252-9274-1

Cataloguing-in-Publication data:

Names: Cockerill, Gareth Lee, author. | Bartholomew, Craig G., foreword.

Title: Yesterday, today, and forever : listening to Hebrews in the twenty-first century / by Gareth Lee Cockerill ; foreword by Craig G. Bartholomew.

Description: Eugene, OR: Cascade Books, 2022

Identifiers: ISBN 978-1-7252-9272-7 (paperback) | ISBN 978-1-7252-9273-4 (hardcover) | ISBN 978-1-7252-9274-1 (ebook)

Subjects: LCSH: Bible. Hebrews—Criticism, interpretation, etc. | Bible. Hebrews—Commentaries.

Classification: BS2775.2 C635 2022 (print) | BS2775.2 (ebook)

05/20/22

To my paternal grandparents, Mr. Welby H. Cockerill and Mrs. Nellie M. Cockerill; my maternal grandparents, the Rev. Charles R. Mateer and Mrs. Daisy E. Mateer; and, especially, to my father and mother, the Rev. W. Lee Cockerill and Mrs. D. Virginia Cockerill. I hope God will use this book to awaken in others the love for Scripture that I received from them.

Contents

Foreword by Craig G. Bartholomew | xi

Preface | xv

Introduction | xix

Abbreviations | xxv

WEEK ONE–*God Has Spoken in One Who Is Son.* Heb 1:1—2:18 | 1

    DAY ONE: God Has Now Spoken Through His Son.
(Heb 1:1–4) 1

    DAY TWO: The Incomparable Majesty of the One through
Whom God has Spoken—Son, Firstborn, and God;
Worshipped by the Angels. (Heb 1:5–9) 4

    DAY THREE: The Incomparable Majesty of the One Through
Whom God has Spoken—Lord, Creator, Judge; Seated
at God's Right Hand. (Heb 1:10–14) 8

    DAY FOUR: Give Undivided Attention to What God is Saying
in His Son! (Heb 2:1–4) 10

    DAY FIVE: Jesus, the Incarnate Son—"made a little lower than
the angels." (Heb 2:5–9) 13

    DAY SIX: "The Pioneer of Our Salvation"—"made perfect
through suffering." (Heb 2:10–13) 16

    DAY SEVEN: "A Merciful and Faithful High Priest"—
"made like his brothers and sisters in every way."
(Heb 2:14–18) 19

WEEK TWO–*A Disobedient Generation and a New High Priest.*
Heb 3:1—5:10 | 22

DAY ONE: Jesus, Moses, and the House of God.
(Heb 3:1–6)   23

DAY TWO: A Son, a Steward, and the House of God.
(Heb 3:1–6)   25

DAY THREE: Shun the Company of the Disobedient
Wilderness Generation. (Heb 3:7–19)   28

DAY FOUR: Pursue, by faith, the Promised "Rest."
(Heb 4:1–11)   32

DAY FIVE: Exposed before the Living Word of God.
(Heb 4:12–13)   34

DAY SIX: Our "Great High Priest." (Heb 4:14–16)   36

DAY SEVEN: Priesthood Old and New. (Heb 5:1–10)   39

WEEK THREE–*Embrace the One Who is Priest "by the Power of
An Indestructible Life."* Heb 5:11—7:18 | 44

DAY ONE: Awaken from Your Inexcusable Immaturity.
(Heb 5:11–6:3)   45

DAY TWO: Beware the Peril of Apostasy. (Heb 6:4–8)   48

DAY THREE: Join the Faithful People of God.
(Heb 6:9–12)   51

DAY FOUR: Rely Upon the Divine Promise and Oath.
(Heb 6:13–20)   54

DAY FIVE: The Melchizedek Who Met Abraham.
(Heb 7:1–3)   57

DAY SIX: This Melchizedek is Far Superior to Levi.
(Heb 7:4–10)   59

DAY SEVEN: A Priesthood Founded on an "Indestructible Life"
Has Replaced the Priesthood Dependent upon "the Law
of Fleshly Ordinance." (Heb 7:11–19)   62

WEEK FOUR–*A High Priest Perfected Forever.* Heb 7:20—9:22 | 66

    DAY ONE: A Guarantor and an Eternal Priest.
      (Heb 7:20–25)   67

    DAY TWO: A Son Perfected Forever. (Heb 7:26–28)   70

    DAY THREE: A Minister of the Heavenly Sanctuary.
      (Heb 8:1–6)   73

    Day Four: God's Promise of a New Covenant.
      (Heb 8:7–13)   75

    DAY FIVE: An Earthly Sanctuary. (Heb 9:1–10)   79

    DAY SIX: An Effective Sacrifice. (Heb 9:11–15)   81

    DAY SEVEN: A Broken Covenant. (Heb 9:16–22)   85

WEEK FIVE–*Behold, I Have Come . . . to Do, O God, Your Will.*
    Heb 9:23—10:31 | 89

    DAY ONE: A Sanctuary that is "Heaven Itself."
      (Heb 9:23–24)   90

    DAY TWO: A "Once-for-All" Sacrifice. (Heb 9:25—10:4)   92

    DAY THREE: An Obedient Sacrifice. (Heb 10:5–10)   95

    DAY FOUR: A Fully Effective Sacrifice. (Heb 10:11–14)   98

    DAY FIVE: A Covenant that Brings Release.
      (Heb 10:15–18)   100

    DAY SIX: A Great Priest Brings Great Blessings.
      (Heb 10:19–25)   103

    DAY SEVEN: A Great Priest Requires Great Accountability.
      (Heb 10:26–31)   107

WEEK SIX–*A Cloud of Witnesses: a History of the Faithful People of God.*
    Heb 10:32—12:3 | 111

    DAY ONE: "My Righteous One Shall Live by Faith."
      (Heb 10:32–39)   113

    DAY TWO: From Creation to Noah: Faith Defined.
      (Heb 11:1–7)   116

DAY THREE: In the Time of Abraham and Sarah: Faith in
an Alien World. (Heb 11:8–16)   119

DAY FOUR: From Abraham to Joseph: Faith in a God
Who Raises the Dead. (Heb 11:17–22)   123

DAY FIVE: From Moses to Rahab: Faith under Stress.
(Heb 11:23–31)   126

DAY SIX: From Gideon and Barak through the Prophets:
Faith in a "Better Resurrection." (Heb 11:32–40)   130

DAY SEVEN: Jesus: "the Pioneer and Perfecter of the Faith."
(Heb 12:1–3)   134

WEEK SEVEN–*You Have Come to Mount Zion.* Heb 12:4—13:25 | 138

DAY ONE: Legitimate Children Disciplined by Suffering.
(Heb 12:4–13)   139

DAY TWO: Do Not Forfeit Your Birthright!
(Heb 12:14–17)   143

DAY THREE: The Tragic Destiny of the Disobedient and the
Privileges of God's "Firstborn." (Heb 12:18–24)   146

Day Four: "The One Who is Speaking." (Heb 12:25–29)   150

DAY FIVE: A Common Life of "Gratitude and Godly Fear."
(Heb 13:1–6)   153

DAY SIX: The Life of "Gratitude and Godly Fear" in
an Unbelieving World. (Heb 13:7–17)   156

DAY SEVEN: A Sermon Sent by Mail. (Heb 13:18–25)   160

*Appendix A: The Beauty of Hebrews: Art in Service to Truth
and Spiritual Wellbeing* | 165

Appendix B: A Sentence Outline of Hebrews | 175

*Appendix C: Select Books on Hebrews for the College Student
and Serious Lay Reader* | 177

Bibliography | 179

Foreword

O ne of the privileges of my academic life was meeting Brevard Childs. He attended our Scripture and Hermeneutics Seminar in Cambridge in the early 2000s and I remained in sporadic contact with him after that. At our Seminar one evening he told us the story of his journey as a Christian scholar. It was fascinating and I regret that we did not record it. What I loved about Brevard was his humility and his deep concern for reading the Bible for the church. He would ask questions like, "Where can the best Reformed preaching be found today?" In my experience it is unusual to have major biblical scholars raise such topics.

I am told that a student once asked Brevard, "How can I become a better exegete?" His answer: "Become a deeper person!" This is a profound answer and thoroughly counter-cultural if we think of modern academic biblical studies. Mainstream academic biblical studies and, in my view, much serious Evangelical work too, follows modernity in rigidly separating the private from the public. In the West modernity dealt with the vexed issue of religion by privatising it and thus keeping it away from the great public areas of life, including academic biblical studies. Thus we are in a situation where scholarship, including biblical studies, tends to be kept apart from one's personal and religious life.

From a biblical perspective this dualism does not and cannot hold. In the Bible knowing the truth and doing the truth are inseparable. Orthodoxy and orthopraxy go hand in hand. If, as Christians confess, the Bible is God's word written, then it follows that the more we become like God, the more we are fashioned in his image, the more we will listen to and read Scripture truthfully.

In this work Gareth not only refers to the author as "the pastor" but Gareth's own pastoral heart illuminates his work as he sets out for us in a wonderfully accessible way the developing argument of Hebrews. Gareth, we might say, has taken Brevard's advice to heart. This book belies the modern

view that the less committed a reading of the Bible the more accurate it will
be. It is precisely Gareth's commitment to the Bible as God's Word that has led
him to work away on Hebrews for decades including replacing F. F. Bruce's
commentary on Hebrews in the prestigious New International Commentary
on the New Testament Series.[1] For an outstanding scholar like Gareth there is
no dichotomy at all between the most rigorous scholarship and opening the
Bible for God's people. Indeed, the two are integrally related.

If we are to overcome the unhealthy ditch between academic biblical
studies and the church, then we need books like this. Gareth has done the
academic heavy lifting over the years and here he makes available all that hard
work in a wonderfully accessible fashion. Pastors, seminarians, laity, students
and scholars will find this volume of great use. In this book Gareth moves
from the hard academic work to accessibility; we, the readers, are thus put
in the privileged position of being able to make the journey in reverse, with
Gareth's commentary readily at hand when we want more detail.

Finally, a word about why Hebrews is so very important. In the
Gospels, Jesus is rendered to us truly. Acts is the indispensable linchpin
between the Gospels and the missional letters of the New Testament. The
letters are rich in their unpacking of the Christ event for congregations
and individuals. Among the letters Romans has understandably received
major attention, especially in Protestant circles, as Paul unpacks "the gospel of God" (Rom 1:1) in profound detail.

Hebrews has often played second or third fiddle to Romans. However,
in my view it stands alongside Romans as a further, deep unpacking of all
that God has done for us in Christ. Such is the fecundity of the Christ event
that it can be explored and unpacked from multiple angles. Any unpacking
will also be contextual as it seeks to open the treasure of the good news of
Jesus for particular contexts. In Romans Paul uses legal metaphors in particular to explain the gospel of God to the Roman Christians. In Hebrews
"the pastor" uses priestly metaphor in particular to do the same. We need
both, not least as a reminder that today we too will have to find the right
metaphors to unpack the Christ event for our twenty-first-century congregations, after we have listened carefully to Romans *and* Hebrews.

1. Eerdmans, 1988.

Gareth's book is a marvellous resource as we listen to the, at times, complex letter of Hebrews. For pastors I envision it sitting amongst several commentaries on Hebrews, and being the first port of call when the pastor—or student, seminarian, or scholar—is working away on this marvellous book, full as it is of Jesus.

Rev. Dr. Craig G. Bartholomew

Director, Kirby Laing Centre for Public Theology in Cambridge
"Ordinary" Time, August 2021

Preface

In 1973 I asked Professor Mathias Rissi to suggest a topic for my ThM thesis. He suggested that I investigate the relationship between Hebrews chapter seven and 11QMelchizedek, a Dead Sea Scroll that had then only recently been published. Pursuing this topic began a life-long love of the letter to the Hebrews. I discovered the theological depth and pastoral sensitivity of its author and began to see the consistency of his Old Testament interpretation. I came to realize that Hebrews had been carefully arranged to encourage the perseverance of the people of God. It began to shape and deepen my own understanding of the Christian faith. The more I studied, the more I realized that Hebrews had a vital message for the people of God in the twenty-first century.

Thus, I am writing *Yesterday, Today, and Forever* to share the treasure that I have received from Hebrews with God's contemporary people. I hope that you who read what I have written gain a holistic understanding of this rich biblical book that will shape and enrich your lives as members of the Christian community. This kind of understanding comes only from familiarity developed over time. That is why I have divided Hebrews into seven weeks of daily readings (49 days). Each week begins with an introduction that helps maintain the big picture. If you take the time to patiently follow this schedule of daily reading, you will be rewarded with an understanding of Hebrews unavailable to those who want a quick fix. You will also be able to use this book as a reference with greater profit.

Such depth of understanding requires seeing Hebrews as a carefully crafted whole. The writer of Hebrews, whom, as you will see, I call "the pastor," was a literary artist skilled in the ancient art of persuasive speech. He has carefully arranged his material so that it has maximum impact on his hearers. I have surveyed this arrangement in the introduction, and then provided a more detailed analysis in the appendix entitled "The

Beauty of Hebrews: Art in Service to Truth and Spiritual Well-being." I
have also, when appropriate, explained each passage in light of the role it
plays in this overall structure. This approach brings clarity to each passage
and enables the reader to finish this reading guide with an overall vision
of Hebrews and its message.

This analysis of the arrangement of Hebrews is also the foundation of
my NICNT commentary (*Epistle to the Hebrews*, Eerdmans, 2012). In order
to evaluate its effectiveness on the basis of that volume, however, one would
need to read all 638 pages of commentary. Now one can judge by reading
the 163 pages of daily readings in this present volume. Thus, I also offer this
book to my fellow scholars as evidence for the structural arrangement of
Hebrews advocated in my commentary. Does this arrangement bring clarity
to the text of Hebrews? "The proof of the pudding is in the eating."

I have tried to clarify the meaning and significance of each passage
without the distraction of footnotes except for direct quotations or necessary explanations. Anyone who wants to know more about why I interpret
Hebrews as I do should consult the commentary mentioned above. There
you will find the sources I have used and appropriate consideration of alternate views. Time, however, does not stand still. There are a few insights
in this present volume that have come to me since the publication of the
NICNT commentary!

Who, then, should use this reading guide to Hebrews? As noted
above, this book is written for the contemporary people of God. It is thorough enough for use in undergraduate courses on Hebrews. It is accessible
enough for personal or group use in churches or parachurch organiza-
tions. Group leaders or professors will find an additional resource in my
commentary mentioned above. In addition, this reading guide shows
scholars how the structural analysis advocated in my commentary illuminates the text of Hebrews. Hebrews may have been written "yesterday,"
but it is relevant "today," because it tells the story of our all-sufficient High
Priest who "remains forever."

I am always grateful to my dear wife Rosa Cockerill, to our daughters Allene Vinzant, Ginny Cockerill (who formatted the tables in Appendix A!), and Kate O'Donnell, our sons-in-law Carey Vinzant and David
O'Donnell, and our grandchildren Patrick Vinzant, Ada O'Donnell, Benja-
min O'Donnell, and Samuel O'Donnell, for their unfailing love and support.
My best friend, David Lee Steveline, has been a great encouragement. I owe
a debt of gratitude to Professor Rissi, whom I mentioned above, and to the
many biblical interpreters who have helped me understand Hebrews. My
heartfelt thanks to the Rev. Dr. Craig G. Bartholomew for writing the Foreword. Finally, I want to express special appreciation to Dr. Carey Vinzant

for his thorough and helpful editing of this volume. His literary skill has enhanced the effectiveness of this reading guide.

I would like to dedicate this book, however, to my paternal grandparents, Mr. Welby H. Cockerill and Mrs. Nellie M. Cockerill; my maternal grandparents, the Rev. Charles R. Mateer and Mrs. Daisy E. Mateer; and, especially, to my father and mother, the Rev. W. Lee Cockerill and Mrs. D. Virginia Cockerill. I hope God will use this book to awaken in others the love for Scripture that I received from them.

Introduction

Hebrews Forever

I n her engaging book *A Distant Mirror,* author Barbara W. Tuchman invites us to view the reflection of our own times in the tumult of *The Calamitous 14th Century.*[2] She helps us to see the idealism, brutality, social unrest, and sense of foreboding and decline characteristic of our own age in the struggles of that far-off epoch that brought the Middle Ages to an end. In like manner, when we read the ancient letter to the Hebrews, we can, if we know how to look, see our own twenty-first century struggles as the post-Christendom people of God. Our temptation to spiritual indifference and sense of marginalization are not unlike the strains and difficulties faced by the little community of believers to whom this letter was addressed. The way in which the author of Hebrews speaks to their situation with compassion, pastoral insight, theological acumen, and profound biblical understanding has much to offer the people of God today. His message is about Jesus Christ, and is therefore relevant "yesterday, and today, and forever" (13:8 KJV).

Hebrews Yesterday

In recent years Craig Bartholomew has expressed the sentiment of many by claiming that Hebrews is as important as Paul's letter to the Romans.[3] The value of this book is demonstrated by the way in which Christians from earliest times persisted in reading it as Scripture, although they questioned its authorship. Near the end of the first century, 1 Clement, a letter from the church at Rome to the Christians in Corinth, made extensive use of Hebrews. Christians in the Greek-speaking eastern half of the Roman Empire

2. Tuckman, *Distant Mirror.*

3. Bartholomew, *Introducing Biblical Hermeneutics,* 487–88.

recognized Hebrews as Scripture from the earliest days, often including it among the Pauline letters. They suggested that Hebrews might have been originally penned in Hebrew or written by someone like Luke at Paul's direction in order to account for the evident differences from the other Pauline letters. In the third century, Origen, the greatest biblical scholar of antiquity, included Hebrews among the New Testament writings despite his admission that "only God knows" who actually wrote it. One early manuscript attests the assessment of Craig Bartholomew, mentioned above, by locating Hebrews right after Paul's letter to the Romans. We would be immeasurably poorer if this book were not in our Bibles.

Hebrews Today

Unlike believers throughout the ages, some modern Christians fail to take advantage of these riches. They may be discouraged by what some consider the difficulties in this book. It is the only New Testament book that talks about Melchizedek, that strange character who encountered Abraham in Gen 14. It compares Christ and his death to the Levitical priestly/sacrificial system so foreign to modern sensibilities. Its seeming assertion that any who fall away from Christ cannot be restored sounds harsh and out of harmony with the general teaching of the New Testament. Thus, some content themselves with quoting a few choice passages, such as "not forsaking the assembling of ourselves together" (Heb 10:25 KJV), "Jesus Christ the same yesterday, and today, and forever" (Heb 18:8 KJV), and "Now the God of peace, that brought again from the dead our Lord Jesus, that great shepherd of the sheep . . ." (Heb 13:20–21 KJV). Then they skip from the Pauline letters to that useful and practical book, James. It is, however, the very things that sound strange—Melchizedek, priesthood, sacrifice—that contain Hebrews' special treasures. I am writing to help you overcome any perceived difficulties so that you can profit from the legacy left us in this profound book.

Hebrews is, indeed, a sermon sent as a letter to a congregation in crisis by one who has a deep pastoral concern for the people of God. Let me get you started by describing the situation of this congregation, summarizing the content of the sermon, and describing the character of the pastor who wrote it. This information will enable you to understand the relevance of Hebrews for our time and know what to look for as you begin to read. It will give you an appreciation for the pastor/author whom you will meet in its pages.

A Congregation under Stress

From what the author of Hebrews says, we know that—like the church to-day—his congregation was suffering from marginalization, increasing persecution from without, and lethargy within. Their commitment to Christ as the only means of salvation isolated them from both the larger Jewish community and the surrounding Roman world. That pluralistic Roman world was quite happy for them to worship any number of gods, but was intolerant of exclusive loyalty to one God alone. Such loyalty was viewed as subversive and seditious because it separated its practitioners from many civic, social, and business functions that involved acknowledgment of other gods. The Romans only grudgingly tolerated the Jews' exclusive loyalty to the God of Israel. Once followers of Jesus emerged as a distinct group, they were excluded by everyone.

Those who first received Hebrews may have begun to wonder if God had truly revealed himself in his Son. To the Greeks and Romans the idea of God revealing himself in history was absurd. Jews who did not follow Christ accepted only what is today our Old Testament. Had God actually spoken in Christ? Had he spoken at all? It appears that the author's congregation was suffering from fatigue and laxity. They had been believers for some time. The way of Christ had become difficult. Was Christ *really* the only way of salvation? Was he *really* God's ultimate self-revelation? They were growing tired of the struggle. Wouldn't their lives be easier if they abandoned this loyalty to Christ and either blended into the Jewish community or conformed to the tolerant lifestyle of the society around them? In our secularized culture that denies God's speaking this scenario feels disturbingly familiar. It presages our "pluralistic" world that tolerates no absolutes. It describes our contemporary religious climate that approves of belief in "God" but is militantly hostile to the exclusive claims of Christ.

A Sermon Addressed to their Situation

Let me summarize the answer given by Hebrews. The writer of this sermon addresses his hearers' situation by reminding them of who they are: "But we do not belong to those who shrink back and are destroyed, but to those who have faith and are saved" (Heb 10:39, TNIV). "We" do not belong to that disobedient, faithless wilderness generation described in Heb 3:1—4:13. That generation refused to trust God's promise of future blessing and to rely on his present power to bring them into that future. No, "we" belong to the faithful people of God throughout history, whose story is at the heart of Heb 10:26—12:3. This grand company lived as if

God's promise of ultimate "rest" in the "heavenly City" was certain and relied on his power to sustain them in obedience until arrival at that destination. "We" who suffer as an isolated and persecuted minority are in reality members of this grand company—if we persevere.

In Heb 1:1—2:18 the writer tells us why "we" who believe in Christ are the heirs of God's faithful people of old. The God who spoke in the Old Testament (referred to as "the prophets" in Heb 1:1) has now spoken in Christ, the Son. Through his incarnation, obedient suffering, and exaltation the eternal Son of God has become the "Source of eternal salvation" (Heb 5:9) and thus the ultimate revelation of God. Thus, we who faithfully follow Christ walk in the steps of those who obeyed before us. Those who "neglect such a great salvation" (Heb 2:1–4) reject the fulfillment of God's self-revelation in his Son. They will suffer ultimate loss with the faithless wilderness generation of Heb 3:1—4:13.

In Heb 4:14—10:25, the heart of this sermon, the writer expands the foundation he has laid in Heb 1:1—2:18. Through his incarnation, obedience, suffering, and exaltation the eternal Son has fulfilled everything anticipated by the sacrificial system so central to the Old Testament. He has offered the one and only sacrifice sufficient for cleansing from sin. He has become the ultimate High Priest who provides access into God's presence. He guarantees the New Covenant of obedient fellowship with God. He is "the Pioneer and Perfecter of the faith" who brings the faithful to their eternal destination (Heb 12:2). He guarantees God's promise of ultimate "rest" and he is the source of God's power for daily perseverance. "We" who draw near to God through him avoid the wilderness generation who "shrink back and are destroyed" (Heb 3:7—4:11) by joining the victorious company who "have faith and are saved" (Hebrews 10:25–12:17). The secret of our success is to keep our eyes focused on this Savior seated at God's right hand.

The author brings his message to a climax in Heb 12:18–29 by reminding his hearers that the God who "spoke" through the Son's incarnation and exaltation (Heb 1:1—2:18) will bring all to its eternal consummation by "speaking" again at the Son's return. At that time "we" certainly will not want to be among "those who shrink back and are destroyed." In Heb 13:1–25 the author makes application, addresses several concerns, and gives greetings, reiterating the key themes of his sermon as he does so: There is a sure word from God. The danger of eternal loss awakens us from our lethargy. The promised reward is worth all hardship. Our Savior and High Priest is more than sufficient to meet our need.

This summary of Hebrews' content suggests the careful way in which the writer has arranged his material in order to encourage the perseverance of his hearers. We might outline this arrangement as follows: God has spoken in his Son, now seated at his right hand, by providing "such a great salvation" (Heb 1:1—2:18). Therefore, we must avoid the fate of the unbelieving wilderness generation (Heb 3:1—4:13), by embracing the full sufficiency of the eternal, incarnate, now exalted Son our High Priest at God's right hand (Heb 4:1—10:25), so that we can join the great company of the faithful who persevere (Heb 10:28—12:17), and thus be among those who participate in the "unshakable kingdom" when God speaks once again through his Son at the Judgment (12:18–29). I have provided a fuller presentation of this careful arrangement in Appendix A: "The Beauty of Hebrews: Art in Service to Truth and Spiritual Well-being."[4] The commentary throughout this book highlights, where appropriate, the contribution of each passage to this overall arrangement. If you give careful attention, you will have a holistic picture of the beautiful tapestry that our author has woven for us when you finish this reading guide.

A Pastor Concerned for the People of God

I, like Origen long before me, do not know the author's name. But I feel like I know him! I have studied his legacy in depth for more than thirty-five years. I have listened carefully to what he has to say. I have laid aside, as best I could, my preconceptions, that I might understand and obey the truth of God thus revealed. The author of Hebrews writes with a burdened pastor's heart. He has a deep concern that his hearers appropriate the full sufficiency of Christ for perseverance in faithful, obedient living until they reach the end of their pilgrimage. That is why I refer to this nameless writer as "the pastor," Hebrews as his "sermon," and the hearers as his "congregation." I feel like I am introducing you to my friend, rather than explaining a book.

This pastor is a deeply insightful biblical scholar who has thought long about how Christ fulfills the Old Testament. He has gained profound insight into the unity and wholeness of God's plan of salvation fulfilled in Christ. He is a theologian who has a clear grasp of Christian truth. Finally, he is a preacher who has skillfully employed the resources of ancient persuasive speech (rhetoric) as an aid in presenting the truth. He writes this way urging us to appropriate the complete sufficiency of Christ and find in him all that we need to persevere. It is well worth listening to this pastor, so passionate about Christ, so compassionate toward his hearers, so insightful in the things of God. As you read this book I ask you to let him be your pastor so that you might derive maximum benefit from his

---

4. If you would like a more extensive analysis of the way Hebrews is arranged, see "The Sermon's Rhetorically Effective Structure" in Cockerill, *Hebrews*, 60–81.

sermon, as I have done. As we read Hebrews together we will be taking our place among the company "of those who through faith and patience are inheriting the promises" (Heb 6:12).

The Purpose and Plan of this Reading Guide

I have divided this reading guide into seven weeks of daily readings so that you will have the time to be formed and shaped by prayerfully encountering God's word. You might want to read together with friends, or perhaps use this book as the basis for an in-depth class on Hebrews. My commentary, *The Epistle to the Hebrews*, provides additional resources for teachers or anyone else with further questions. I have used the translation of Hebrews from that commentary in this present book (with occasional modification). You can begin with week one, day one, at any time.

I want you to experience the impact not only of each individual passage but of the pastor's sermon *as a whole*. I want you to understand the role that each passage plays in that whole. I want you to grasp the careful way in which the pastor has put his book together in order to stress the sufficiency of Christ and the crucial importance of perseverance. I hope the message of Hebrews will shape your mind and heart. Most of all, I invite you, by attending to Hebrews, to "draw near to God" (Heb 10:22) through his Son who "is able even to save completely those who come to God through him, because he is always living to make intercession for them" (Heb 7:25). And so, through the "Spirit of Grace" (Heb 10:29), you will take your place among the "we" who "are not of those who shrink back" (10:39). Now, in order to receive the pastor's answer to our own spiritual needs and to some of the pressing concerns of our time, let us begin to meditate on the Letter to the Hebrews.

Scripture Abbreviations

Old Testament:

Gen	Judg	Neh	Song	Hos	Nah
Exod	Ruth	Esth	Isa	Joel	Hab
Lev	1–2 Sam	Job	Jer	Amos	Zeph
Num	1–2 Kgs	Ps (pl. Pss)	Lam	Obad	Hag
Deut	1–2 Chr	Prov	Ezek	Jonah	Zech
Josh	Ezra	Eccl	Dan	Mic	Mal

New Testament:

Matt	Acts	Eph	1–2 Tim	Heb	1–2–3 John
Mark	Rom	Phil	Titus	Jas	Jude
Luke	1–2 Cor	Col	Phlm	1–2 Pet	Rev
John	Gal	1–2 Thess			

Abbreviations for English Translations of the Bible

ESV	English Standard Version
KJV	King James Version
TNIV	Today's New International Version
NAB	New American Bible
NASB	New American Standard Bible (1995)
NRSV	New Revised Standard Version

God Has Spoken in One Who Is Son

Hebrews 1:1—2:18

Introduction

T he pastor appeals to our imagination. In this first week's readings
(Heb 1:1—2:18), he invites us to identify with God's Old Testament
people gathered around Sinai. As they heard God's word at Sinai so we
have received God's word in "one who is Son." In next week's Scripture
(Heb 3:1—4:13) he warns us against disobedience by painting a vivid
picture of how those who once stood around Sinai rebelled at Kadesh
Barnea. Taken together, I have described these first four chapters as "A
Short History of the Disobedient People of God."

Two important assumptions underlie these pictures. First, God's final
self-revelation in "one who is Son" seated at his right hand is the fulfillment of God's awe-inspiring, angel-mediated revelation at Mount Sinai
(Heb 2:1–4). The Sinai revelation was essential preparation for the "great
salvation" (Heb 2:3) available through the incarnate-now-exalted Eternal
Son. Second, we who hear God's word in the Son are heirs of those who
heard God's speak at Sinai. We are called to respond to God's word with
faith and obedience just as they were. We seek the same ultimate homeland and we have the same Savior. We differ in possessing greater privilege
and thus greater responsibility.

∾ Day One: God Has Now Spoken Through His Son (Heb 1:1–4)

> [1] *At various times and in various ways of old God spoke to the
> fathers by the prophets,* [2] *but at the end of these days he has spoken
> to us by one who is Son, whom he established as heir of all things,*

through whom he also made the worlds. [3] *As the radiance of God's glory and the exact representation of God's very being, and as the one who bears all to its intended end by the word of his power, the Son, by making purification for sins, sat down at the right hand of the Majesty on high.* [4] *Thus he became as much superior to angels as the name he has inherited is more excellent than theirs.*

In *Waiting for Godot,* Samuel Beckett pictures the modern world waiting in vain for a word from God. The pastor who wrote Hebrews announces good news: "God has spoken." We are not left to grope our way through life. We are not, to borrow from Paul, "without hope and without God in the world" (Eph 2:12 TNIV). There is a true north by which we can set our compass. God has spoken. Verses 1–2a describe the scope of God's speaking; verses 2b–3, the climax of God's self-revelation in the Son and the means by which the Son discloses the character of God. Verse 4 supports the dignity of the Son by introducing the comparison with the angels in verses 5–14.

Verses 1–2a. These verses describe the breath-taking panorama of God's comprehensive and accessible self-revelation. His conversation with his people began in the "prophets" and climaxes in the exalted "Son" who continues to address God's people today through the Scripture.

"Prophets" is a fitting term to encompass the entire Old Testament and affirm its divine origin. Moses himself was often considered the greatest prophet. "At various times" and "in various ways" describes the great variety within the Old Testament. Each of these expressions translates a single Greek word. These two words sound alike and are almost indistinguishable in meaning. By their pleasant-sounding combination the pastor celebrates the bounty of the various times, places, ways, and methods used in God's Old Testament revelation. Furthermore, "of old" affirms the antiquity and, thus, in the ancient mind, the integrity of Scripture. God's self-revelation, rich in diversity, long in the making, is no afterthought. We stand in awe of God's ancient word just as his people did at Sinai.

The term "Prophets," however, also conveys the anticipatory nature of the Old Testament. The Old Testament looks forward to fulfillment. The terms that describe the profound diversity and venerable authority of God's Old Testament word also expose its incomplete and preparatory role when compared with God's final word spoken "at the end of these days." The time of fulfillment has come. The diversity of the old has been given focus and fulfillment by God's self-disclosure in "one who is Son." The Son is the key that unlocks God's Old Testament revelation so that its richness can be seen. He brings together all of its various threads. As the pastor will explain in the rest of his sermon, the old is preparation for and a picture of the Son as "the Source of eternal salvation" (Heb 5:9) and of the "great salvation" (Heb 2:3) that he has provided. The entire Sinai Covenant, rightly understood, was "prophetic" of what God has now done in his Son (see week two, day one, 3:1–6 below). Without the "prophets" we would not understand the "Son." It is only in the "Son" that we comprehend the full meaning of the "prophets." The pastor writes in order to help us understand the full conversation.

Verses 2b–3. In these verses the pastor turns our attention to "one who is Son." Because of the quality and character of his Sonship he, and he alone, fulfills the prophetic word as God's final self-revelation. The pastor's insight into the nature of the Son is deep and rewarding.

The key to understanding these verses is the relative clause that immediately follows the word "Son": "Son, whom he [God] established as heir of all things." Inheritance is the appropriate fulfillment of what it means to be a "son." Thus, the Son fulfills his Sonship when, at the invitation of the Father, he takes his seat as the "heir of all things" "at the right hand of the Majesty on High." This he does "by making purification for sins." The incarnate obedience of God's eternal Son by which he obtained our salvation is the way in which he has become "heir of all things" in fulfillment of his Sonship. At this fulfillment he publicly inherits the name "Son" that has been his from eternity (v. 4 below).

We are brought to our knees when we realize that his saving work was not something external to his person. He fulfilled what he had always been as the eternal Son of God by taking his seat at God's right hand through his incarnation, obedience, and suffering on our behalf—"enduring the cross, despising the shame" (Heb 12:3). Certainly, he is worthy of our trust and obedience.

It is by thus fulfilling his Sonship that the eternal, incarnate, obedient, now exalted Son of God provides the ultimate revelation of God. He is "the radiance of his [God's] glory and the exact representation of his [God's] very being." God's "glory" is his revealed nature (Lev 9:23; Num 14:21–22; Isa 40:5), often pictured as resplendent with light (Exod 24:16–17; 40:34–35; 1 Kgs 8:11). By his saving work the Son is the "out-shining" of who God really is. As an impression on wax is the "exact representation" of the seal that made it, so the eternal, incarnate, now exalted Son is the perfect "imprint" of the "very being" of God. These two complementary expressions, "the radiance of God's glory" and "the exact imprint of God's very being," preserve the distinctness of the Son's Person while affirming that the finality of his revelation is based on his identity with the God he reveals. The all-sufficient "Source of eternal salvation" that he has become (Heb 5:9) is the full revelation of God.

The sovereign deity of the Son is confirmed by the fact that he is not only the universal heir and the agent of creation, but also the one who sustains the universe, "bearing all by the word of his power." By fulfilling his Sonship through becoming the "Source of eternal salvation" the Son "bears" or "directs" the creation to its God-intended goal at his return "for the purpose of bringing salvation to those awaiting him" (Heb 9:28). The pastor's prayer is that those who hear his sermon will persevere as part of this people who are "awaiting," with expectation, the return of the Lord.

Thus, from the very beginning, the pastor focuses our attention on "the Son, [who] by making purification for sins, sat down at the right hand of the Majesty on high." We are brought to our knees in adoration when we realize that our salvation is not merely the result of the divine will but the ultimate revelation of the divine nature.

His full exercise of the inheritance that he has received at God's right hand will become evident at his second coming "when his enemies are made a footstool for his feet" (Heb 1:13; 2:5–10; 9:28) and the faithful enter their inheritance through him (Heb 1:14).

Verse 4. The Son, as we have seen, fulfills the Sonship that has been his from all eternity through his incarnation and exaltation. Thus, it was appropriate to say that he publicly "inherited" the title "Son" at the exaltation when his Sonship was revealed to the world. We, however, are still left with the question of how he "became superior" to the angels at his exaltation? What follows in Heb 1:5—2:18 explores the great mystery of how the eternal—and thus always infinitely superior—Son of God became "lower" than the angels by assuming humanity in order that he might become "superior" to them in a new way as our Savior. The following contrast with angels only accentuates and enhances the awesome mystery of the eternal, incarnate, and exalted Son.

✑ Day Two: The Incomparable Majesty of the One through Whom God has Spoken—Son, Firstborn, and God; Worshiped by the Angels (Heb 1:5–9)

> [5] *For to which of the angels did God ever say, "Son of me you are, today I have begotten you," or again, "I will be to him a father and he will be to me a Son." [6] And again, when he introduces the First-born into the world he says, "Let all God's angels worship him."*
>
> [7] *And on the one hand in regard to the angels he says, "The one who makes his angels winds and his ministers a flame of fire." [8] But on the other hand to the Son he says, "Your throne, O God, is forever and the scepter of uprightness is the scepter of your*

kingdom. ⁹ *You have loved righteousness and hated lawlessness, therefore, O God, your God has anointed you with the oil of gladness beyond your companions.*

It is as if the pastor is saying to his hearers, "you haven't yet grasped the full significance of the fact that God has now spoken "in one who is *Son.*" The pastor's way of getting his point across is to contrast the Son with the angels. Angels stand in God's heavenly presence. They worship around his throne. They are his attendants awaiting his command. They govern nations and sometimes control the forces of nature. Moreover, they were present as intermediaries when God spoke at Sinai. Now, however, he has spoken in "one who is *Son.*"

God's speaking in the Son reaches fulfillment when the eternal, incarnate, now exalted Son takes his seat at God's right hand. Envision the Son assuming this place of authority surrounded by myriads of worshiping angels. On this occasion God speaks to the Son acknowledging his Sonship and his deity, confirming his incarnate obedience, announcing his enthronement, and inviting the Son to take his seat at God's right hand. At the same time, he commands the myriads of angels, his created servants, to worship the Son in the same way that they worship the Father.

The words with which God addresses the Son are not new. Most of them God once addressed to the heir of the Davidic throne on the occasion of his enthronement (2 Sam 7:14; Pss 2:7, 45:7–8, 110:1). They now find fulfillment at the cosmic enthronement of David's ultimate heir as the all-sufficient Savior of the people of God. As at the creation, the word of God brings into being what it affirms. The Son has become the ultimate Savior of God's people, and thus the full revelation of God through obedience to the word of God (Heb 10:5–10).

And yet, God's address to the Son on the occasion of his enthronement is ever-present. The Son continues to be the eternal, incarnate, exalted Son at God's right hand *who is fully adequate to meet his people's need.* The pastor would not fix his hearers' gaze on the earthly Jesus. He would not have them linger at the exaltation. He points them to the ever-present reality of the "Great High Priest who has passed through the heavens, Jesus, the Son of God" (Heb 4:14).

The three-part contrast with the angels in Heb 1:5–14 reveals the Son's eternity, exaltation, session,[1] and divine sovereignty. The continuation of this contrast in Heb 2:5–18 underscores the saving significance of the

---

1. "Exaltation" refers to the Son's return in triumph to God's presence after his resurrection. Sometimes it also includes the Son's "session." "Session," however, is used specifically to describe the Son's taking his seat at God's right hand.

Son's incarnation, suffering, and death. The pastor contrasts the Son with the angels (1:5–6, the Son inherits the name "Son"), the angels with the Son (1:7–12, the Son's deity and divine sovereignty), and then, again, the Son with the angels (1:13–14, the Son's exaltation and session).

Verses 5–6. Let's focus on the first contrast between the Son (v. 5) and the angels (v. 6) and on the divine declarations through which the Son inherits the all-important name "Son."

Verse 5 establishes the father/son relationship between God and the one he addresses: "*Son* of me you are, today I have begotten you" (Ps 2:7, italics added) and "I will be to him a father and he will be to me a *Son*" (2 Sam 7:14, italics added). God's words in Ps 2:7 to David's heir on the occasion of his coronation find fulfillment in the coronation of God's eternal Son. God's promise of Sonship to David's heir in 2 Sam 7:14 also finds fulfillment on that occasion. The translation of Ps 2:7 above that begins with the word "Son" preserves the emphasis of the Greek text. Taken together Ps 2:7 and 2 Sam 7:14 begin and end with the word "Son." The pastor would leave this word ringing in our ears.

But God's declarations of Sonship assume that he is "Father." "Today I have begotten you" and "I will be to him a father." The "Today" of God's begetting was the occasion when the Son took his seat at God's right hand. It was the day when the Son entered into the fulfillment of what he had always been as the "only begotten" Son, but it was also the beginning of a new epoch. God continues to speak what he has spoken. God's words to the Son on the occasion of his exaltation and session continue in force so long as the Son sits in authority at his right hand. Thus, the "Today" of God's begetting is the "Today" for hearing God's "voice" (Heb 3:7–8). The "today" of the Son's session as all-sufficient Savior is the "today" for our obedience as his faithful people.

"Let all the angels of God worship him" in verse 6 comes from Deut 32:43.[2] This verse calls on all heavenly beings to worship God because he has accomplished the salvation of his people. Now these words become God's instructions to the angels to worship the exalted Son as the "Firstborn" who has become the all-sufficient Savior.

2. This line is absent from Deut 32:43 in the King James Version. However, in the light of new textual evidence from the Dead Sea Scrolls, it is included in the ESV and the NRSV. See "bow down to him, all gods" and "worship him, all you gods" in Deut 32:43 of the ESV and NRSV respectively. The term "gods" with a small "g" refers to heavenly beings. Thus, the Greek translation used by Hebrews translated this word as "angels." See the TNIV footnote: "and let all the angels worship him." For further discussion of this issue see Cockerill, *Hebrews*, 104–8.

This worship of the son as "Firstborn" by the highest heavenly beings confirms his deity as well as his triumph as Savior. "Firstborn" underscores the unique and unparalleled nature of his relationship with the Father. God never addressed a single angel as "son" (v. 5), but this one is his "Firstborn."

However, he is also the "Firstborn" of God's faithful children, God's "sons" (with a small "s") and daughters (Heb 2:10, 13). As such he is the heir (v. 1) who brings all the family into its inheritance. By taking his seat at God's right hand in the eternal "world" he opens the way for all who persevere to join him in the "world to come" (Heb 2:5). The pastor gives us a tantalizing glimpse of that world and its inhabitants in Heb 12:22–24. This world of salvation is a present reality, in it the "spirits of the just made perfect" find rest, but it is also the ultimate destiny of the resurrected people of God at Christ's return (Heb 9:28, 12:25–29).

Verses 7–9. The second contrast between the angels and the Son is in verses 7–12. Verse 7 emphasizes the creaturely nature and servant status of the angels. Verses 8–9, the deity and sovereignty of the Son as Savior. Verses 10–12, the deity and sovereignty of the Son as Creator and Judge.

Who are these angels whom God commands to worship the "First-born"? Verse 7 clarifies their relationship to God by quoting Ps 101:4: "The one who makes his angels winds and his ministers a flame of fire." God is the one who created them. He can change "his angels" into "winds" and "his ministers" into a "flame." What is more ephemeral than wind and flame? The angels are temporal and malleable creatures made by the eternal, unchanging God.

The Son, however, is God. The Father addresses the Son as "God" in verse 7 and affirms the sovereign rule that the Son has assumed at God's right hand. God's declaration to David's heir in Ps 45:6–7 is fulfilled when directed to the Son at his enthronement: "Your throne, O God, is for ever and ever." This psalm also suggests that the Son has entered into this sovereign rule because of his earthly obedience. "The scepter of uprightness is the scepter of your kingdom" par excellence. "You have loved righteousness and hated lawlessness." It is for that reason that God has "anointed you with the oil of gladness above your fellows" as Sovereign Savior seated at the Father's right hand. We will hear of earthly obedience again in Heb 2:5–18, for both the Son's eternal deity and his obedient humanity are essential for him to become "the Source of eternal salvation" (Heb 5:9). This "great salvation" (Heb 2:3) we have in Christ alone.

∾ **Day Three:** The Incomparable Majesty of the One through Whom God has Spoken—Lord, Creator, Judge; Seated at God's Right Hand. (Heb 1:10–14)

> [10] And "You, from the beginning, Lord, founded the earth, and the heavens are the works of your hands. [11] They will perish, but you remain, and they will all wear out like an article of clothing, [12] and as a cloak you will roll them up, and as an article of clothing they will be changed. But you are the same and your years will never cease."
>
> [13] And to which of the angels has he ever said, "Sit at my right hand until I make your enemies a stool for your feet." [14] Are they not all ministering spirits sent out for service on behalf of those who are about to inherit salvation?

Verses 10–12. The pastor joins Ps 102:25–27 to Ps 45:6–7 with a mere "and" as the Father's additional proclamation to the Son. The Father addressed the Son as "God" in Ps 45:6. So now the Father can address him with words originally directed to God. He who confirmed the Son's title as "Son" and addressed him as "God," now speaks to him as "Lord," the sovereign, unchangeable Creator of the universe: "You, from the beginning, Lord, founded the earth, and the heavens are the works of your hands" (Ps 102:25). The Father addresses the Son "through whom he created the worlds" (Heb 1:2) as the Creator, not merely of the angels, but of the entire created order, "the earth" and "the heavens."

In verses 11–12 the Deity of the Son stands in stark contrast not merely with the creaturely nature of the angels but with the temporal, finite character of the entire created order. It will be helpful to arrange the text of these verses as follows:

> A "They will perish, but you remain,
>
> > B and they will all wear out like an article of clothing,
> >
> > > C and as a cloak you will roll them up,
> >
> > B[1] and as an article of clothing they will be changed.
>
> A[1] But you are the same and your years will never cease."

The first and last lines, "A" and "A[1]," assert the unchanging eternal deity of the Son. The second and fourth lines, "B" and "B[1]," the contrasting temporal nature of the creation. It will "wear out" just like the ratty old clothing in your rag bag. The emphasis, however, is on line "C" at the center: "and as a cloak *you* will roll them up" (italics added). The Son is eternal and the creation temporal. But there is something more. *He* is the one who will bring the universe to an end. *He* will "roll up" heaven and earth. He founded it, and he will bring it to a conclusion. We are reminded that he "bears all to its intended end by the word of his power" (Heb 1:3). Perhaps the pastor is thinking of the Son as the one who will "shake" and remove the temporal world so that the eternal will remain as described in Heb 12:25–29. He is the final judge. He has the first word and the last. The one who is the "Pioneer and Perfecter of the [way of] faith" (Heb 12:3) is also the Founder and Finisher of Creation.

It is clear by now that the pastor affirms the eternity and the deity of the Son as *necessary* if the Son is to be the all-sufficient Savior and final revelation of God. The Father has proclaimed him to be "Son" (Ps 2:7), addressed him as "God" (Ps 45:6–7), and now hailed him as "Lord" (Ps 102:25–27). The Father himself bears witness to the Son as Creator, Sustainer, and Judge of the creation. At the same time, the pastor does this without diminishing the initiative of the Father; indeed, it is the Father's words that bring the Son to the fulfillment of his Sonship. It is the Father who "begets" the Son (Heb 1:5). It is the Father who grants him the inheritance of the name "Son" (Heb 1:4). It is the Father who "anoints" the Son "above his fellows." And, thus, it is the Father who speaks in the eternal, incarnate, now-exalted Son. Furthermore, as we saw when discussing "whom he made heir of all things," the Son's obedience to the Father is necessary for him to fulfill his Sonship (see also Heb 10:5–10). We, with the angels, bow in awe before the eternal Son who assumed our humanity in order to become our all-sufficient Savior.

Verses 13–14. We can feel the intensity of the pastor's enthusiasm as he reaches his climax at this third and final contrast in support of the Son's majesty. We might ask, after verses 10–12, what more could be said? But a key question remains: how do we know that the Son has taken his seat at God's right hand? The pastor gave us a hint in verse 3 when he said that the Son had "sat down at the right hand of the Majesty on high," but he has kept the word of God that answers this question in reserve until now. For the verse in question is Ps 110:1: "Sit at my right hand until I make your enemies a stool for your feet." This psalm, like Ps 2:7 and Ps 45:6–7, finds fulfillment at the Son's exaltation because it was addressed to the heir of David's throne. God never said anything like this to an angel. The Son has taken his seat at God's right hand in response to the Father's invitation. The Son's position is established by the oracle of God.

We have already seen that the being of the Son is as superior to the being of the angels as eternal Creator is superior to temporal creature. At the public declaration of his Sonship they were commanded to worship him (Heb 1:5–6). We would expect, then, that the Son is also infinitely superior in his ministry. He is *seated* at God's right hand by God's invitation. They are *sent out* by divine fiat. He has taken his seat at God's right hand as our all-sufficient Savior. Hebrews will call him "the Source of eternal salvation" (Heb 5:9) and refer to the salvation he provides as "such a great salvation" (Heb 2:3). The angels, on the other hand, mighty though they be, have "been sent out to serve those who will inherit" the salvation that the Son provides.

The pastor has saved Ps 110:1 for the climax of this contrast because he wants to keep our gaze fixed on the eternal, incarnate, exalted Son *now seated* at the Father's right hand. For the same reason he will allude to Ps 110:1 over and over again at crucial points throughout his sermon (Heb 1:3; 8:1; 10:12, 13; and 12:2). It is *this* Son who cleanses us from sin. It is *this* Son who enables us to persevere. He will exercise this authority until his second coming when the Father will "make [his] enemies a stool for [his] feet" (see Heb 9:28). The season of his session as our all-sufficient Savior is the time of our perseverance in faithful obedience. Thus, before explaining how the Son came to this place of exaltation "by making purification for sin" (Heb 1:4), the pastor pauses to warn us lest we take our eyes off the Son and neglect "such a great salvation." That warning, found in Heb 2:1–4, is the subject of tomorrow's meditation.

⟡ Day Four: Give Undivided Attention to What God is Saying in His Son! (Heb 2:1–4)

[1] *On account of this it is necessary for us to give much greater attention to the things heard, lest we drift away.* [2] *For if the word spoken through angels proved valid, and every transgression and disobedience received a just reward,* [3] *then how shall we escape if we neglect such a great salvation? This salvation had its beginning by being spoken through the Lord and was validated for us by those who heard him,* [4] *God adding his witness to theirs by signs and wonders and various miracles and apportionments of the Holy Spirit according to his will.*

Verse 1. The pastor cannot restrain himself. He must impress upon his hearers the urgency of listening to God's ultimate revelation in this Son whom he has been describing in Heb 1:1–14. He begins, "On account of" God's superior self-revelation in the Son "it is necessary for us to give much greater attention to the things heard, lest we drift away." This first exhortation expresses the heart of the pastor's concern and lays a foundation for all the exhortations to follow (Heb 3:7—4:13; 4:14–16; 5:11—6:20; 10:19–39; 11:1–40; 12:1–29).

What are the "things heard"? God's revelation in his Son, of course, introduced in 1:1–14. Stay tuned, however, for the pastor will continue to expand our understanding of these "things heard" in 2:5–18; 3:1–6; 5:1–10; and 7:1—10:18, for they constitute the "great salvation" that is at the heart of his message. How urgent it is, then, to truly "hear" what we have "heard" by responding with obedience: "Today, if you hear his voice, do not harden your hearts" (Heb 3:7).

Two more phrases catch our attention: "to give much greater attention" and "lest we drift away." The pastor urges us to give a degree of attention that is appropriate for nothing less than God's ultimate revelation of "such a great salvation" in his Son. Nothing could be more tragic than for his hearers to "drift away" from *this* salvation. The pastor fears that they might "drift away" little by little from fatigue, inconvenience, indifference, distraction, peer pressure, social exclusion, and/or growing persecution. As the hearers drift, the "things heard" begin to fade. The more the "things heard" fade from their memory, the more they drift. Heedlessness and drifting raise the threating specter of falling "away from the living God" (Heb 3:12). On the other hand, if they give "much greater attention" to the "things heard" they will hold "firm" to their confession of Christ (3:6, 14), by drawing "near" to God through their great High Priest (Heb 4:16, 10:22), and thus "run the race" (12:1) set before them.

Verses 2–3a. These verses underscore the importance of paying attention to the "things heard" by comparing the preparatory Old Testament revelation with God's ultimate self-revelation in the Son: if it was important to heed what was preparatory, how much more the fulfillment.

The pastor who described God's Old Testament revelation in 1:1 as what God spoke "in the prophets," now describes it as "the word spoken through angels." As noted above, "the prophets" included the entire Old Testament and emphasized the fact that it looked forward to a greater fulfillment. "The word spoken through angels" refers more specifically to God's revelation at Sinai (Gal 3:19; Acts 7:38, 53), the heart of the Old Testament upon which all else depended. Its angelic, rather than prophetic, mediation underscored its central importance. Its absolute validity, demonstrated by the fact that *every* infraction received due punishment, was confirmed by the prophets.

The fulfillment of this "word spoken through angels" is described as "such a great salvation." The pastor is whetting his hearers' appetite and awakening their curiosity. He will spend much of the rest of this sermon explaining the nature and magnitude of this salvation. The point at hand, however, is the absolute certainty of punishment for those who "neglect" this "great salvation." If the punishment of those who violated the "word

spoken through angels" was certain, how *much more* certain the consequences for those who "neglect" this "great salvation." Those who "neglect"
it effectively deny its importance. They, then, are the ones who "drift away."
The fruit of neglecting this salvation is its rejection. "How shall we escape
if we neglect such a great salvation?"

Verses 3b–4. These verses substantiate the magnitude of this "great
salvation" by contrasting its source with the "angels" through whom God's
word was spoken at Sinai. First, this salvation had its beginning, its source,
not in angels but in "the Lord." As noted above, God proclaimed Christ
"Son" (1:5–6), "God" (Heb 1:8), and "Lord" (Heb 1:10) at his exaltation.
The judgment that fell upon violators of the angel-mediated "word" demonstrated its validity. This "great salvation," however, is valid beyond doubt
because it has been accomplished through and is proclaimed by the incarnate, obedient, and risen "Lord" seated at God's right hand.

Second, it was reliably attested and "validated" to both the pastor and
his hearers "by those who heard" the Lord. The pastor is in harmony with
the rest of the New Testament in his affirmation that the Gospel is based on
the testimony of those who knew Jesus. This "great salvation" is built on valid
testimony to historical fact. The recipients of Hebrews, along with other first
generation Christians, received this testimony directly from those who were
with Jesus. It is likely that the pastor and his hearers could have named those
who had been witnesses to Jesus' life and had confirmed the truth to them.
We, of course, receive this "great salvation" through the New Testament,
which is the legacy and testimony of "those who heard Him."

Finally, God himself bears witness to the authenticity of this "great salvation." He has not only "spoken" this salvation into existence through his
Son the risen "Lord," but he has validated the witness of "those who heard"
the Lord with "signs and wonders and various miracles and apportionments
of the Holy Spirit." These "signs and wonders and various miracles" not only
validate the truth of this "great salvation," they confirm it as the fulfillment
of God's Sinai revelation, which was also attended with "signs and wonders"
(Deut 4:34; 6:22; Ps 135:9; Jer 32:20–21). They affirm its identity with the
ministry of Jesus (Acts 2:22) and with the gospel as preached throughout
the world (Rom 15:19; 2 Cor 12:12; Gal 3:5).

It is no surprise that the pastor associates "apportionments of the
Holy Spirit" with these "signs and wonders." These confirming "signs and
wonders" are the work of the Holy Spirit whom the exalted Son of God has
poured out on the church. The Holy Spirit was not subject to conjuring or
human manipulation. The Spirit and the "signs and wonders" performed
by him were "apportioned" according to God's "will" in order to authenti-
cate "such a great salvation." The pastor is also referring to the confirming

testimony of the Spirit received by his hearers. God's Spirit still attests the "great salvation" found in God's word to those who "give much greater attention to the things heard."

The pastor begins the exhortations of this sermon with warning, "How shall we escape if we neglect such a great salvation?" This strategy, however, is no superficial manipulative appeal to fear, for the danger is very real, as will be demonstrated by the example of the wilderness generation (Heb 3:7—4:13). The pastor intends this warning to awaken his hearers and dispel their lethargy so that they will embrace the grace available to them through Jesus "the Source of eternal salvation" (Heb 5:9) and attain the glorious destiny of the people of God on Mount Zion (Heb 12:22–24).

The pastor continues the story begun in chapter one in Heb 2:5–18. He describes how the eternal Son entered his inheritance at God's right hand as exalted Son. As such, the Son became, for the faithful, the "Pioneer of their salvation" (Heb 2:10) through his obedient incarnation and death "on behalf of everyone" (Heb 2:9).

∾ Day Five: Jesus, the Incarnate Son—"made a little lower than the angels." (Heb 2:5–9)

5 For it is not to angels that he has subjected the world to come of which we are speaking. 6 For someone has attested somewhere saying,"What is man that you remember him, or the son of man that you visit him.[3] 7 You have made him a little lower than the angels, with glory and honor you have crowned him. 8 All you have subjected under his feet." By subjecting everything he left nothing unsubjected to him. But now we do not yet see all things in a state of subjection to him. 9 But we do see the one who has been made a little lower than the angels, Jesus, because of the suffering of death crowned with glory and honor, so that by the grace of God on behalf of everyone he might taste death.

We can never grasp the incomparable majesty of the exalted Son (Heb 1:1–14), or the greatness of the salvation he has provided (Heb 2:1–4), apart from the wonder of the incarnation by which the eternal Son took his seat at God's right hand (Heb 2:5–18)! With the quotation of Ps 110:1 in Heb 1:13–14 the pastor left us gazing at the eternal Son seated at God's right hand awaiting the time when God would make his enemies a stool for his

---

3 I have retained the singular "man" and "son of man," as in the Greek text, because terms like "humanity," "human beings," or "mortals" (see the TNIV and NRSV) obscure the fact that the pastor's primary reference is to Jesus, the incarnate Son of God.

feet. Here, in Heb 2:5–9, the pastor introduces Ps 8:4–6 in order to show that it was by the Son's obedient incarnation and death that he assumed this place at God's right hand. By so doing he fulfilled his Sonship and became "the Pioneer" of our "salvation" (Heb 2:10).

The pastor intentionally introduces Ps 8:4–6 with "For someone has attested somewhere saying" (Heb 2:6). This psalm is the "attested" word of God. However, it is not one of the Old Testament Scriptures with which the Fathers addresses the Son in Heb 1:1–14, nor is it one of the Scriptures with which the Son answers the Father in Heb 2:10–13. Instead, this psalm is the hinge that makes this Father-Son conversation possible. It reveals that the incarnation was the road to the Son's taking his seat at God's right hand. The Father addresses the Son, affirming his eternity and exaltation; the Son responds, affirming his incarnate obedience as the path to exaltation. As noted above, this divine conversation at the Son's session continues to address us as the people of God through the ever-present Son seated at God's right hand.

Verse 5. Everything that has already been said up to this point suggests that the "world to come" has been subjected to the Son. At the end of the last chapter the pastor left us with (1) the Son seated at God's right hand and (2) the angels sent out to serve "those who are about to inherit salvation" (Heb 1:13–14). Thus, it is certainly not *the angels* to whom "God has subjected the world to come of which we are speaking." It must, then, be the eternal Son, already enthroned in that "world to come" (Heb 1:6). This "world" is the "salvation" that the faithful are "about to inherit." It appears that it has been "subjected" to the one *seated at God's right hand.* As the "Pioneer of their salvation" (Heb 2:10), he grants the faithful their inheritance.

Verses 6–8a: The quotation of Ps 8:4–6 in Heb 2:6–8a, however, calls this interpretation into question: "What is *man* that you remember him, or the *son of man* that you visit him. . . ." (italics added). Ps 8 is, after all, a description of the glorious way in which God has made *humanity* in his image. We can hear the pastor's audience thinking: "What is he saying? We thought that this 'world to come' had been subjected to the Son? Is the pastor saying that it has been subjected to human beings?" The pastor has created this ambiguity to reengage his hearers after the exhortation in Heb 2:1–4, and to awaken their curiosity: "What is he going to say about this psalm?"

Verses 8b–9. The pastor gradually resolves this ambiguity as he interprets the three lines of Ps 8 quoted in verses 7–8b: (1) "You have made him a little lower than the angels," (2) "with glory and honor you have crowned him," and (3) "All you have subjected under his feet." When the pastor is finished we will know that the first line refers to the Son's incarnation; the second, to his exaltation and session at God's right hand (Ps 110:1a); but the third awaits the time when God will "make" his "enemies a stool for his feet" (Ps 110:1b).

First, however, a qualification in verse 8a: "all things" means "all things." Everything has been subjected to this "him." Then the pastor affirms that we, however, do not yet "see" with our eyes "everything in a state of subjection to him." (Can you hear the pastor's congregation thinking: "who in the world are you talking about—the Son or humanity?"?) Finally, the fog begins to lift and the ambiguity begins to clear: "But we do see the one who has been made a little lower than the angels," yes, so, who is that? *Jesus*. This is the first time the pastor has used this name. He reserves the name *Jesus* for the *incarnate* Son of God, for the Son of God who has taken on our humanity.

It is with the eyes of faith that we see "Jesus, because of the suffering of death crowned with glory and honor." The pastor writes Hebrews with the burning desire that we will keep our eyes of faith focused on this Jesus, the ultimate Savior, the eternal, incarnate Son seated at God's right hand (see Heb 3:1; 8:1–2; 12:1–3). He alone enables our perseverance.

The Son is, then, the one who through "the suffering of death" as the incarnate Jesus was "crowned with glory and honor" so that he could fulfill Ps 8:4–6 by bringing humanity to its God-intended destiny. For, by the "grace" and goodness of God he tasted death "for everyone."

The expression "taste death" underscores the reality of Jesus' experience. "Taste" does not mean that he sampled death. It means that he experienced death to its fullness. He experienced its pains, its horrors, and its desolation. His experience of death was multiplied beyond imagining because he experienced it "for everyone." As noted in the introduction, the pastor who wrote Hebrews is concerned primarily with encouraging the *perseverance* of beleaguered believers rather than with the evangelization of humanity. As will be noted below, he emphasizes the fact that Jesus became human because God's people were human (Heb 2:14). Nevertheless, the pastor affirms a gospel according to which the eternal, incarnate, exalted Son seated at God's right hand has, by God's grace, drunk the bitter dregs of death for *every human being*. Only such a gospel is sufficient for the perseverance of the people of God.

And so, the eternal Son of God, who "became a little lower than the angels" by assuming our humanity as "Jesus," is now enthroned at God's right hand as "Jesus." The pastor presents us with the awe-filled reality of the incarnation. By becoming a "little lower than the angels" the Son of God added a new dimension to his superiority over the angels. It is he alone, and not they, who have become, for humanity, "the Source of eternal salvation" (Heb 5:9).

Some have tended to separate the Son's eternal deity/exaltation from his humanity by saying that Heb 1:1–14 refers to the former and Heb 2:5–18 to the latter. Heb 2:5–18, however, focuses on the *incarnation* of the *eternal, exalted* Son. Hebrews never discusses the "humanity" of the Son in isolation from his eternity and exaltation.

The quotation from Ps 8:4–6 began by marveling that God would "remember" or "visit" humanity (v. 6 above). He has "remembered" us and "visited" us by providing for our eternal salvation through the incarnate suffering of his Son. He continues to "remember" and "visit" us through the grace available through the eternal, incarnate, exalted Son—all praise to his name. We must not "neglect such a great salvation" (Heb 2:3).

∽ Day Six: "The Pioneer of Our Salvation"—"made perfect through suffering." (Heb 2:10–13)

> [10] *For it was fitting to him, for whom are all things and through whom are all things, in order to bring many sons and daughters[4] into glory, to perfect the Pioneer of their salvation through suffering.* [11] *For both the one making holy and those being made holy are all from one. For which reason he is not ashamed to call them brothers and sisters,* [12] *saying, "I will announce your name to my brothers and sisters. In the midst of the congregation I will praise you."* [13] *And again, "I will put my trust in him." And again, "Behold I and the children whom God has given me."*

The pastor has just affirmed that the incarnate Son experienced death for all human beings. In these verses he boldly asserts that the Son's "suffering" was "fitting" to the divine character and purpose (v. 10), and appropriate for God's relationship with his people (v. 11). In verses 12–13 the Son responds with appropriate Scripture to the words addressed to him by the Father in Heb 1:5–14. The Son's responses confirm the beautiful appropriateness of his suffering for the redemption of the people of God.

Verse 10. This verse boldly asserts the appropriateness of the Son's "suffering." "Suffering" is a comprehensive term for all that the incarnate Son endured. This "suffering" reached its full intensity and climax in the experience of death affirmed in verse 9. The Son's incarnate "suffering" was "fitting" for no one less than the God "for whom are all things and

---

4. In Greek "sons and daughters" is literally "sons." In the world contemporary with Hebrews "sons" were heirs. Thus, by using "sons" for both men and women the pastor included all the faithful among those who would inherit salvation (compare Heb 1:14). We have used "sons and daughters" here and elsewhere to make this inclusiveness clear. See also "brothers and sisters" in verses 11 and 12.

through whom are all things." It was in full accord with the redemptive purposes of the God who created the universe, for its purpose was "to bring many sons and daughters into glory."

It is important to understand how Hebrews uses filial language, such as "sons and daughters" or "brothers and sisters." Hebrews does not use this language to describe the new life that comes through faith in Christ. According to Hebrews, the faithful people of God throughout history have always been his "children" (Heb 2:14). The problem was not how they could become children of God. The problem was how God's sinful people would be able to enter their inheritance as the "sons and daughters" of God. Thus, the Son became incarnate and suffered in order "to bring many sons and daughters into glory."

In order to achieve this purpose, it was "fitting" for the God of creation and redemption "to perfect the Pioneer of their salvation through suffering." Notice that the pastor does not begin with what the Son's suffering has done for *us*. He begins with what it has done to *him*. We have a "great salvation" (Heb 2:3) *only* because we have a fully sufficient Savior—"the Source of eternal salvation" (Heb 5:9). We have salvation in union with him.

A "pioneer" is one who opens the way for others to enter a new land by overcoming difficulties and entering himself. This term reminds us of Moses leading the people of God into the promised land. The incarnate Son, however, is the one who leads God's people into "glory," another name for the "salvation" they are inheriting (Heb 1:14). Hebrews agrees with the rest of the NT: although the eternal Son is without defect, he had to be "perfected," that is, made fully competent, as the Savior of God's people through the incarnation and all that it entailed. At the same time, this "perfecting" is the fulfillment of what it means for him to be Son (Heb 1:3).

The rest of Hebrews, especially Heb 4:14—10:25, will explain how the Son's incarnate suffering equipped him to be "the Source of eternal salvation." (5:9). Through his *obedient* suffering he became the all-sufficient sacrifice for sin, the fully competent High Priest able to bring God's people into God's heavenly presence, and the Mediator of a New Covenant of obedience. As such he is more than able to sustain his people in obedient faithfulness until they enter "glory." But that is getting ahead of the story. The pastor will explain all of this in due time.

Verse 11a. The Son's incarnate suffering was appropriate because of the relationship that this God had with his people. The "one making holy" is the Son. "Those being made holy" are the "sons and daughters" of God. Both the Son and the "sons and daughters" are "of one." Both have a filial relationship with God! The one relationship is eternal, the other by grace, but both relationships are filial. For this reason it was appropriate for the

Son to assume the humanity of the "sons and daughters" in order to enable their faithful perseverance. The Son's incarnation was appropriate because a gracious God considered his people to be his "sons and daughters."

Notice that the work of the Son is to make the "sons and daughters" "holy." He is the Sanctifier. Hebrews understands salvation not merely as forgiveness (though that is included), but as cleansing from sin and empowerment for obedience. The life of the faithful is a life that is continually "being made holy."

Verses 11b–13. The Son willingly bore the awful shame of the cross (Heb 12:1–3) because he was not "ashamed" to identify with God's "sons and daughters." The Son acknowledges his filial relationship with the people of God and affirms his assumption of their humanity by his threefold response to the Father in these verses.

In Heb 1:5 the Father openly addresses the Son as the Son who has fulfilled his Sonship by entering his inheritance at the exaltation. The Son responds, here in verse 12, with Ps 22:22: "I will announce your name to my brothers and sisters. In the midst of the congregation I will praise you." Jesus quoted the first verse of this psalm on the cross in the bitterness of suffering: "My God, my God, why have you forsaken me?" (ESV). In verse 22 the sufferer of verse 1 praises God for his deliverance. Thus, it is an appropriate response as the incarnate, exalted Son takes his seat at God's right hand. On this grand occasion he is not "ashamed" to own the people of God, whose humanity he has assumed, as his "brothers and sisters." As the fully adequate Savior he proclaims God's "name" (his gracious character) to them and invites them to join him in praise. The exalted Son has not abandoned us.

In Heb 1:8–12 the Father addresses the Son as "God" and affirms his divine sovereignty with Pss 45:6–7 and 102:25–27. The Son answers in words that come from both victorious King David (2 Sam 22:3, Greek translation) and distressed Isaiah (Isa 8:17): "I will put my trust in him." In response to God's declaration of the Son's sovereignty, the incarnate Son affirms his complete dependence upon God. He is indeed the "God" whom, according to Ps 45:6–7, God has exalted because he "loved righteousness and hated lawlessness." He is God who is also a fully obedient human being. His life of obedience is both the means of his people's salvation and a pattern, through his mediation, for their behavior.

We have already noted that Ps 110:1 (Heb 1:13) is the climax of the contrast between the Son and the angels in Heb 1:4–14. This verse from the psalms is the Father's invitation for the incarnate Son to take his seat at God's right hand. How does the Son respond to this invitation? He uses Isa 8:18: "Behold I and the children whom God has given me." The Son accepts the invitation to sit at God's right hand—for himself *and for his* "children." The Son has not abandoned us after identifying with us by living a fully human life. No, on the occasion of his victory he presents us to the Father as his children invited to enter God's presence and join the Son in his inheritance. We respond with awe, praise, and obedience.

❧ Day Seven: "A Merciful and Faithful High Priest" — "made like his brothers and sisters in every way." (Heb 2:14–18)

> [14] *Therefore, since the children share blood and flesh, he himself in like manner became a partaker with them, in order that through death he might destroy the one who has the power of death, that is, the devil,* [15] *and set free those who by fear of death throughout their lives were subject to bondage.* [16] *For clearly it is not angels that he has taken hold of, but the seed of Abraham he has taken hold of.* [17] *Therefore, it was necessary for him to be made like the brothers and sisters in every way, in order that he might become a merciful and faithful High Priest in things pertaining to God, to make atonement for the sins of the people.* [18] *Because he himself has suffered when he was tested, he is able to help those undergoing testing.*

We can summarize these verses in this way: "The incarnate Son's suffering for the sons and daughters of God was an appropriate expression of God's faithfulness (vv. 10–13) because it corresponded to their fallen human condition: captive through sin (vv. 16–18) to the fear of death (vv. 14–15)."[5]

Verses 14–15. God's "children share blood and flesh." "Blood and flesh" describe humanity in its weakness, frailty, and mortality. God's "children" share in the mortality that is the inescapable lot of the human race and the deepest angst of every human heart. All human beings feel the impact of the pastor's description of our situation as "subject to bondage" throughout our entire lives "by fear of death."

God's people, here called God's "children" ("sons and daughters" in verse 10 above), were human and thus by nature shared this condition with all human beings. Thus, it was *appropriate* for the Son to "become a partaker with them" of this fragile, broken, dying humanity in order to deliver them from their greatest enemy. We have already been told that the incarnate Son experienced the fullness of death for every human being (Heb 2:9). Now we learn that it was by that very "death" that he destroyed "the one who has the power of death, the devil." The death of the incarnate Son of God is the key to the deliverance of the human sons and daughters of God.

How did the devil acquire the "power of death" over us, and how does the incarnate Son's death destroy that power? Remember God's words

5. Cockerill, *Hebrews*, 146.

to Adam and Eve: "For in the day that you eat of it you shall die" (Gen 2:17 NRSV). The apostle Paul reminds us that death came into the world "through sin" (Rom 5:12 ESV) and that "the wages of sin is death" (Rom 6:23 ESV). By enticing to sin the devil has subjected the human race to life-long "fear of death." This fear is so intense because death is followed by "judgment" (Heb 9:27) on sin. Verses 16–18 will make it clear that the Son of God delivers from the fear of death by removing the sin that incurs the judgment of God. The mortal "sons and daughters" of God may still be subject to physical death, but its terror has been removed.

By beginning his description of the salvation provided by the incarnate Son with deliverance from the fear of death the pastor (1) insures that his message will have the broadest and deepest appeal, (2) exposes the horror of sin as the source of death, and, most important of all, (3) prepares his hearers to persevere even in the face of death. The pastor will make it plain that the faithful of chapter 11 have a destiny that transcends death because they serve a God who "was able to raise from the dead" (Heb 11:19). They live in anticipation of the "better resurrection" (Heb 11:35) as they await Christ's return with "salvation" (Heb 9:28) for those patiently anticipating his arrival.

Verses 16–18. The Son of God, then, is not concerned with the angels but with the heirs of salvation whom the angels have been sent to serve (Heb 1:14). He is concerned about God's human "children" (Heb 2:14) who, by faith, are "the seed of Abraham" and heirs of the Abrahamic promise (Heb 6:12–20). Long ago God took "hold" of his people by the hand and led them through the wilderness toward the promised land. So, now the Son of God takes the people of God by the hand and shepherds them toward their eternal homeland (see Jer 31:32 quoted in Heb 8:9). Remember, he is the "Pioneer of their salvation" who opens the way for them and leads them to their destiny (Heb 2:10).

In order to do this "it was necessary for him to be made like the brothers and sisters in every way." There was nothing superficial or temporary about the humanity he assumed. At the incarnation he took upon himself and redeemed our broken and marred humanity. It was only by becoming one of us (Heb 5:1) that he could represent us "in things pertaining to God" as our "Merciful and faithful High Priest." As the pastor will reveal (Heb 9:11–14; 10:5–10), by his faithful obedience "he made atonement for the sins of the people" and thus became the conduit of God's mercy. Furthermore, we can depend on the mercy thus offered because our High Priest is ever faithful.

The pastor is whetting his hearers' appetite by describing the incarnate Son as the "Merciful and faithful High Priest" who makes "atonement for the sins of the people." He will satisfy their curiosity in Heb 4:14—10:25. There they will discover the magnitude of this atonement and the "great salvation" it provides. By his once-for-all obedient sacrifice the incarnate Son "cleanses our consciences from dead works to serve the living God" (Heb 9:11–14; 10:5–10). By thus dealing with sin he became their High Priest, seated at God's right hand who ushers them into God's presence (Heb 9:23–24, 10:19–22). Furthermore, by taking upon himself the divine sin-curse he releases them from impending judgment and brings them into a New Covenant of obedience which he guarantees (Heb 9:15–22; 10:14–18).

For the moment, however, it is crucial to realize that the incarnate Son is, even now, our "Merciful and faithful High Priest in things pertaining to God." He is, right now, able to minister to God's people in their hour of need. "Because he himself has suffered when he was tested, he is able to help those undergoing testing." "Testing" involves more than what most of us would include under "temptation." The pastor is referring to everything that would deter God's people from the path of faithful obedience. Resistance to the forces that would distract our attention and impede our obedience often involves suffering. Jesus' life of perfect obedience (Heb 10:5–10) was a life of suffering that culminated in his atoning death. He overcame every test, whatever the suffering involved, including the cross (Heb 12:1–3). Thus, as our "Merciful and faithful High Priest" at God's right hand, he empowers us to endure whatever suffering we might face in order to persevere as God's obedient children, the faithful "seed of Abraham." We can depend on him for the mercy of forgiveness and the grace for obedience.

In this opening section of Hebrews (1:1—2:18) the pastor has shown us that by his incarnation and death the eternal Son of God has "made purification for sins" and become our "Merciful and faithful high priest." By thus providing "such a great salvation" (Heb 2:3) he fulfills his Sonship and his role as the full revelation of God. The pastor first warned us lest we drift away from this "great salvation" through neglect (Heb 2:1–4). He balances that warning by concluding this opening section of Hebrews with assurance that our "Merciful and faithful High Priest" offers forgiveness for sin and empowerment for obedience. He enables us to persevere as God's faithful people despite suffering. He tenderly "takes hold" of God's people and guides them on their way.

These words of encouragement fortify us for today's trials and prepare us for what is coming in chapters 3 and 4. There the pastor will expand the warning of Heb 2:1–4 by introducing the account of the faithless wilderness generation. He will, then, follow that warning with his grand explanation of the all-sufficiency of our Savior in Heb 4:14—10:25.

A Disobedient Generation and a New High Priest

Hebrews 3:1—5:10

Introduction

D uring the first five days of this week we will complete our study of "A Short History of the Disobedient People of God." As already noted, the account of that history began at Sinai in Heb 1:1—2:18. Just as God's people of old heard him speak at Sinai, so we have heard him speak in the eternal, incarnate, exalted Son seated at his right hand. Those, however, who stood at Sinai became the faithless wilderness generation who rebelled at Kadesh Barnea and forfeited God's "rest" (Num 14:1–45; Ps 95:7b–11). In Heb 3:1–6 the pastor assures us that both we who have heard God's word in the Son and that Sinai generation are part of God's one "House" or "household." We are the one people of God. Christ is the Son "over" that House, while Moses is the "Steward" in that household. Just as Moses in Deuteronomy warned the children of the wilderness generation, so the pastor warns us lest we follow the wilderness generation's example of disobedience (Heb 3:7–19), before urging us to pursue what they forfeited (Heb 4:1–11). The pastor then concludes this "short history" with a reminder of our accountability before the word of God (Heb 4:12–13). The history of the disobedient is "short" because it has no future. It ends in judgment.

The pastor wants us to avoid the wilderness generation's fate (Heb 3:1—4:13) by following in the steps of the faithful people of God whom he will introduce in chapter 10 and begin to describe in Heb 11:1–40. We will only be able to emulate them and obtain the promised "rest," however, if we embrace the eternal, incarnate, exalted Son of God as our fully sufficient High Priest. As God's people in the wilderness approached him through the Old Testament priesthood, so we enter the true heavenly Most

Holy Place through our "Great High Priest" (Heb 4:14). The pastor will explain all of this to us in Heb 4:14—10:25.

On day six of this week we will "taste" the sample of that priesthood that the pastor gives us in Heb 4:14–16. That taste only makes us want more. Then, on day seven we will examine the outline in Heb 5:1–10 of the way in which our "Great High Priest" (Heb 4:14) both fulfills and supersedes the pattern established by the Old Testament high priest. This outline provides the context for the rest of the pastor's grand explanation of the Son as the "Source of eternal salvation" (Heb 5:9), the one and only all-sufficient High Priest and Savior able to bring us into God's presence.

∾ Day One: Jesus, Moses, and the House of God. (Heb 3:1–6)

¹ *Therefore, holy brothers and sisters, partakers of the heavenly calling, consider the Apostle and High Priest of our confession, Jesus,* ² *as one faithful to the one who appointed him, just as Moses also was faithful in all his House.* ³ *For this one has been considered worthy of more glory than Moses to as great a degree as the one who establishes a house has more honor than the house.* ⁴ *For every house is established by someone, but the one establishing all things is God.* ⁵ *And on one hand Moses was faithful in all his House as a steward for a witness of things yet to be spoken,* ⁶ *but Christ as a Son over his House, whose House we are if we hold fast our boldness and our boasting in hope.*

As we have seen, the pastor began his sermon by affirming that God's word in his Son fulfills the word that he spoke in the Old Testament through "the prophets" (Heb 1:1–4). He also implied that we who hear God's Son-mediated word are the heirs of the "fathers" who received that Old Testament revelation. The God who spoke to them at Sinai has now spoken to us in "one who is Son."

In Heb 3:1–6 the pastor brings these relationships into sharper focus. He will show the relationship between the Son and the person who mediated the Sinai revelation, the greatest "prophet," Moses. He will also clarify how we who hear God's word in the Son relate to the people whom Moses brought to Mount Sinai and then led through the wilderness to the promised land. We often call them the "wilderness generation." These relationships are fundamental to everything the pastor has to say.

You will be richly rewarded with a deeper understanding of Hebrews if you give this passage prayerful, careful attention. Hebrews 3:1–6 is so important for the following chapters that we are going to spend two days meditating on it. Today's reading focuses on verses 1–3, tomorrow's on verses 4–6. If you just can't wait, no one will stop you from reading both meditations in one day!

Verse 1–2a. The pastor begins, as is his habit, by calling attention to Jesus: "Therefore" refers to everything said about the Son thus far. The eternal, incarnate, exalted Son who has defeated death by giving his life as an atonement for sin deserves the undivided attention of the people of God. As the faithful people of God we are "holy brothers and sisters." We are the "brothers and sisters" of the Son and therefore "sons and daughters" of the Father, set apart by the death of Jesus as "holy" unto God. As such, we are "partakers of the heavenly calling." This "calling" comes to us from God's eternal, incarnate, exalted Son enthroned at his right hand in heaven. This "calling" also beckons us to approach God in his heavenly sanctuary. It invites us to persevere until we enter the "heavenly Jerusalem" (Heb 12:22–24).

And so, since we have, in the Son, a heavenly origin and destiny, it is only proper that we give him our full attention. Here the pastor urges us to give consideration to "the Apostle and High Priest of our confession, Jesus, *as one faithful to the one who appointed him*" (Italics added). As we will see, it is by the Son's incarnate faithfulness to God that he procured our salvation (Heb 2:18; 9:11–14; 10:5–10). His utter faithfulness is also the grand example for us to follow (Heb 12:1–3) because we know we can depend on him, even now, to sustain us in every test (Heb 2:18).

Amid life's struggles, meditate on his faithfulness, for he is "the Apostle and High Priest of our confession." Hebrews gives us a rich understanding of the Son by describing him with a number of terms, such as "Pioneer" (Heb 1:10; 12:1–3), "Forerunner" (Heb 6:20), and "Apostle," that are not used elsewhere in the New Testament. The pastor, however, uses these terms with great care. "Apostle" fits well with this passage's emphasis on faithfulness. An "apostle" was one "sent" as the fully authorized representative of another. The very essence of being an "apostle" is faithfulness to the sender. In John's Gospel Jesus often speaks of himself as the one "sent" by, and thus obedient to, the Father. The pastor uses "Apostle" here to underscore the unique role of the Son as the one who has revealed the Father through his faithfulness. As usual, the pastor reserves "Jesus" for the final, emphatic, position. Together "Apostle and High Priest" remind us that he has become the ultimate revelation of God by providing "such a great salvation" (Heb 2:3) through his faithful obedience as the incarnate "Jesus." It is as "the Source of eternal salvation" (Heb 5:9) that he is "the radiance of God's glory and the exact representation of God's very being"

(Heb 1:3). The "partakers of the heavenly calling" joyfully confess and freely acknowledge Jesus as their "Apostle and High Priest."

Verse 2b–3. ". . . just as Moses was faithful in all his house." The pastor is going to compare and contrast this "Apostle and High Priest . . . Jesus" with Moses. First, comparison: this affirmation of Moses' "faithfulness" in God's "House" comes from Num 12:7, which the pastor will quote in verse 5 below. On the basis of this Scripture, the pastor affirms that both Moses and Jesus ("the Apostle and High Priest of our confession") were faithful to God. This faithfulness was carried out within their roles as mediators of God's word to his people, here called God's "House." These two mediators, past and present, can be compared because both were faithful.

However, "This one has been considered worthy of more glory than Moses." The pastor uses "this one" in order to reserve "Son" for verse 6. This somewhat awkward expression refers to everything that the pastor has said about "the Apostle and High Priest . . . Jesus." *He* "has been considered worthy" by God the Father "of more *glory* than Moses" because, as God's ultimate self-revelation, he is the very "radiance of God's *glory*" (Italics added).

How great is his superiority to Moses? The pastor answers with what might have been a common proverb: ". . . to as great a degree as the one who establishes a house has more honor than the house." Nevertheless, within this context the terms of this proverb have special reference. As will become evident from the verses that follow, "the one who establishes a house" refers to Christ. "House" refers to the people of God. Most English translations read "the one who builds a house" or "the builder of a house" (but see "founder of a house" in NAB). The verb in question, however, often refers to someone who brings something to completion. It can refer to the one who completes a house, makes it ready for habitation, and furnishes it. This meaning is appropriate for Christ's role in Hebrews. He is the one who enables the people of God to enter their inheritance and thus reach their destiny. As we will see below, Moses may have played an important part in the household of God, but he was but a member of the household that God's Son "established."

"Consider" him in all his "glory." Adore "the Apostle and High Priest whom we confess, Jesus," who is seated at God's right hand.

∾ Day Two: A Son, a Steward, and the House of God. (Heb 3:1–6)

[1] *Therefore, holy brothers and sisters, partakers of the heavenly calling, consider the Apostle and High Priest of our confession,*

Jesus, [2] as one faithful to the one who appointed him, just as Moses also was faithful in all his house. [3] For this one has been considered worthy of more glory than Moses to as great a degree as the one who establishes a house has more honor than the house. [4] For every house is established by someone, but the one establishing all things is God. [5] And on one hand Moses was faithful in all his House as a steward for a witness of things yet to be spoken, [6] but Christ as a Son over his House, whose House we are if we hold fast our boldness and our boasting in hope.

Yesterday we focused on the first three verses of this passage. The pastor began to show us the relationships between Moses, Jesus, and the people of God, whom he referred to, in the language of Num 12:7, as God's "House." Both Moses and Jesus were faithful as mediators of God's word to his people. Jesus, however, "the Apostle and High Priest of our confession," was considered worthy of "more glory than Moses" because he was the very "radiance of the glory of God." He is the one who "established" God's people by cleansing them from sin and enabling them to enter their inheritance and God-intended destiny. Moses, on the other hand, was a member of the people of God whom Jesus thus "established."

Verses 4–6 bring greater clarity to the relationship between "this one" and Moses by affirming that the one is "Son" over God's House while the other was a "Steward" within God's House. They also make it plain that we who are "holy brothers and sisters, partakers of the heavenly calling" are the heirs of those addressed by Moses and, with them, constitute the one people of God.

Verse 4. This verse has puzzled many Bible readers. Taken by itself, it is a mere truism: "For every house is established by someone, but the one establishing all things is God." Of course, every house has been completed by someone. From beginning to end the Bible asserts that "the one establishing all things is God." However, taken within its context here in Hebrews, this verse becomes very significant. The first clause, "For every house is established by someone" lays the groundwork for the second and crucial clause: "but the one establishing all things is God."

How might the writer of Hebrews have intended us to understand "the one establishing all things"? We have just been told that "the Apostle and High Priest of our confession," has established the "House" (people) of God. In Heb 1:10–12 the pastor asserted that this same person is the Creator of everything and the one who brings the creation to its destiny. If we have interpreted Heb 1:3 correctly, it is by accomplishing the salvation of the people of God that he brings the creation to its "intended end." Thus, "the one establishing all things" is a reference to the Son of God, who not only created the universe, but brings it to its intended end by ushering the people of God into their inheritance. The pastor, then, is not affirming a truism. He is saying that the Son who "established all things" is God. He is affirming the Son's deity in anticipation of the contrast between Moses as "Steward" and the Son as "Son" in verses 5 and 6. At the same time, he reserves the word "Son" for the climax of this contrast in verse 6.

Verses 5–6a. No one in the Old Testament was greater than Moses. He "was faithful in all his [God's] House as a steward for a witness of things yet to be spoken." In Num 7:12 God himself affirmed that Moses his servant or steward was "faithful in all my House." The word "steward," which the pastor takes from the Greek translation of Num 7:12, is an accurate description of Moses' place. No other servant of God is to be compared with Moses as the "Steward" in charge of God's entire household. In Num 12 God also affirmed that Moses was the only one with whom he spoke "face to face." Thus, it is not surprising that the pastor interprets Moses' faithfulness as "Steward" in terms of the reliability of God's revelation through him as a faithful "witness of things yet to be spoken."

Christ, however, was faithful not as a "steward," but "as a Son"; and not "in," but "over" God's "house," The pastor has told us that Moses was faithful as "a witnesses," but he has not disclosed the nature of the Son's faithfulness. Heb 4:14—10:25 clarifies both the content of Moses' witness and the character of the Son's faithfulness. By establishing the Sinai covenant, priesthood, and sacrifice Moses was, a *faithful* witness to what God has now spoken and accomplished through the *faithful* obedience of his incarnate Son, who has become our merciful and *faithful* High Priest at God's right hand.

The Sinai system established by Moses was, then, inadequate as a means of salvation. Any attempt to perpetuate it would be a denial of fulfillment in the Son. But, as God's word, it was and is an indispensable "witness" to the Son as all-sufficient sacrifice (Heb 9:14), heavenly High Priest (Heb 8:1–2), and Guarantor of the New Covenant (Heb 7:22). Without that "witness" the death and resurrection of Jesus would have no discernable meaning for the people of God.

Verse 6b: "Whose House we are" reminds us of our privileged place. As the Son's "brothers and sisters, partakers of the heavenly calling," we are, with God's people of old, members of this blessed household. There is only one household in which Moses served as "Steward" and over which the Son reigns as "Son." This household is also united by the fact that God's revelation in his Son fulfills the Sinai revelation. The members of this household reach their eternal destiny through the Son, whether they lived before or after he assumed our humanity (Heb 11:39–40, 12:22–24). Since, then, there is one household of God throughout time, the pastor is going to use the disobedience of the wilderness generation (Heb 3:7—4:13) as a dire warning of impending loss. This warning is, if possible, more urgent for those of us who come after Christ because we enjoy the "great salvation" (Heb 2:3) that he has provided.

In Heb 2:1–4 the pastor warned us lest we "drift away" through "neglect." Now he urges us to continue as the people of God by holding "fast our boldness and our boasting in hope." The pastor is going to explain how through Christ the faithful have been given "boldness" to enter God's presence in order to receive the grace necessary for perseverance (Heb 4:14–16, 10:19–25). "This 'boldness' is not a mere feeling but the right or privilege of access to God provided and validated by Christ's high priesthood as described in Heb 8:1—10:18."[1] The grace thus received enables us to boldly persevere in the profession of our faith despite the opposition of the world around us and to "boast" in the "hope" of the future that will be ours at Christ's return (see Heb 9:27–29, 12:25–29). The faith that perseveres is no timid affirmation. It is courageous living in the reality of present grace and by the certainty of future hope. The pastor's overriding concern is that we will persevere in this life of faithfulness.

∾ Day Three: Shun the Company of the Disobedient Wilderness Generation. (Heb 3:7–19)

> [7] *Therefore, as the Holy Spirit says: "Today if you hear his voice,* [8] *do not harden your hearts as in the rebellion according to the day of testing in the wilderness,* [9] *where your fathers tested me with proving and saw my works* [10] *for forty years. Therefore, I was angry with this generation and said: they always go astray in heart, and they have not known my ways,* [11] *as I swore in my anger: 'they shall never enter my rest.'"*
>
> [12] *Be alert, brothers and sisters, lest there be in any of you an evil heart of unbelief through turning away from the living God,* [13] *but exhort one another day by day, while it is called 'today,' so that none of you might be hardened by the deceit of sin—*[14] *for we have become participants in Christ, if we hold the beginning of our steadfastness firm until the end—*[15] *while it is said: "Today if you hear his voice, do not harden your hearts as in the rebellion."* [16] *Now who, although they had heard, rebelled? Was it not all those who came out of Egypt through Moses?* [17] *And with whom was he "angry for forty years"? Was it not those who sinned? Whose corpses fell in the desert?* [18] *And concerning whom did he "swear*

1. Cockerill, *Hebrews*, 173.

that they shall never enter into" his "rest," if not those who dis-obeyed? [19] Thus we see that they were unable to enter in because of unbelief.

God's Sinai revelation mediated through his "Steward" Moses was a "witness" to God's ultimate self-revelation in his Son. The one people of God throughout history (God's "House"), then, consists of both those who received God's Old Testament revelation and those who have embraced its fulfillment in the Son. Sinai was an ever-present reality to all the succeeding generations of God's people (see Deut 5:1–4). Through the eternal, incarnate, exalted Son at God's right hand the ever-present word of God addresses God's people with heightened intensity. In particular, God's Old Testament warnings against faithlessness, far from becoming obsolete, receive new urgency.

It was natural, then, for the pastor to move from the faithfulness of Moses in Num 12:7 (Heb 3:5) to the faithless wilderness generation in Num 13:1—14:45. On the Plains of Moab Moses had cautioned the children of that generation lest they follow their parents' example of apostasy (Deut 1:35, cf. Num 32:13). The author of Ps 95:7–11 confirmed that wilderness generation as the quintessential example of apostasy for succeeding generations of the people of God.

The pastor uses this faithless wilderness generation as an example by quoting Ps 95:7–11 in verses 7–11. That generation is a picture of the judgment anticipated by the pastor's question in Heb 2:1–4: "How shall we escape if we neglect such a great salvation?" In verses 12–14 the pastor focuses on "Today" and "do not harden your heart." Then, in verses 15–19 he recites again the warning with which the psalm began and focuses on its final, ominous word—"rebellion."

Verses 7–11. The pastor introduces the quotation of this psalm with "the Holy Spirit says." The Holy Spirit who inspired Scripture directs its words to the people of God with conviction. The psalm begins with an urgent invitation, "Today, if you hear his voice," but ends with a sentence of judgment on those who refuse the invitation: "'they shall never enter my rest.'"

Compare verse 8 with the TNIV of Ps 95:8: "Do not harden your hearts as you did at *Meribah*, as you did that day at *Massah* in the wilderness" (italics added). The pastor quotes the Greek Old Testament that translated the place names "Meribah" and "Massah" according to their meaning, "rebellion" and "testing" (see the NIV footnotes on Ps 95:8, which translate these words as "quarreling" and "testing"). The Greek translators made a good choice. This psalm focuses on the wilderness generation's rebellion at Kadesh

Barnea in Num 13:1—14:45, not on the events that took place at "Meribah" and "Massah" in Exod 17:1–7. That generation's entire time in the wilderness was a time of "rebellion" and of "testing" God by their disobedience. Their "testing" God climaxed with the ultimate "rebellion" when they refused to trust God and enter the promised land at Kadesh Barnea.

Both the Greek and Hebrew versions of this psalm omit the "therefore" from verse 10 and join the "for forty years" with what follows: "For forty years I was angry with this generation." The addition of "therefore" does two things. First, it joins the "for forty years" with what has gone before: "your fathers tested me with proving and saw my works for forty years." Instead of the forty years of wandering that followed Kadesh Barnea being described as the time of God's anger, it is now described as a time of continued disobedience. There was no true repentance after the rebellion at Kadesh Barnea. Second, the "therefore" makes it clear that the rebellion of the people was the cause of God's anger and resulting judgment.

Verses 12–14. The pastor explains what the psalmist meant when he said that the wilderness generation always "went astray *in heart*" (Italics added). Their heart was "evil" because of "unbelief." With many signs and wonders God had delivered them from Egypt, revealed himself to them at Sinai, and protected and sustained them on their journey to the promised land of Canaan. Now, the time has come. They are at Kadesh Barnea on the very border of that land, ready to enter. Throughout this journey they have often failed to trust in God's promises and power to fulfill those promises. What will they do now? At this, the climax of their journey, despite having witnessed the many demonstrations of God's power, they flatly *refused* to trust God. They refused to believe that God had the power to overcome the Canaanites and thus that he would keep his promise of giving them the land. They wanted to choose their own leader and go back to Egypt. They had, indeed, "turned away from the *living* God" (Italics added) by acting as if he were dead—powerless and undependable.

Sin produces such an "evil heart" by deceit. Sin focuses our eyes on the world around us and causes us to doubt the reality of God. All the wilderness generation could see was the might of the Canaanites. Moses, on the other hand, "endured as seeing the Unseen One" (Heb 11:25). The pastor wants us to keep our eyes ever on the eternal, incarnate Son of God seated at God's right hand as our High Priest (Heb 3:1; 12:1–3). Thus, the pastor urges us to exhort and warn each other daily lest such an "evil heart" arise during the "today" of opportunity. He is aware that the evil report of ten spies led the whole congregation of God's people astray at Kadesh Barnea. Neglect and gradual drift can lead to turning away "from the living God."

The antidote is "true hearts in fullness of faith" (Heb 10:22) upon which God's laws have been inscribed (Heb 10:16).

The pastor concludes this section by reminding his hearers, the "holy brothers and sisters" of the Son, that they have become "participants in Christ" with all the privileges that entails. This privileged relationship, however, will be of no avail unless they maintain the steadfast life of faith in God's promises and power with which they began their journey.

Verses 15–18. The pastor reinforces what he has said by reintroducing the urgent exhortation with which the psalm began and then by focusing on the gravity of its final word—"rebellion": "Today if you hear his voice, do not harden your hearts as in the *rebellion*" (Italics added). He drives his message home with a series of questions underscoring the identity and accountability of those who rebelled, the seriousness of their sin, and the dire consequences of their disobedience. Those who rebelled were none other than the people whom God delivered from Egypt "through Moses" and who "heard" God speak at Sinai. Although they had experienced God's grace in such powerful ways, they definitively refused to trust him, "disobeyed" him, and decided to do things their own way. That is what made their sin "rebellion." Because of their rebellion God "swore that they would not enter into" his "rest." What they suffered as a result of this rebellion under the divine oath was terrible, but not as bad as what they lost! They suffered God's wrath for the remaining forty years of their lives and their "corpses" fell unattended in the desert, but they lost the blessing for which God had redeemed them from Egypt!

Verse 19. The pastor brings his message home by putting it in one word: "they were unable to enter in because of *unbelief*" (Italics added). "Unbelief" is not merely the denial of certain propositions, but the failure to trust in the power and promises of God and to live accordingly. "Unbelief" always involves disobedience because "unbelief" and unfaithfulness are inseparable—as are their opposites, faith and faithfulness. The pastor would turn us away from such unbelief/unfaithfulness by showing us its dire results. He has painted this picture of the wilderness generation as preparation for renewed warnings in Heb 6:4–8. Notice that in this final verse of chapter three the pastor gives no name to the destiny that "they were unable to enter." In Heb 4:1–11 he will show that the "rest" they forfeited was far more than real estate in Canaan and thus worthy of our utmost pursuit.

❧ Day Four: Pursue, by Faith, the Promised "Rest." (Heb 4:1–11)

¹ *Therefore let us fear, since a promise remains of entering his rest, lest any of you should be found to have fallen short.* ² *For we also have had good news proclaimed to us just as they, but the word that they heard did not profit them because they had not joined themselves to those who heard with faith.* ³ *For we are in the process of entering this rest, we who have believed.* ⁴ *As he has said, "As I swore in my wrath, they shall never enter into my rest," although his works had been completed since the foundation of the world. For he has spoken somewhere concerning the seventh day thus, "And God rested on the seventh day from all his works."* ⁵ *And in regard to this again, "They shall never enter into my rest."* ⁶ *Because, therefore, it was necessary for some to enter into it, and those who first had the good news proclaimed to them did not enter through disobedience,* ⁷ *he again designated a certain day as "today." He made this designation by speaking through David after so long a time, as it has already been said: "Today if you hear his voice, do not harden your hearts."* ⁸ *For if Joshua had given them rest, he would not have spoken after these things concerning another day.* ⁹ *Therefore a Sabbath rest remains for the people of God.* ¹⁰ *For the one who enters into his rest has himself rested from his works just as God rested from his.* ¹¹ *Let us be diligent, then, to enter into this rest, lest anyone fall by the same example of disobedience.*

Verse 1. In Heb 3:1–19, as we have seen, the pastor warned us against falling into the "unbelief" of the wilderness generation. He focused our attention on the tragedy of their "rebellion" motivated by "an evil heart of unbelief." In Heb 4:1–11 he reinforces his warning by turning our attention to the magnitude of the "rest" that they forfeited. The exhortations with which he begins in verse 1 and ends in verse 11 remind us that the magnitude of the reward only adds urgency to the tragedy of loss. In verses 2–10 the pastor substantiates the premise of verse 1, "a promise remains of entering his rest," by demonstrating the continuing availability and nature of this "rest." This premise is the essential foundation for his exhortations to "fear . . . lest any of you should be found to have fallen short" (v. 1) and, finally, to "be diligent . . . to enter into this rest" (v. 11).

    Verses 2–3. "For we also have had good news proclaimed to us just as they": once again the pastor asserts the unity of we who have received God's word in the Son with those who stood before Sinai—we both belong to the one people of God. The "good news" that God has now spoken in his Son is the fulfillment of the "good news" revealed to that earlier generation at Sinai (see on Heb 3:5 above). We, of course, enjoy the benefits brought by our "Great High Priest" (Heb 4:14) which they could only anticipate. However, at this point in the pastor's argument, the essential distinction between us is not our place in salvation history but our response to the promise of God. He describes that generation by saying, "the word that they heard did not profit them because they had not joined themselves to those who heard with faith." They did not join themselves to Joshua and Caleb who believed in both the promise and power of God to give them Canaan. They distanced themselves from the company of people described in chapter 11 who lived "by faith" in God's promises and power. True faith involves identification with the people of God. We, however, are "those who have believed." We have the privilege of trusting in the promises and power of God guaranteed and made available through his Son. The pastor is urging us to persevere *because* "we are in the process of entering this rest" from which they have been excluded due to "unbelief" (Heb 3:19).

Verses 4–5. The pastor can describe the faithful as "in the process of entering this rest" because "a promise remains of entering his rest" (v. 1). In verses 4–10 the pastor uses Scripture to support the continuing validity of this promise and to clarify the nature of the "rest" that has been promised. First, he cites the necessary Scriptures in verses 4–5, explains them in verses 6–9, draws conclusions in verses 9–10, and applies them in the exhortation of verse 11.

The last phrase of Ps 95:11 is the pastor's primary Scripture, cited at the beginning of verse 4 and again at the end of verse 5: "they shall never enter into my rest." The natural place to discover what the psalmist meant by "*my* (*God's*) rest" would be Gen 2:2: "And *God rested* on the seventh day from all his works" (Italics added). And so the pastor quotes this verse in the first part of verse 5. The "rest" of the psalm, which God invited his people to enjoy, was the eternal "rest" that he entered at the culmination of creation on the "seventh day." Clearly, then, he established this "rest" with the intention that his people would share it.

Verses 6–10. Let's follow the logic of the pastor's interpretation. His major premise is that God established this rest with the purpose that his people would share it with him. His minor premise is "those who first had the good news proclaimed to them did not enter through disobedience." He draws this conclusion: "therefore it was necessary for some to enter it." And so, God through the Holy Spirit (Heb 3:7) "designated another day" of opportunity when he inspired David to write this psalm urging the succeeding generations of God's people not to "harden" their "hearts" but to "hear" God's "voice" and persevere until they should "enter" God's "rest." For those of us who come after Christ, this "today" is indeed the "today" of great privilege established by the Son's taking his seat at God's right hand (Heb 1:5).

In verse 8 the pastor anticipates a possible objection in the minds of his readers: "But we thought that Joshua gave them 'rest' when he brought them into the promised land?" The pastor deals with this objection in a summary but adequate manner. He will not be diverted from pressing home the urgency of perseverance by an extended discussion of the Promised Land as a type or picture of God's eternal "rest." The fact that God issued this Ps 95 invitation to enter his rest by David long after Joshua was decisive. The "rest" involved could not have been mere real estate in Canaan.

And so, a "Sabbath rest remains for the people of God." Heb 12:22–24 gives us a tantalizing glimpse of what this grand "Sabbath rest," established by God on the seventh day of the creation week, might look like. The eternal destiny that God has for his people both transcends creation and is creation's goal. God established and entered into that "rest" after completing the "works" of creation. We, according to verse 10, enter it when we have completed the "works" of this life by persevering in faith, whatever the difficulties we must endure.

Verse 11. The pastor concludes by asserting that the surpassing worth of this "rest" warrants all diligence to enter it. He reinforces this exhortation by recalling once again the tragedy of the wilderness generation from Heb 3:1–19: "lest anyone fall by the same example of disobedience." The cause of their tragedy can be described as both "unbelief" (Heb 3:19) and "disobedience." As noted above, "unbelief" is also "unfaithfulness." On the other hand, "disobedience" is crystalized "unbelief." "Unbelief" and "disobedience" are two sides of the same coin. We cannot have one without the other.

The pastor arouses us to renewed diligence through both hope and appropriate fear by showing us the tragic end of those who through careless "drifting" and "neglect" (see Heb 2:1–4) abandoned their trust in God. Do not let adversity deter you from the way of faith so that you turn away from the "living God" in disobedience.

❧ Day Five: Exposed before the Living Word of God. (Heb 4:12–13)

> [12] *For the word of God is living and active; sharper than any two-edged sword; penetrating until it divides life and spirit, even joints and marrow; and judging the thoughts and intentions of the heart.* [13] *And no created thing is hidden before him, but all things are naked and prostrate to the eyes of him to whom we must give account.*

This first grand section of Hebrews (Heb 1:1—4:13) began with the declaration that the God who spoke through the "prophets" has now spoken in "one who is Son" (Heb 1:1–4). It concludes appropriately in these verses with a reminder of our accountability before the all-penetrating word that God has spoken.

The pastor has carefully prepared us for this warning. First, he announced that God has spoken "in these last days" by providing "such a great salvation" through the obedient suffering, death, and exaltation of his eternal Son (Heb 1:1–14; 2:5–18). Then he warned us by comparing the consequences of neglecting this "great salvation" with the consequences of rejecting God's earlier revelation at Sinai. If the consequences for rejecting what God spoke at Sinai were certain, then the consequences for neglecting this final revelation in the Son are tragically more certain in proportion to the greatness of this salvation (Heb 2:1–4)! The pastor reinforces this warning by describing the fate suffered by the disobedient "wilderness generation" who stood before Sinai (Heb 3:1—4:11). Together we and they are the one people of God (Heb 3:1–6). Avoid the fate they suffered (Heb 3:7–19) and pursue the "rest" they forfeited (Heb 4:1–11) for you are inescapably accountable before the word of God (Heb 3:12–13).

Verse 12. The Greek sentence emphasizes the word "living." The true and "living God" (Heb 3:12; 9:14; 10:21) speaks a "living" word. He fulfills all that he has said in the prophets by speaking to us "today" in "one who is Son" and urging us "do not harden your hearts." Thus, this "living" word is not a passive word that can be ignored without consequence. The fate of the wilderness generation (Heb 3:7—4:11) is evidence that God's word is "active"—it always accomplishes his purpose. This "sharper," "penetrating" word is ultimately "discerning." When God reveals himself he also exposes the depths of the human heart.

The pastor begins with a visceral description: "sharper than any two–edged sword; penetrating until it divides life and spirit, even joints and marrow." He wants us to feel in our bodies the intrusive power of God's word. It is so much "sharper than any two–edged sword" that it penetrates until it divides what cannot be divided. How can one divide "life" from "spirit" or "joints and marrow"? Bone "marrow" suggests the innermost secret sanctum of the human person. God's word is such an invasive surgical procedure that it exposes that inner sanctum with perfect accuracy, for it "judges the thoughts and intentions of the heart." "Thoughts and intentions" is a comprehensive expression that includes all human motives and plans to achieve the goals of those motives.

How does God's word "judge," "discern," or expose the hearts true "thoughts and intentions" with all their rationalization and self-justification? Let's have a look at the wilderness generation. How did God's word expose their "evil heart of unbelief" (3:12)? By calling them to "hear" with faith and obedience. When we truly "hear" the word of God it *always* confronts us with an *unavoidable* decision. Will we "hear" with faith and obedience, or with unbelief and disobedience? Will we act as if God's promise of entering his "Sabbath rest" is certain and his grace is sufficient for us to persevere until that day? Or will we act as if he was unfaithful and impotent, thus denying that he is the "living God"? God's word elicits our response, and then pronounces judgment upon it. His ruling is either "they shall never enter into my rest" (Heb 3:11, 19; 4:4–5) or "a Sabbath rest remains for the people of God" (Heb 4:9).

Verse 13. God's word, then, makes what is in the heart public by requiring a response. There is no question about God's judgment, or appeal from his verdict, because his knowledge is accurate. The pastor underscores this sobering truth by focusing on God's role as Creator and ultimate Judge of the universe. "No created thing is hidden" before the Creator of all things (Heb 1:2, 11–13; 11:1–3). Furthermore, "all things are naked and prostrate to the eyes of him to whom we must give account." "To whom we must give account" translates a Greek idiom, which we might render literally as "to whom in relation to us a word." We cannot avoid giving a "word" of account to the "word" that God has spoken in his Son. "Today, if you hear his voice . . ."

The pastor, who began by telling us that God's penetrating word was "sharper than a two–edged sword," continues his appeal to our physical senses. "All things" are like a naked body lying flat on the ground with head pulled back and throat exposed before the very "eyes" of the person to whom we owe ultimate accountability. The pastor thus concludes by focusing everything that he has said in this first major section of Hebrews, 1:1—4:13, on our inescapable responsibility before the living God. He has pressed us with the dire seriousness of our situation so that we will gladly embrace our "Great High Priest" (Heb 4:14) whose complete sufficiency for our need as the "Source of eternal salvation" (Heb 5:9) he will eloquently portray in the next major section of his sermon, Heb 4:14—10:25. Don't stop reading here!

∾ Day Six: Our "Great High Priest." (Heb 4:14–16)

[14] *Therefore, because we have a Great High Priest who has gone through the heavens, Jesus the Son of God, let us hold firmly to our confession.* [15] *For we do not have a high priest who is unable to sympathize with our weaknesses, but we have one who has been tempted in every way, just as we are, yet without sin.* [16] *Therefore,*

let us approach the throne of grace with confidence, so that we
may receive mercy and find grace to help us in time of need.

Heb 4:14–16 parallels 10:19–25. The former introduces the description of the magnitude and benefits of the Son's high priesthood in Heb 5:1—10:18 as the means of avoiding the fate of the faithless wilderness generation (Heb 3:7—4:13). The latter is a glorious summary of Heb 5:1—10:18 as means and motivation for joining the faithful of Heb 11:1–40.

The pastor reintroduces the subject of priesthood with a concise, two-part description. Verse 14 is part one, followed by part two in verses 15–16. Each part begins with a statement about the High Priest that "we have" (vv. 14a, 15), followed by an exhortation to take advantage of the benefits he provides (vv. 14b, 16). The first part (v. 14) builds on Heb 1:1–14 by focusing on the greatness of our High Priest as the exalted Son at God's right hand. The second, recalls Heb 2:4–18 by focusing on the obedience of the incarnate Son of God, "Jesus."

Verse 14. Heb 3:1—4:13 has shown the urgent need for perseverance. The "therefore" with which this verse begins reintroduces the Son as High Priest, whom we first met in Heb 2:16—3:1, as the answer to this need.

The first half of this verse affirms that "we," the faithful people of God, "have" in the present, a "Great High Priest." The Hebrew expression "high priest" could be translated into Greek either as "high priest" or "great priest."[2] The pastor uses this expanded term, "Great High Priest," to underscore the unprecedented greatness and all-sufficiency of the priest "who has gone through the heavens, Jesus, the Son of God."

This comprehensive but concise sketch is crafted to impress the pastor's hearers with this "Great High Priest's" exceeding greatness. This sketch is comprehensive because it includes the Son's exaltation ("has passed through the heavens"), incarnation ("Jesus"), and eternal deity ("Son of God"). Yet by giving "has passed through the heavens" and "the Son of God" the first and last emphatic positions, this description focuses our attention on the eternal exalted Son *of God* seated at God's right hand. The pastor is building on what he said about the Son's exaltation and eternal Sonship in Heb 1:1–14. He will show the significance of exaltation and eternal Sonship for priesthood in Heb 7:1–28. At this point, however, there is no better way to emphasize the *greatness* of this High Priest as motivation for holding "firmly to our confession" (v. 14b) than by drawing our attention to the eternal exalted One.

---

2. "High priest" (literally "archpriest") is the more common translation in Hebrews, but "Great Priest" is a more literal rendering of the Hebrew.

The wilderness generation failed to enter God's "rest" because they did not "hold fast" to their "confession" that God's promise of entrance was certain and his power to fulfill his promise was real. Since, however, we have this "Great High Priest," the pastor urges us to persevere in faithful obedience by maintaining our firm commitment to and public proclamation of his trustworthiness and power. The grand presentation of Christ's high priesthood that follows (Heb 5:1—10:18) is meant to fortify us in perseverance by expounding the meaning and significance of our "confession" of him as all-sufficient High Priest at God's right hand.

The pastor always wants to keep our eyes fixed on the one "who has gone through the heavens" (Heb 1:14; 3:1; 7:26; 8:1; 12:1–3). The Son of God who has accomplished our salvation and permanently taken his seat at God's right hand is the only one able to meet our need. Yet the pastor will never let us forget that this one at God's right hand is "Jesus." He has accomplished our salvation only through his human obedience. While the humiliation of the Son of God might not be as immediately impressive as his deity and exaltation, it is perhaps the most amazing ingredient of our High Priest's adequacy as the one and only "Source of eternal salvation" (Heb 5:9).

Verse 15. Thus, in verses 15–16 the pastor turns to the significance of "Jesus," the incarnate Son of God. As verse 14 built on what the pastor had already said about the eternal, exalted Son in Heb 1:1–14, so verses 15–16 build on what he has said about the incarnate Son, Jesus, in Heb 2:5–18. The pastor will elaborate on the significance of the Son's incarnate obedience for his high priesthood in Heb 8:1—10:18.

As noted above, the pastor's immediate purpose for describing the glory of the exalted, eternal Son in verse 14 was to emphasize the Son's greatness as motivation for perseverance. His immediate purpose for describing the obedient, incarnate Son of God is to demonstrate that he is the source of *mercy and grace* that will enable us to persevere by holding firm to our confession (note the "for" at the beginning of verse 15). The pastor wants us to know that the God before whom, according to Heb 4:12–13, we are exposed and accountable, has mercifully and generously provided the grace necessary for perseverance in faithful obedience.

The contrast in verse 15a between the high priest that we "do not have" and the one that we "have" leaves the reality and significance of the incarnation beyond doubt. "For we do not have a high priest" like the Aaronic high priest (Heb 5:2) "who is unable to sympathize with our weaknesses." The pastor means more than the normal understanding of "sympathize." This High Priest can actually *help* us in our "weaknesses." "Weaknesses" encompasses everything about our broken human condition that makes us subject to sin. Our High Priest can provide this aid because he assumed our humanity with its "weaknesses" and faced all the kinds of temptations that we face, whether they come from fear of persecution or desire for illicit pleasure. He can do this because, unlike the Aaronic high priest, he was not "*beset* with weakness" (Heb 5:2 again!). He did not yield to sin!

The pastor knows that reintroducing the subject of high priesthood from Heb 2:16–18 only makes his hearers more anxious to raise several questions: "How does the Son's high priesthood fit in with the Aaronic high priesthood established by Moses at Sinai? What Scriptural proof do you have that the Son has replaced the Aaronic high priesthood?" He will provide an initial answer in Heb 5:1–10 by giving Scriptural proof and outlining how the old priesthood typified, but the Son fulfilled, the essentials of effective high priesthood. Then follows a lengthy exhortation to gain their full attention (Heb 5:11—6:20). After obtaining their attention, he will explain in detail, on the basis of the Old Testament, how the Son's eternal deity/exaltation (Heb 7:1–28, building on 1:1–14; 4:14), and incarnate obedience (Heb 8:1—10:18 building on 2:5–18; 4:15–16) have made him the all-sufficient High Priest.

The pastor, however, cannot wait to impress upon his hearers the benefits of the Son as High Priest. By his obedience the incarnate Son has turned God's throne into a "throne of grace," a true "mercy seat." Thus, he has authorized us to draw near in order to find the "mercy" of cleansing from sin and the "grace" for victory over temptation *whenever we need it.*

ꙮ Day Seven: Priesthood Old and New. (Heb 5:1–10)

¹ *For every high priest taken from among human beings is appointed for human beings in things pertaining to God, in order that he might offer gifts and also sacrifices for sin.* ² *He is able to deal gently with those who are ignorant and going astray because he himself is also beset with weakness.* ³ *Because of this he must offer for sins on his own behalf as well as on behalf of the people.* ⁴ *And no one takes this honor for himself but is called by God just as also Aaron was called.*

⁵ *Thus also Christ did not glorify himself to become High Priest, but the one who said to him, "You are my Son, today have I begotten you,"* ⁶ *also spoke thus in another place, "You are a priest forever according to the order of Melchizedek."*

⁷ *In the days of his flesh he offered both prayers and petitions to the one who was able to save him out of death with loud cries and tears, and he was heard because of his godly fear.* ⁸ *Although being One who is Son, he learned obedience through what he*

> *suffered.* ⁹ *And having been perfected, he became to all who obey*
> *him the Source of eternal salvation,* ¹⁰ *having been designated by*
> *God High Priest according to the order of Melchizedek.*

Heb 5:1–10 presents Aaron as a type of the one who is "High Priest forever according to the order of Melchizedek" (Heb 5:10). Verses 1–4 show how, as type of the one to come, Aaron exhibits, but fails to fulfill, the four essentials of high priesthood. Verses 5–10 show how the Son, as "priest according to the order of Melchizedek," not only exhibits, but also fulfills to the fullest extent every requirement and thus becomes "the Source of eternal salvation" (v. 9). The pastor begins and concludes his description of the Son's high priesthood in Heb 5:5–10 with its long–awaited Scriptural foundation from Ps 110:4.

Verse 1. The pastor uses the general description "every high priest" in order to introduce the four essential characteristics of high priesthood: *humanity* ("taken from among human beings), divine *appointment* ("appointed"), effective *ministry* ("for human beings in things pertaining to God"), and *sacrifice* for sin ("in order that he might offer gifts and sacrifices for sin"). In verses 5–10 he will describe the Son's supreme fulfillment of these requirements.

Nevertheless, by the time we get to "Aaron" in verse 4 we realize that the pastor has had him in mind from the beginning. This description already contains the seeds of the old priesthood's ineffectiveness. "Aaron" was only "taken from among human beings" and had to offer repeated "gifts and sacrifices." By assuming our humanity the Son infused his priesthood with divine power (Heb 7:16) and offered a single all-sufficient sacrifice (Heb 7:27; 9:25–28; 10:11–14). The pastor proceeds to affirm that the old high priesthood's *ministry* was ineffective (v. 2a), because of his sinful *humanity* (v. 2b), as evidenced by the twofold nature of his *sacrifice* (v. 3).

Verse 2–3. The old high priest's *ministry* (v. 2a) was ineffective. Unlike the Son of God (Heb 4:15), he could offer no real help. He could do no more than "deal gently" with the people of God, here described as "those who are ignorant and going astray." This description reminds us of the recalcitrant wilderness generation about whom God said "They always go astray in heart, and they have not known my ways" (Heb 3:10). The old high priest could do little more than acknowledge that it was difficult not to sin and urge them to try to do better. His ministry was thus limited because his *humanity* (v. 2b) was "beset with weakness." As noted when commenting on Heb 4:15 above, "weakness" denotes everything about fallen humanity that makes us subject to sin. The Son assumed our humanity with its "weaknesses" but never yielded to sin. The old high priest's humanity, however, was determined by this "weakness" and therefore sinful. His sinful humanity, and thus the ineffectiveness of his ministry, is proven by the fact that he had to offer *sacrifice* (v. 3) "on his *own* behalf" (italics added) as well as for the people.

In some contexts the word translated "beset" can mean "clothed." Sirach, a popular work written in the second century before Christ, depicted the high priest in all his splendor as he prepared to enter the Most Holy Place (Sir 45:6–7). We might think of Hebrews as picturing him clothed with "weakness," subjected to sin, and therefore unable to enter God's eternal presence.

Verse 4. Aaron, as legitimate high priest, did have a divine appointment. The inferiority of his appointment only becomes clear when compared with the Father's summons for the Son to assume his place as High Priest at God's right hand in verses 5–6.

Let's summarize this description of Aaron as type in verses 1–4: the old high priest had an ineffective *ministry* (v. 2a) because of his sinful *humanity* (v. 2b) as demonstrated by his need to offer *sacrifice* for his own sin (v. 3), even though he had been *appointed* by God (v. 4).

Now let's preview the Son's fulfillment of this type as described in verses 5–10: God's *appointment* of the eternal Son as High Priest (vv. 5–6), enabled him to offer himself as a fully sufficient *sacrifice* (v. 7), because of his perfectly obedient *humanity* (v. 8), and thus obtain a fully effective *ministry* (v. 9).

Verses 5–6. By returning to Ps 2:7 (Heb 1:5), "You are my Son, today have I begotten you," the pastor recalls the Father's address to the Son in Heb 1:1–14. Then he adds Ps 110:4 to show that God's *appointment* of the Son as High Priest is an integral part of that address. The God who publicly proclaims his Sonship with Ps 2:7 at the occasion of his exaltation, and invites him to take his seat at God's right hand with Ps 110:1, uses Ps 110:4 to appoint him "a priest forever according to the order of Melchizedek." As Heb 7:1–28 will make clear, the Son's eternal Sonship (v. 15; Ps 2:7) is the foundation of the all-sufficiency of this Priest, seated at God's right hand "according to the order of Melchizedek" (Heb 7:15; Ps 110:4).

Verse 7. The pastor begins his discussion of the Son's *sacrifice* by contrasting his assumption of the frail mortality ("In the days of his flesh") shared by all humanity (Heb 2:13–15), with the God "who was able to save him out of death." His offering "both prayers and petitions . . . with loud cries and tears" depicts this utter dependence on the God "who was able to save him out of death." His offering was a life of such faithful reliance upon God, culminating with his prayer of obedience in the garden and then offered to God on the cross (Heb 10:5–10). Abraham was able to sacrifice

Isaac because he believed in a God who "was able to raise from the dead" (Heb 11:19). The Son was able to offer himself because he relied on a God who "was able to save him out of death." The pastor describes this obedient reliance as "godly fear." The incarnate Son's actions fully demonstrated his absolute trust in the promises and power of the "living God." Because of his obedience "he was heard"—his sacrifice was accepted by God as completely sufficient and effective.

Verse 8. The Old Testament high priest's sacrifice (v. 2b) confirmed the sinfulness of his humanity (v. 3). However, the Son's obedient *humanity*, described here in verse 8, assured the effectiveness of his sacrifice (v. 7). What is the pastor's point in saying "although being One who is Son"? At the very least he makes it clear that we cannot separate the Son's humanity from his deity. As shocking and wonderful as it may seem, the one who "learned obedience through what he suffered" ("in the days of his flesh") is the one the pastor described in Heb 1:1–14 as Son, God, Creator, Judge of Creation, and Lord seated at the Father's right hand. He did not "learn" to be obedient by "suffering" punishment as correction for disobedience. He "learned" what it meant to be a completely obedient human being through life-long obedience despite resistance from the powers of evil, culminating in the cross. Suffering established the quality of his obedience. The pastor passionately desires his hearers' continued obedience despite resistance.

Verse 9. "And having been perfected" describes the result of the Son's absolute obedience despite suffering. By this obedience he has been "perfected" as "the Source of eternal salvation." The eternal Son of God, who was without defect, has become perfectly and completely able to save. His *ministry* is completely effective. The pastor underscores the effectiveness of the "great salvation" of Heb 2:3 by calling it "eternal salvation." In Heb 7:1—10:18 he will describe this salvation as deliverance from sin, access to God, and life in a New Covenant of obedience that will culminate at Christ's return (Heb 9:28) in the "Sabbath rest" (Heb 2:9) of "Mount Zion" (Heb 12:22–24). Through his incarnate obedience the eternal Son has entered into his inheritance at God's right hand (Heb 1:2) as the one and only all-sufficient High Priest and thus the "Source" of eternal salvation to all those who are in union with him through obedience. "Those who obey him" is an invitation to emulate the Son's obedience through availing oneself of the grace the Son provides (see Heb 4:16).

Verse 10. The pastor concludes with a return to the Scriptural warrant for the Son's high priesthood: "having been designated by God High Priest according to the order of Melchizedek." After the exhortation of Heb 5:1—6:20 he will explain the significance of God's *appointing* him "according to the order of Melchizedek in Heb 7:1–28. Then in Heb 8:1—10:18 he will show how his *obedience,* as a *human being* established the effective *ministry* of this High Priest.

Embrace the One Who is Priest "by the Power of An Indestructible Life"

Hebrews 5:11—7:18

Introduction

In Heb 1:3 the pastor affirmed that the Son of God had "made purification for sins." In Heb 2:17–18 he introduced the subject of the Son's high
priesthood. In Heb 4:14–16 he allowed us to taste the benefits of our "Great
High Priest." In Heb 5:1–10 he introduced Ps 110:4 as scriptural substan-
tiation for the Son's priesthood "according to the order of Melchizedek,"
and outlined the typological relationship between Aaron and this "Great
High Priest." We can almost hear the thoughts of his listeners, "Please,
explain how the Son is this 'High Priest forever according to the order of
Melchizedek' (Heb 5:10)!"

The pastor, however, is afraid that his hearers are spiritually unpre-
pared to receive this teaching. He has no interest in speculation—only in
edification. He fears that through "neglect" they have been drifting and become insensitive to the grandeur of "such a great salvation" (Heb 2:1–4). It
is imperative that they grasp what he has to say with both mind and heart if
they are going to persevere. Thus, in Heb 5:11—6:20 he has carefully com-
posed a four–part exhortation to awaken their spiritual sensitivity. After this
necessary preparation, he will return to Ps 110:4 and explain the "Priest
according to the order of Melchizedek" in Heb 7:1–28.

This exhortation in Heb 5:11–6:20 bears all the marks of the pastor's
literary skill and insight into human nature. He begins by rebuking them
for their inexcusable immaturity (Heb 5:11—6:3), and warning them lest it
lead to apostasy (Heb 6:4–8), before reminding them of their past faithfulness (Heb 6:9–12) as motivation to join those who trust in the oath-backed
promise of God (Heb 6:13–20). As usual, the pastor moves them from

negative to positive. He would awaken them from their present immaturity (Heb 5:11—6:3) by reminding them of their past faithfulness (Heb 6:9–12). He rescues them from the peril of apostasy (Heb 6:4–8) by focusing their attention on the promise/oath of God (Heb 6:13–20).

We have the opportunity to prepare our own hearts by listening to this exhortation during the first four days of this week. Then we will be ready, on days five and six, to see how the pastor interprets Ps 110:4 in terms of Abraham's encounter with Melchizedek in Gen 14:17–21. On day seven we will discover that this "priest according to the order of Melchizedek" is, indeed, of a totally different "order," because his priesthood is made effective by "the power of an indestructible life" (Heb 7:16).

∾ Day One: Awaken from Your Inexcusable Immaturity. (Heb 5:11—6:3)

¹¹ Concerning which we have an extensive message, but it is difficult to explain because you have become dull of hearing. ¹² For although you ought to be teachers on account of the time, you again have need of someone to teach you the basic elements of the beginning of the words of God; you have become people who have need of milk rather than solid food. ¹³ For everyone living on milk is unskilled in the word of righteousness, for he is immature. ¹⁴ But solid food is for the mature who on account of their mature state have their senses trained for the discrimination of both what is appropriate and what is evil.

⁶:¹ Therefore let us leave the elementary Christian message and let us press on to maturity, not laying again a foundation of repentance from dead works and faith in God, ² of teaching about washings and laying on of hands, of resurrection of the dead and eternal judgment. ³ And this we will do, if indeed God permits.

The pastor shows the shamefulness of spiritual regression (Heb 5:11–13) as motivation for going on to the "maturity" so necessary for perseverance (Heb 6:1–3). His audience's immaturity is a serious barrier to their embracing what the pastor has to teach about the Son as all-sufficient High Priest (Heb 7:1—10:18). At the same time, proper appropriation of this teaching is what will bring maturity.

Verse 11. The "extensive message" about what it means for the Son to be High Priest "according to the order of Melchizedek" is the heart of the pastor's sermon (Heb 7:1—10:18). God's "message" or "word" always calls for obedient response, just as it did at Sinai (Heb 2:1–4) and in the wilderness (Heb 4:2). However, the pastor fears that his hearers will not understand this "word." Their problem is not intellectual but spiritual. Through neglect of God's "great salvation" they have "become dull of hearing." "Dull of hearing" recalls the wilderness generation's refusal to "hear his voice" (Heb 3:7) as well as many other Scriptural warnings (Isa 6:9–10, Matt 13:13). The pastor is anxious because of the direction their lives appear to have taken: they once were spiritually receptive, but have become and remain "dull of hearing."

Verse 12. The pastor describes the severity of their malaise with emphasis on "again" and "the basic elements of the beginning of the words of God." It is neither necessary nor possible to identify with precision these "basic elements." The pastor's point is that his hearers need to be taught the *most* basic principles of the faith, the very "A, B, C's." And, they need to be taught them *again*. They had been instructed in these things, and they have been believers long enough that they should be teaching others. However, their retrogression is so severe that once *again* they require the most elementary instruction. The pastor helps us to visualize what he is saying by using the contrast between "milk" and "solid food." His hearers are old enough in the faith to be eating the "solid food" of the Son's High Priesthood, but they have regressed to spiritual infancy and need the "milk" of the simplest teaching.

Verses 13–14. The pastor adds color to this metaphor by contrasting the immaturity of those who live on the "milk" of the most elementary truths with the "mature state" of those who live on the "solid food" that the pastor is going to feed them. The immaturity of the first group is described as "unskilled in the word of righteousness." The "mature state" of the second, as having "their senses trained for the discrimination of both what is appropriate and what is evil."

The pastor calls God's revelation in the Son the "word of righteousness" because it enables the faithful to make the choices that are necessary to live a righteous life, that is, to persevere in the life of faith. The "immature" are, however, "unskilled" in this "word" because they have not been practicing receiving it with obedience. Those new to the faith may not have had opportunity to develop this skill. However, the pastor's hearers have squandered their opportunity by treating "the word of righteousness" with careless "neglect" (Heb 2:1–4).

On the other hand, the "mature" have had their "senses trained" by being careful to both hear this "word" and obey it. Through this practice of careful obedience they have developed the ability to discriminate not only between good and evil, but between "what is appropriate and what is evil." They are not concerned about what is "permissible," but about what is "helpful." The chief goal of the mature is to strengthen their own perseverance and encourage the faithfulness of the people of God. May God help us to live by such discernment.

Chapter 6, verse 1a. The pastor has painted this vivid picture of spiritual regression in order to arouse all who hear his sermon and awaken desire for the "solid food" of the mature. He wants his hearers to respond, "No, we are not as immature as you suppose, we are ready to go on to maturity." He urges them, "let us leave the elementary Christian message and let us press on to maturity."

Notice the pastor's tactful use of the first-person plural. "Let us . . . press on to maturity." The pastor invites us to join him on this journey. He will feed and we will eat the "solid food" that brings maturity. He will explain the truth about our "Great High Priest" through whom we will "draw near" to God. This is a journey of "hearing" God's word with faithful obedience. It is a journey of coming to understand and appropriate the privileges available through our "Great High Priest." Though it requires all diligence, it is possible only through the one who is "the Source of eternal salvation" (5:9). "Let us . . . press on to maturity" could be translated, "Let us . . . be carried on to maturity [by our High Priest]."

Verses 1b–2. The pastor believes that there is one people of God throughout history. Thus, it is not surprising that his description of "the elementary Christian message" is applicable to the faithful both before and after Christ. Let's examine the three pairs of phrases used to describe this elementary teaching. It is by "repentance from dead works and faith in God" that we become part of the people of God. On the other hand, "resurrection of the dead and eternal judgment" refers to the final destiny of the people of God. It is less clear what the pastor has in mind with "teaching about washings and laying on of hands." The "solid food" that the pastor is offering them fills these "elementary" teachings with Christ. He is the one, for instance, who will "cleanse their consciences from dead works" (Heb 9:11) and return with "salvation" for those expecting him at the Last Judgment (Heb 9:28).

Verse 3. The pastor concludes with an affirmation of hope, "this we will do," and a warning, "if indeed God permits." The first anticipates the words of comfort in verses 9–12. The second, the dire warning that immediately follows in verses 4–8.

The affirmation of hope, "And this we will do," affirms the pastor's commitment to teach, and his conviction that his hearers will accept, the "solid food" that brings maturity. He has been feeding them this food since the beginning of his sermon in anticipation of the feast he will serve in Heb 7:1—10:18. Maturity, however, comes by a life of hearing with obedience.

The warning, "if indeed God permits," recalls the fate of the wilderness generation (Heb 3:7–19), who, because of their rebellion (Heb 3:8, 16), were not permitted (Heb 4:5) to enter God's "Sabbath rest" (Heb 4:9).

❧ Day Two: Beware the Peril of Apostasy. (Heb 6:4–8)

> [4] *For it is impossible to renew again to repentance those who have once been enlightened,* [5] *who have also tasted the heavenly gift, and have become partakers of the Holy Spirit, and have tasted both the good word of God and the powers of the coming age,* [6] *and who have fallen away. Renewal is impossible because they are re–crucifying for themselves the Son of God and holding him up to public disgrace.* [7] *For land that drinks the rain that often falls upon it and produces fruit useful to those for whom it is farmed receives a blessing from God.* [8] *But if it produces thorns and thistles, it is unprofitable and subject to a curse. Its destiny is to be burned.*

The pastor follows "if God permits" (Heb 6:3) with "For it is impossible to renew again to repentance." If unchecked, the spiritual regression and dullness of hearing that come from drifting along in unconcern and neglect may result in apostasy. In verses 4–6a the pastor describes those who "have fallen away" (v. 6a). In verse 6b he gives reason for the impossibility of their renewal. He concludes in verses 7–8 by visualizing this terrible danger in a parable laden with Old Testament covenant language. If his hearers will only embrace the one and only fully sufficient High Priest to be described in Heb 7:1—10:18, they will be able to avoid this fate.

Verses 4–6a. "Who have once been enlightened" (v. 4b) and "who have fallen away" (v. 6a) refer to the same group of people. The pastor is not describing believers who might fall away but the terrible tragedy of believers who have fallen away. "Once" (cf. Heb 9:26; 10:2; 12:26–27) underscores the definitive nature of their conversion here described as enlightenment.

The three clauses in verse 5 are an elegant description of the rich spiritual privileges of those who have been "enlightened." The pastor begins appropriately with the "heavenly gift" that we now enjoy and concludes with the "powers of the age to come" toward which he would have us persevere. You "have become partakers of the Holy Spirit" is the heart of this description. The pastor shares the common Christian conviction that through the gift of the "Spirit of grace" (Heb 10:29) all the benefits of Christ are mediated to the people of God (see also Heb 2:1–4). Thus, those who are "partakers of the Holy Spirit" share in the heritage of the people of God and the source of all spiritual blessings.

Only "taste" (see on Heb 2:9 above) could describe the fullness and intimacy with which the "enlightened" experience the "the Heavenly Gift," "the good word of God," and "the powers of the age to come." "The Heavenly Gift" is nothing less that the "great salvation" that the pastor continues to describe throughout this sermon. This gift is "heavenly" because it comes from God and opens the way to life in the presence of God (Heb 12:22–24). We receive it only as God's gracious "gift."

The "enlightened" have also "tasted" the "word of God" and discovered that it is "good" and fully satisfying. The "word of God" by which he created the world (Heb 11:3) found ultimate fulfillment in the eternal, incarnate Son seated at God's right hand and the "eternal salvation" of which he is "Source" (Heb 5:9). Those who "taste" this word know the faithfulness of God

The pastor who began this description by calling attention to their heavenly destiny concludes by directing their thoughts toward "the age to come" in which they will enjoy the fullness of that destiny. The "powers" of the coming "age" of salvation, which will arrive in its fullness at Christ's return (Heb 9:28), are already available through our "Great High Priest." These "powers" include "signs and wonders" like those experienced by the recipients of Hebrews at their conversion (Heb 2:1–4), participation in the Holy Spirit, and life as the people of God under the New Covenant of obedience (Heb 10:15–18).

By concluding with "the age to come" the pastor focuses our attention on the goal of our pilgrimage. By reminding us of its "taste" he awakens within us a longing and determination to persevere until its arrival. He underscores the tragedy of apostasy by mentioning this blessed goal just before referring to those "who have fallen away."

Verse 6b. The impossibility of restoration confirms this falling "away" as apostasy. By explaining the reasons for this impossibility the pastor clarifies the nature of the offense involved. Restoration is "impossible" because of the greatness of the salvation rejected, the definitiveness of the rejection, and the character of God.

These apostates "are re–crucifying for themselves the Son of God and holding him up to public disgrace." The pastor had no stronger language in his vocabulary to describe their offense. The very mention of crucifixion evoked horror and revulsion. There is nothing in our experience as modern people that compares with the awful public shame associated with this cruelest means of execution. They have "re–crucified" and thus brought utter "public disgrace" upon the one who "endured a cross" on their behalf, "despising the shame" (Heb 12:2). By their rebellion they have completely cut themselves off from and despised the fulfillment of all that God said in the prophets and the one and only all-sufficient Savior that he has provided—the very *Son of God*. To whom will those who have so de-finitively rejected God's once-for-all most gracious gift of salvation turn? Would we expect God to provide another way of salvation for those who have so cut themselves off from his largesse?

It is important to note the present tense of the verbs in this statement. The pastor did not say "re–crucified" and "held . . . up" but "they *are* re–crucifying the Son of God and holding him up to public disgrace" (italics added). Their utter rejection was the beginning of a life that continued to heap public disgrace upon the "Son of God" by treating his cross as if it were nothing. Let's recall three aspects of the wilderness generation's sin. First, their refusal at Kadesh Barnea was the culmination of a long history of unbelief, disobedience, and rebellion. Second, it was definitive. God had brought them out of Egypt in order to bring them into the promised land. If they refused to enter, what else could he give them? Third, their rejection was followed by forty years of continual complaining and disobedience, which began with their decision to enter the Land after God had pronounced judg-ment upon them. In the same manner, the falling "away" in this passage is the end result of carelessness, neglect, and turning aside from the way of God. This history of drifting has then resulted, perhaps when things became tough, perhaps out of desire for pleasure, in a definitive rejection of God's only provision for salvation, followed by a life lived as if the crucifixion were of no count. (I could hardly write those last words!)

There is nothing here that need disturb the sensitive conscience. The people described have no concern for their relationship with God. Nor is the pastor providing guidance for excommunication or for re–admitting to the fellowship of the church the repentant who once denied Christ. *He is showing his hearers the possible (probable?) result of laxity, carelessness, and drifting due to neglect of the things of God in order to awaken them. He would move them to diligent perseverance in faith. Such perseverance is the way of those who appropriate God's provision in his Son, soon to be dramatized in Heb 7:1—10:18.*

Verses 7–8. The pastor is bringing home the force of his initial warn-ing: "How shall we escape if we neglect such a great salvation?" (Heb 2:3). Those who received but then rejected the "good news" at Sinai did not es-cape (Heb 3:7—4:11). How much more certain the fate of those who have experienced but abandoned God's provision in his Son (Heb 6:4–6). The pastor brings this truth home with the powerful parable of the "land that drinks the rain that often falls upon it" in verses 7–8. The more we are im-mersed in the language of the Old Testament, the greater the impact this parable upon us. It evokes the rich Old Testament imagery of the people of God as his "vineyard" (Isa 5:1–7) and makes abundant use of covenant language, such as "useful," "unprofitable," "blessing," and "curse."

It is important not merely to interpret this parable but to feel the impact of its imagery. The "land that drinks the rain that often falls upon it" can be nothing other than the people of God who receive his abundant grace. Their faithful perseverance in obedience is the "fruit useful to those for whom it is farmed." At one level, of course, this land "is farmed" for God and he is the one who pronounces the verdict "useful." And yet this "fruit" is very "useful" for the people of God, who on the basis of God's judgment receive the eternal "blessing" that is the ultimate reward for covenant faithfulness. On the other hand, if this grace-blessed "land" produces the "thorns and thistles" of persistence in faithless disobedience, it will be judged by God as "unprofitable" and thus "subject to a curse." The final words, "Its destiny is to be burned" confirm the ultimate character of this "curse."

"Subject to a curse" intensifies the threat. The pastor prepares his hearers for what he is about to say in Heb 6:9–12 by leaving them with the inevitable "curse" hanging over the heads of the faithless. He anticipates how relieved they will be when he assures them, that, on the basis of their past conduct, he is "persuaded" of "better" things in their case. He expects that they will be ready to avoid neglect and disobedience and live up to their past record.

∾ Day Three: Join the Faithful People of God. (Heb 6:9–12)

> [9] *But we are persuaded in your case, beloved, of things that are better and pertain to salvation, even if we thus speak.* [10] *For God is not unjust to forget your work and the love which you demonstrated for his name by having ministered to his saints and by ministering to them.* [11] *But we yearn for each of you to demonstrate the same zeal for the full assurance of faith until the end,* [12] *in order that you might not become dull, but might become imitators of those who through faith and patience are inheriting the promises.*

The pastor has painted this terrible picture of spiritual regression (Heb 5:11—6:3) that leads to apostasy (Heb 6:4–8) so that his hearers will grasp the hope he now offers and join the company of the faithful who persevere with diligence until they inherit "the promises." He will buttress this appeal in verses 13–20 below by affirming the certainty of the promises of God fulfilled in the "High Priest according to the order of Melchizedek" whom he will present in Heb 7:1—10:18.

Verse 9. Heb 6:8 left the hearers under the threat of God's "curse, destined to be burned." It is wonderful, then, to hear the pastor say, "But we are persuaded in your case, beloved, of things that are better and pertain to salvation." By addressing them as "beloved" the pastor not only confirms his love but comforts and encourages them by affirming their identity as the people of God. Their life need not be a life of regression and apostasy, but of "things that are better." Not the "curse" of Heb 6:8, but the "blessing" of 6:7.

What are these "things that are better"? For a full answer we must wait until the pastor tells us about a "better hope" (Heb 7:19), a "better covenant" (Heb 7:22) based on "better promises" (Heb 8:5), a "better sacrifice" (Heb 9:23), "better possessions" (Heb 10:34), and finally, a "better country" (Heb 11:16) and a "better resurrection" (Heb 11:35). All of these things are "better" because they "pertain to salvation." This "salvation" encompasses all that our High Priest has done to cleanse the people of God from sin, bring us into God's presence, and empower us to live under the New Covenant of obedience (see Heb 10:5–18). It climaxes with the final entrance of the people of God into God's "Sabbath rest" (Heb 4:9; 12:22–24) when God's Son appears "a second time . . . for the purpose of bringing salvation to those awaiting him" (Heb 9:28). It includes final entrance into joyous celebration in the presence of God (Heb 12:22–24) and all of God's provision to persevere until that entrance (Heb 10:19–25). The pastor encourages his hearers by affirming that he believes they are on their way to this ultimate "salvation," "even if" he has been talking about regression and apostasy to rouse them from the lethargy he feared was overtaking them. Heb 7:1—10:18 will reveal how, as High Priest, the Son is the "Source" of this "eternal salvation" (Heb 5:9) from beginning to end. It can be described as nothing less than "such a great salvation" (Heb 2:3).

Verse 10. The pastor's confidence in the perseverance of his hearers is based on the faithfulness of God, about which he is certain, and the faithfulness of his hearers, for which he has both good hope and reason for concern. We can be sure that a faithful God will not overlook their "work," their past faithfulness, as described in Heb 10:32–34. That faithfulness is best evidenced by "the love which" they "demonstrated for" God's own "name." Their past and present "ministry" to the people of God is clear evidence of their devotion to God and passion to be identified by his "name." The pastor is probably referring to their support of and identification with believers who were suffering persecution from the unbelieving world (Heb 10:33–34). The risk involved proved the quality of their love for God. The fact that this ministry continues is a most hopeful indication of their continued devotion.

Verse 11. Every true pastor feels the beat of this pastor's heart. He *"yearns"* for the perseverance of *"each"* member of his congregation (Italics added). Past and present faithfulness reassure the pastor's hearers that they are not among the apostate and provide motivation for, but no guarantee of, future perseverance. Thus the pastor earnestly "yearns" that they will continue to live a life that demonstrates "the same zeal" that they have evidenced "for the full assurance of faith until the end." Be zealous to continue fully trusting the certainty of God's promise of "Sabbath rest" and the reality of the grace necessary for perseverance until preliminary entrance into that "rest" at death (see on Heb 12:22–24) or final entrance at Christ's return (Heb 9:28). For it is our "Great High Priest" "according to the order of Melchizedek" who both guarantees the promise and is the only source of grace for perseverance. (Heb 7:1—10:18).

Verse 12. The pastor concludes with a two-line sketch that impresses the contrast between the life of disobedience and the life of perseverance on his hearers' hearts. Those who fail to live as if God' promise is certain and his power is real become "dull" in hearing (cf. Heb 5:11). They are in danger of imitating the faithless wilderness generation whose fate has been so vividly portrayed in Heb 3:16–19. Those, however, who persevere in obedience, trusting in the promise and power of God, "become imitators of those who through faith and patience are inheriting the promises" and who will soon be paraded before our eyes in Heb 11:1–40. The plural "promises" includes promise of present grace, though the emphasis is still on "inheriting" the ultimate promise of "Sabbath rest." "Faith and patience" might be taken as "patient faith," faith that endures through obedience despite opposition or distraction. The pastor is doing all within his power to keep his hearers from relapsing into the dullness from which he has awakened them (Heb 5:11–13) and to encourage their participation in this grand company of the faithful. We live this life of faith conscious that we are part of the faithful people of God.

In commenting on verse 10 above, we mentioned that the pastor's confidence in the future of his hearers was based on the certain faithfulness of God and the hoped-for faithfulness of his congregation. In verses 13–20 the pastor will assure them that the faithfulness of God is an absolutely certain basis for their own trust and faithfulness. Joining this company of the faithful is worthwhile because the God who cannot lie has secured his promise with an oath. The pastor anticipates the heroes of faith in Heb 11:1–40 by introducing Abraham himself as an example of one who proved the faithfulness of God by inheriting what God had promised through patient obedience. Furthermore, this divine promise-oath has been validated and fulfilled by our "High Priest according to the order of

Melchizedek" whose grandeur as the "Source of eternal salvation" (Heb 5:9) will be portrayed with graphic detail in Heb 7:1—10:18. Only then will the pastor be free to transition (Heb 10:19–39) to the grand drama of the faithful (Heb 11:1–40) because they, like us, will only inherit the ultimate promise through this "Great High Priest."

◌ **Day Four:** Rely Upon the Divine Promise and Oath. (Heb 6:13–20)

> [13] For when God made a promise to Abraham, since he had no one greater by whom to swear, he swore by himself, [14] saying, "If I will not certainly bless you and certainly multiply you." [15] And thus by having been patient Abraham obtained what was promised.
>
> [16] For human beings swear by someone greater, and for them an oath is the end of every controversy for confirmation. [17] Because God was desirous of demonstrating the unchangeable character of his plan most convincingly to the heirs of the promise, he mediated it with an oath. [18] He did this in order that through two unchangeable things, in both of which it was impossible for God to lie, we might have strong encouragement, we who have fled for refuge to take hold of the hope laid before us. [19] We have this hope as a sure and steadfast anchor of the soul, a hope that enters into the inner place behind the curtain,[1] [20] where the forerunner on our behalf has entered in, Jesus, according to the order of Melchizedek having become High Priest forever.

The pastor has awakened his hearers by warning them lest present lethargy (Heb 5:11—6:3) result in final apostasy (Heb 6:4–8). He now encourages them to persevere based on their past faithfulness (Heb 6:9–12) and the certainty of the promises of God (Heb 6:13–20) that find fulfillment in the "High Priest according to the order of Melchizedek" (Heb 6:20). His purpose from beginning to end is expressed by the last verse of Heb 6:9–12: that his hearers might be among those "who through faith and patience are inheriting the promises" (Heb 6:12). Heb 6:13–20 brings the exhortation begun in Heb 5:11 to its climax by demonstrating both the certainty of God's promises and the ultimate desirability of inheriting what has been promised.

Verse 13–15. Mention of God's promises recalls Abraham, who received God's promise of blessing for the world. The pastor has already identified the faithful people of God as the "seed of Abraham" (Heb 2:17), the ones who

---

1. I have followed the ESV in much of verse 19.

"through faith and patience are inheriting the promises" (Heb 6:12), the ones who "take hold of the hope laid before us" (Heb 6:18). Their perseverance is the ultimate fulfillment of God's promise that he would multiply Abraham's seed, made in Gen 12:1–3, 7, and reaffirmed in Gen 15:1–21.

In order to reassure us of this promise's absolute dependability, however, the pastor takes us to Abraham's sacrifice of Isaac on Mount Moriah in Gen 22:1–19. There God backed his promise of many descendants with an oath: "If I will not certainly bless you and certainly multiply you." Furthermore, this oath is even more certain because, "since he had no one greater by whom to swear," God swore this oath "by himself." God himself calls God to witness.

Furthermore, Abraham confirms this promise. During his lifetime the promise of descendants was focused on the birth of Isaac, in whom his "seed" would "be called" (Heb 11:18). After trusting God patiently for twenty–five years "Abraham obtained what was promised" at the birth of Isaac, and once again when God returned Isaac to him on Mount Moriah (Heb 11:17–19). The God who began the fulfillment of this promise in the birth of Isaac will bring it to ultimate fulfillment when the people of God enter into the "hope laid before" them (Heb 6:18). Like Abraham, we persevere toward this hope with patient trust in God.

Verses 16. Why did God swear this oath to Abraham? Verse 16 provides needed background information by explaining the function of an oath in human society. Verse 17 gives us God's motive; and verse 18, his purpose.

God used an oath because of the oath's significance in human society. An oath was the ultimate way for a person to affirm his integrity. When one swore an oath one called on "someone greater" (God) to attest one's faithfulness and to punish one's unfaithfulness with death. The ancients took oaths very seriously. There was no greater way to convince others of one's honesty and faithfulness.

Verse 17. This being so, we can understand God's motive for swearing an oath. "Because God was desirous" of impressing the "heirs of the promise" with "the unchangeable character of his plan" of redemption in the most convincing way, he used an oath. "God was desirous" is emphatic. His "plan" of bringing his faithful people into the ultimate "Sabbath rest" as the culmination of creation is absolutely "unchangeable" in its essence. Thus, it is necessary for the "heirs" of this promise to be assured of its validity. In this context "mediated" implies guaranteed (see Heb 7:20–22). God *guaranteed* what had been promised to "the heirs of the promise" by swearing an "oath." However, this oath is no ordinary oath. Because there is no one greater, God swore "by himself." The almighty Creator called on himself to attest his integrity, he called on himself to judge his own faithfulness. Fall in worship before this God who accommodates himself to human weakness for our assurance.

Verse 18. God has condescended to the level of our human understanding in order to give us the "strongest assurance" of his "plan," which is the "hope laid before us." We might say he makes it doubly certain: (1) It is confirmed by the "unchangeable" promise of a "God who cannot lie." (2) That promise is guaranteed by the "unchangeable" oath of a "God who cannot lie."

Why was God so concerned about assuring us of the integrity of his promise and plan? So that we will keep on fleeing "for refuge to take hold of the hope laid before us" until we enter the "Sabbath rest" that "remains for the people of God" (Heb 4:9).

Nothing describes our present situation as "heirs of the promise" with greater clarity and urgency than "we who have fled for refuge to take hold of the hope laid before us." Throughout this sermon the pastor combines warning against apostasy with encouragement in faithful obedience. The faithful people of God are those who "flee" the one and "take hold" of the other. There is no room for complacency. Life is not about present comfort, convenience, wealth, power, or pleasure. *Because God's promise/ oath is certain* life is about fleeing eternal loss and pursuing "the hope" of entering God's eternal "Sabbath rest," which has been "laid before us" through the saving work of the Son. The pastor pleads with us to feel the urgency of our situation and to self-identify as those "who have fled for refuge to take hold of the hope laid before us."

Verses 19–20. The pastor concludes by illustrating the nature and certainty of this hope before reintroducing the "high priest forever according to the order of Melchizedek" as the fulfillment of God's promise and thus the source of this hope.

He gives us two descriptions of the hope that "we have." First, it is "a sure and steadfast anchor of the soul." Second, it is "a hope that enters into the inner place behind the curtain." The first is a nautical metaphor. The second, reintroduces the theme of priesthood by reminding us of Aaron's entrance into the Most Holy Place "behind the curtain" on the Day of Atonement. The pastor, however, is not referring to the Most Holy Place in the Mosaic Tabernacle, but to the true eternal Most Holy Place, which, according to verse 20, Jesus has already entered as a "Forerunner on our behalf." As our "Forerunner" Jesus brings the faithful into the very presence of God. We might say that the hope which God has promised and Jesus provides anchors our very souls to the throne of God. There is no reason for the faithful to "drift" away through carelessness or neglect (Heb 2:1–4) from this sure and certain divine anchorage.

Our rather awkward translation of verse 20 preserves the emphasis of the Greek text on the words "Forerunner" and "forever." *Forever* anticipates Heb 7:1–28; *Forerunner*, Heb 8:1—10:18. The priest *forever* according to the "power of an indestructible life" (Heb 7:1–28), enters God's heavenly presences as our *Forerunner* through his incarnation as *Jesus* (Heb 8:1—10:18).

The pastor intentionally reintroduces the theme of priesthood with the word "Forerunner," for no term better describes the effectiveness of this "High Priest according to the order of Melchizedek." Aaron was not a "Forerunner." His annual entrance into the earthly Most Holy Place never opened the way for others to follow. However, through his atoning sacrifice and once-for-all entrance into heaven, this new priest has opened the way for *the faithful to enter the divine presence* as the New-Covenant people of God. He is the true "Forerunner."

∾ Day Five: The Melchizedek Who Met Abraham. (Heb 7:1–3)

> ¹ For this Melchizedek, King of Salem, Priest of God Most High, met Abraham as he was returning from the slaughter of the kings and blessed him, ² to whom also Abraham apportioned a tithe from all. First his name is translated as "King of Righteousness," then also he is "King of Salem," which means "King of Peace." ³ Without father, without mother, without genealogy; having neither beginning of days nor end of life; made like the Son of God; he remains a priest forever.

The explanation of Ps 110:4 in Heb 7:1–28 resumes the divine conversation begun in Heb 1:1–14. The God who invited the Son to sit at his right hand and addressed him as Son, God, and Lord, now addresses him, in the words of Ps 110:4, as "priest forever according to the order of Melchizedek." This divine declaration provides scriptural/divine warrant for replacing the Aaronic priesthood with the priest of Melchizedek's order whom Aaron typified. It also shows that this replacement takes place because the former priesthood was based on mortal, sinful humanity; but the latter, on the power of the eternal Son's "indestructible life" (Heb 7:16).

If we want to know what it means to be "a priest forever after the order of *Melchizedek*" (Ps 110:4, italics added), then we need to know about *Melchizedek* and, if possible, his relationship to Aaron. The pastor turns to the only source of such information, the description of the time when Melchizedek "met Abraham as he was returning from the slaughter of the kings" in Gen 14:17–24. In this passage Melchizedek is a divine messenger whose presence reminds Abraham that his faith is in God, not the wealth offered him by the King of Sodom. Melchizedek then disappears from the pages of Scripture as mysteriously as he appeared. Some people have felt that the Melchizedek of Hebrews, especially of Heb 7:1–3, was even more mysterious than the Melchizedek of Genesis. I will do my best to help you understand this enigmatic fellow!

Verses 1–2a. The pastor begins by recalling the information from Melchizedek's meeting Abraham (Gen 14:17–22) that he needs for his argument. First, he reminds us of Melchizedek's name and titles: (1) "Melchizedek," (2) "King of Salem," and (3) "Priest of God Most High." Then he focuses our attention on two events that happened on this occasion: (1) Melchizedek was the one who "blessed" Abraham, and (2) the one "to whom also Abraham apportioned a tithe from all." The pastor fails to mention Melchizedek's offering Abraham bread and wine because it is without relevance for his argument.

The pastor is going to show us how Melchizedek was superior to Aaron (Heb 7:4–10) in order to show us how Melchizedek foreshadowed the Son's superiority to the Aaronic priesthood (Heb 7:11–25). He reserves the two events of blessing and tithing to demonstrate the former in Heb 7:4–11. In verses 2b–3 he interprets Melchizedek's name and titles as preparation for the latter. It is important to remember that these verses are not describing the Son of God. They are describing the Melchizedek who met Abraham as the Melchizedek who foreshadowed the eternity of the Son of God.

Verse 2b. "King of Righteousness" was a common translation of the name "Melchizedek." "Melchi" comes from the Hebrew word for King, and "zedek," from the word for "righteousness." Philo, the Jewish philosopher, and Josephus, the first-century Jewish historian, both understood "Melchizedek" in this way. "Salem" resembles the Hebrew word for "peace." "Righteousness" and "peace" are often attributed to the Messiah. The pastor, however, makes no further use of the meaning of these names. We almost feel that he wanted to get them out of his way so that he could address the really important issue of Melchizedek's priesthood in verse 3. Nevertheless, they enhance the greatness of Melchizedek and subtly suggest the character of the one who will come "according to" his "order."

Verse 3. The pastor celebrates Melchizedek's greatness and explains the significance of his being "Priest of the Most High God" with this four-line poem, which we will letter a–d:

a. "Without father, without mother, without genealogy;

b. "having neither beginning of days nor end of life;

c. "made like the Son of God;

d. "he remains a priest forever."

Let's focus our attention on the first two lines. When we go to Genesis we discover that Melchizedek was without recorded father, mother, or genealogy. This is striking because the validity of an Aaronic priest depended on the *record* of his descent from Aaron. Here we have a priesthood that was recognized by Abraham but was "without genealogy." Clearly, this priesthood was not dependent upon human descent. "Without father" and "without mother" might be interpreted as no more than "without genealogy." However, in other contexts these expressions were used to describe deity. Thus, they suggest the next line, "having neither beginning of days nor end of life," which is clearly a description of eternal deity. Both lack of Aaronic genealogy (Heb 7:11–14) and divine eternity (Heb 7:15–19) are crucial characteristics of the "priest according to the order of Melchizedek."

But how could divine eternity apply to Melchizedek? Let's have a look at line "c" of this poem: "made like the Son of God." The Melchizedek of Genesis has been carefully crafted as a picture of the Son of God. Although he is a historical person, he reminds us of the Angel of the Lord (e.g. Gen 16:7–11; 22:11–15; Judges 6:11–22). Melchizedek appears unexpectedly without genealogy or connection as God's special messenger and then, just as mysteriously, disappears. In this way he has become a picture of the priesthood of the *eternal* Son of God. Thus line "c," "made like the Son of God," is crucial. Only a Melchizedek that foreshadows, but does not rival, the eternity of the Son of God fits the pastor's argument.

By the time the pastor gets to line "d" he is no longer thinking about Melchizedek but about the "priest after the order of Melchizedek," the Son of God, who "remains a priest forever." As we will learn below, the "indestructible life" of the eternal Son of God is the foundation of his fully effective, unending high priesthood. The fact that Ps 110:4 prophesied a new High Priest without Aaronic descent demonstrated the insufficiency of the old priesthood (Heb 7:11–14). The fact that this verse prophesied a "priest forever" affirmed the full sufficiency of the one who "remains a priest forever" (Heb 7:15–19).

∾ Day Six: This Melchizedek is Far Superior to Levi. (Heb 7:4–10)

⁴ *See, then, how great this one is, to whom even Abraham gave a tithe from the spoils, Abraham the Patriarch.* ⁵ *And those from the*

sons of Levi receiving the priestly office have an ordinance accord-
ing to the law to tithe the people, that is, their brothers and sisters,
although they also have come out of the loins of Abraham. [6] *But*
the one not reckoning his genealogy from them has received tithes
from Abraham and has blessed the one who has the promises. [7]
Now without any contradiction the inferior is blessed by the su-
perior. [8] *And here dying men received tithes, but there one about*
whom it is witnessed that "he lives." [9] *One might even say that*
through Abraham Levi the one receiving tithes paid tithes [10] *for*
he was still in the loins of his father when Melchizedek met him.

The pastor wants us to feel "how great this one is" so that we will grasp the magnitude of the priest "according to the order of Melchizedek." It is easy for us to get lost in the technicalities of the pastor's argument and miss their cumulative effect. It was indeed an astounding fact that someone should receive a tithe from *Abraham* and pronounce a priestly blessing upon *him*. Abraham, who was "the *Patriarch*," Abraham, who had "*the* promises" of God (Italics added). Some ancient Jewish sources attempted to explain away this troubling subordination of Abraham to Melchizedek by identifying Melchizedek with Abraham's ancestor Shem.

The mysterious meeting between Melchizedek and Abraham, as sum-marized in verses 1–3, demonstrated Melchizedek's superiority to Abraham, and thus, to the Levitical (Aaronic) priesthood. Verse 4 identifies the most obvious sign of this superiority—Abraham paid a tithe to Melchizedek. Since collecting tithe was a priestly function, it becomes the basis for the two following contrasts between Melchizedek and Levi, the first in verses 5–7, the second in verse 8. In the first, Melchizedek's blessing Abraham supplements the tithe; in the second, the tithe is merely the framework for something greater. The first is dependent on Melchizedek being "without genealogy" (v. 3a); the second, on his being "without beginning of days or end of life" (v. 3b). Perhaps, however, we will understand the argument bet-ter if we recognize that there are three stages, each greater than the previous: (1) Abraham paid tithe to Melchizedek, (2) Melchizedek blessed Abraham, and, finally, (3) "about whom it is witnessed that he lives."

Verse 4. "*Even* Abraham" "the Patriarch," gave Melchizedek "a tithe from the spoils" of war. One could not imagine a human being greater than Abraham, because he was "the Patriarch," the *Father* of all the people of God, and the recipient of God's promises of blessing for the world. He had just returned from a great military victory with "the spoils" of war. And yet, this Abraham paid a tithe from these spoils to Melchizedek. "See" then, "how great" this Melchizedek is!

Verses 5–6. Let's compare the Levitical priests' authority to collect tithes with Melchizedek's authority. In both cases it is important to note who collects tithe, from whom, and by what authority. Verse 5 describes the Levitical priests; verse 6, Melchizedek.

The descendants of Aaron were "those from the sons of Levi receiving the priestly office." They had authority to collect tithes from their "brothers and sisters," the other descendants of Abraham. "Out of the loins of Abraham" emphasizes the literal, physical nature of this shared descent. There was an "ordinance" in the Mosaic "law" that gave them the right "to tithe the people" because of their special descent from Aaron/Levi and because of their common descent from Abraham with those from whom they received tithes.

On the other hand, Melchizedek, who did not reckon "his genealogy from" Levi or Abraham, "received tithes from Abraham" who, as "Patriarch," was the ancestor of both the Levitical priests and those from whom they received tithe. By apportioning him this tithe Abraham acknowledged his authority.

Verse 7. Furthermore, Melchizedek confirmed his superiority to Abraham by pronouncing a priestly blessing upon him. Is it true that "without any contradiction the inferior is blessed by the superior"? Sometimes the word "bless" is used as a synonym for "praise." We might think of Ps 103:1 that calls on us to "bless the Lord." Clearly it is the inferior who praises the superior. However, it was always the superior person who pronounced a *priestly* blessing upon an inferior. Thus, it was truly amazing that the priest Melchizedek blessed Abraham in the name of "God Most High," especially since Abraham was the one person who had God's "promises" of blessing for the world.

Verse 8. Tithe, blessing, but there is more. The Levitical priests descended from Aaron were obviously mortal since the "ordinance" that granted them their "priestly office" was based on descent. Thus, it was as continually "dying men" that the Levitical priests collected tithes. But the new priest is "one about whom it is witnessed that 'he lives.'" The pastor is thinking about "without beginning of days or end of life" in verse 3b, about "a priest forever" in Ps 110:4, and about the marvelous way in which Melchizedek appears as God's messenger, exercises such authority over Abraham, and then disappears from Scripture. The pastor mentions this feature as the climax of his discussion of Melchizedek because it finds its fulfillment only in the "priest according to the order of Melchizedek" whom he is about to describe. We will see how it applies to the one whom God has declared "a priest forever according to the order of Melchizedek" in verses 15–19 below.

Verses 9–10. The pastor concludes this section by returning to the foundational point with which he began—Abraham's giving Melchizedek "a tithe of the spoils" (v. 4). He wants to rivet our attention on the superiority of Melchizedek to Levi (rather than Abraham) so that in the following verses he can show the superiority of the priest "according to the order of Melchizedek" to the Aaronic priests descended from Levi. He puts it all in this soundbite: "One might even say that through Abraham, Levi (the one receiving tithes) paid tithes." "One might even say" introduces, but does not weaken, this statement. As "Patriarch" Abraham's actions represented the entire people who would "come out of" his "loins" (v. 6). Thus, representatively, Levi "was still in the loins of his father when" on that fateful day, "Melchizedek met him."

Are you ready to meet the one who was declared "priest according to the order of Melchizedek" by the divine oath (Heb 7:21)? Keep reading through verse 28! You have met him before, for he is the one whom God acknowledged as his eternal Son (Heb 1:5; Ps 2:7) when he invited him to sit at the Father's right hand (Heb 1:13; Ps 110:1) as "God" (Heb 1:8; Ps 45:7) and "Lord" (Heb 1:10; Pa 102:25).

∾ Day Seven: A Priesthood Founded on an "Indestructible Life" has Replaced the Priesthood Dependent upon "the Law of Fleshly Ordinance." (Heb 7:11–19)

[11] *If, then, there had been perfection through the Levitical priesthood, for on the basis of it the people received the law, what need would there have been for a different priest to arise according to the order of Melchizedek and not one designated according to the order of Aaron?* [12] *For a change of the priesthood is of necessity a change of the law.* [13] *For the one about whom these things are said has taken part in a different tribe, from which no one has ever attended to the altar.* [14] *For this is clearer because our Lord arose from the tribe of Judah. Moses has said nothing about priests in regard to that tribe.* [15] *And this is even clearer, if a different priest arises according to the likeness of Melchizedek,* [16] *who has not come to be priest according to the law of fleshly ordinance but according to the power of an indestructible life.* [17] *For it is attested that "you are a priest forever according to the order of Melchizedek."* [18] *For on the one hand the abolition of the foregoing ordinance has become a reality because of its weakness and uselessness* [19] *(for the*

law has perfected nothing); on the other hand is the bringing in of
a better hope through which we draw near to God.

The explanation of Gen 14:17–22 in verses 1–10 has laid the necessary foundation for the pastor's long-awaited, phrase-by-phrase explanation of Ps 110:4. Verses 11–19 expound "according to the order of Melchizedek." Verses 20–22, "the Lord has sworn and will not change his mind"; and verses 23–25, "you are a priest forever." Today's passage, verses 11–19, shows why this new, effective priest has replaced his ineffective predecessor. Verses 11–14 show the significance of the fact that this promised priest was "without genealogy" (v. 3a), that is, "*not* designated according to the order of Aaron" (italics added). Verses 15–19 show the significance of the fact that he was "without beginning of days or end of life," that he has *arisen* "according to the *likeness* of Melchizedek" (italics added).

Verses 11–14. The pastor does not begin with the fulfillment of Ps 110:4, but with the fact of its existence in the Old Testament. Apart from how it was to be fulfilled, Scripture promised the coming of a non–Levitical priest. The very fact that Scripture foretold the coming of a priest "not designated according to the order of Aaron" showed that there was no "perfection through the Levitical priesthood." The purpose of priesthood was to bring people into God's presence by making atonement for sin. This provision for access into the divine presence was the "perfection" of a priesthood. Scripture would not have promised a new priesthood if the Levitical priests had been able to provide an atonement sufficient for their people to enter the heavenly presence of the eternal God. They failed in the essential function of priesthood.

Furthermore, remember, that "the people received the law" "on the basis of" the Levitical priesthood (v. 11). The law was dependent on the functioning of the Levitical/Aaronic priesthood. So, if the priesthood was inadequate, and thus must be changed, as Ps 110:4 demands, then the entire Levitical system must be changed (v. 12).

Verse 13 clenches the argument. This promise of a new priest in Ps 110:4 was obviously addressed to someone who "has taken part" in a *non*–Levitical, *non*–priestly tribe. Although the pastor is not yet speaking directly about the Son of God, the phrase "has taken part" reminds us of the Son's assuming humanity for our sakes (Heb 2:14). This inadequacy of the entire Levitical priesthood and the Sinai system *as a means of approaching God* was essential to its ultimate and continuing function *as a type or picture of the fully-sufficient priest* who was to come.

By mentioning "our Lord" verse 14 transitions to the fulfillment of Ps 110:4 in verses 15–19. However, the crucial point is not yet our Lord's person but simply that he "arose from the tribe of Judah" and not the tribe of Levi. Moses, through whom God established the whole Sinai system, said *nothing* about priests from Judah. Notice, the old priests were "designated." They "descended." But "our Lord *arose*" (italics added). Bottom line: Since the promise of a new priest in Ps 110:4 was directed to someone who was not of the tribe of Levi, in fact, to "our Lord" who was of the tribe of Judah, a change is inevitable. The old priesthood and all that went with it must be replaced.

Verses 15–19. Now the pastor turns to the fulfillment of the Ps 110:4 oracle, to the actual appearance of a "different priest" who "arises according to the *likeness* of Melchizedek" (italics added). This One is not a priest "by descent." He "arises" in fulfillment of God's words to him in Ps 110:4. What does it mean to be a priest like Melchizedek? It means that he was not a priest "according to the law of fleshly ordinance but according to the power of an indestructible life." "Power" contrasts with "law," "indestructible" with "fleshly," and "life" with "ordinance." This priest is the eternal Son of God (Heb 1:1–14, remember how the pastor brought Ps 110:4 and Ps 2:7 together in 5:5–6?). This priest was foreshadowed by one "having neither beginning of days nor end of life" (v. 3b), by one about whom it was witnessed that "he lives" (v. 8). As the eternal Son of God his priesthood was empowered by the very "life" of God. Death on the cross did not conquer life. The "indestructible life" of God conquered death. By contrast, "fleshly" emphasizes the weakness, mortality (and sinfulness) of the old priests. By being based on a law of descent their priesthood was based on *mortality* and human weakness.

Some have suggested that "you are a priest forever," quoted from Ps 110:4 in verse 17, refers only to eternity future. The pastor, however, has made the importance of the Son's divine eternity clear from the beginning (Heb 1:1–14). He has affirmed Melchizedek as a picture of one "without beginning of days or end of life" (v. 3a), one who is priest "by the power of an indestructible life" (v. 16). Thus, it is clear that the pastor understood "you are a priest forever," taken directly from Ps 110:4, as "you are an eternal priest." Your priesthood has a radically different *quality* because it is based on the eternal deity of the Son of God.

The existence of the Old Testament oracle (Ps 110:4) showed that the priesthood had to be "changed" (vv. 11–12). The fulfillment of that oracle, however, by an eternal priest has "abolished" the old priesthood (vv. 18–19). It was only a "foregoing" or temporary "ordinance." It has been abolished as a means of approaching God because of its "weakness and uselessness." It was, as we have seen, "fleshly," that is based on mortal, sinful human "weakness." Because of that it was useless. That is, it could not provide true atonement that brought worshipers into the ultimate presence of God. For you will remember, "the law made nothing perfect" (see comment on "perfection" in verse 11 above).

However, that "foregoing ordinance" has been replaced by a "hope" that is "better" because through it we actually can "draw near to God." As we will see, the new priesthood has offered a "better sacrifice" (Heb 9:23), and has established "a better covenant" (v. 22), based on "better promises" (Heb 8:6). In Hebrews "better" describes the new order that truly atones for sin and brings God's people into his eternal presence. The pastor begins, however, with "a better hope" because he wants us to look forward. His goal is that we flee "to take hold of the hope laid before us" (Heb 6:18). It is worth persevering in faithful obedience until we receive this "hope." In the meantime, keep your focus on the one to whom God said, "you are an eternal priest." In the rest of chapter 7 the pastor begins to paint a glorious panorama of the benefits that this priest brings to "those who come to God through him" (v. 25 below).

A High Priest Perfected Forever

Hebrews 7:20—9:22

Introduction

When we read Hebrews 1–2 we had the privilege of "overhearing" the Scriptural conversation between the Father and the Son that occurred on the occasion of the Son's triumphal session at God's right hand. In Heb 1:5–14 the Father spoke the oracles of Ps 2:7, 2; Sam 7:14; and Ps 45:6–7, 102:25–27, and 110:1 to the Son. He addressed the Son as Son, God, Creator, Lord, and Judge and invited him to sit at his right hand. The Son's reply in Heb 2:11–13 was the heart of Heb 2:5–18. He answered the Father with the words of David and Isaiah found in Ps 22:22; 2 Sam 22:3; and Isa 8:17–18. He accepted the Father's invitation by affirming his identity with the human people of God and his dependence upon the Father.

This conversation resumes with the introduction of Ps 110:4 in Heb 5:5–6 and reaches a conclusion in 7:1–10:18. In Heb 7:1–28 the Father speaks the oracle of Ps 110:4 to the eternal Son at his right hand, declaring that he is "a priest forever according to the order of Melchizedek." At the heart of Heb 8:1—10:18 is the sons answer, in the words of the writer of Ps 40:7–9 (Heb 10:5–10), affirming that he attained this priesthood by coming into the world as a human being and doing the will of God.

In our study of Heb 7:1–19 we have already heard the Father address the Son as a Priest "according to the likeness of Melchizedek." We have seen how this effective, eternal Priest has replaced the ineffective Aaronic priesthood by which he was prefigured. Heb 7:20–25, the passage for day one of this week, makes sure that we understand the benefits that this priest brings. Heb 7:26–28, day two, is a majestic summary of what has been said in Heb 7:1–25 and an appetite-whetting introduction to what follows in Heb 8:1—10:18.

The Son's response to the Father in the words of Ps 40:7–9 (as recorded in Heb 10:5–10) is the key to Heb 8:1—10:18. This section describes the Son's obedient incarnation, death, exaltation, and session as the means of his responding to Ps 110:4 and becoming High Priest at God's right hand. Heb 8:1—10:18 is a symphony in three movements. I've entitled these three movements "The New Promised" (Heb 8:1–16), "The Old Antiquated: the New Foreshadowed" (Heb 9:1–22), and "The New Explained" (Heb 9:23—10:18).[1] Each movement goes through the themes of *sanctuary, sacrifice,* and *covenant.* According to the first movement, Heb 8:1–16, the Old Testament promises (Ps 110:4; Jer 31:31–34) that Christ would serve in the heavenly *sanctuary* (Heb 8:1–2) and establish a New *Covenant* (Heb 8:7–13) imply that his *sacrifice* must be very different from the sacrifices of the earthly Tabernacle (Heb 8:3–6). The second movement, Heb 9:1–22, uses the inadequacy of the old Tabernacle *sanctuary* (Heb 9:1–10) and the broken Old *Covenant* (Heb 9:16–22) to highlight the unique nature and effectiveness of Christ's *sacrifice* (Heb 9:11–15). In the final, climactic movement, Heb 9:23—10:18, the symphony reaches its climax in a grand description of Christ's sufficiency: by his obedient self-offering he has provided an all-sufficient atoning *sacrifice* for sin (Heb 9:24–10:14), and thereby has become the all-effective High Priest in the heavenly *sanctuary* (Heb 9:23–24) and the Guarantor of the New *Covenant* of obedience (Heb 10:15–18). We will spend days three (Heb 8:1–6) and four (Heb 8:7–13) on the first movement; and days five (Heb 9:1–10), six (Heb 9:11–15), and seven (Heb 9:16–22) on the second. We must restrain our impatience, however, and wait until next week for the grand finale in movement three (Heb 9:23—10:18).

⮌ Day One: A Guarantor and an Eternal Priest. (Heb 7:20–25)

> [20] And in proportion to how significant it was that he did not become a priest without an oath—for they have become priests without an oath, [21] but he with an oath through the one saying to him, "The Lord has sworn and will not change his mind: you are a priest forever"— [22] To that degree Jesus has become the Guarantor of a better covenant. [23] And on the one hand many have become priests because they have been prevented from continuing by death. [24] But he, because he "remains" forever, has a priesthood that is inviolable. [25] Therefore he is able even to save completely those who come to God through him, because he is always living to make intercession for them.

1. For the titles of these movements see Cockerill, *Hebrews,* 349, 370, and 411.

Verse 19 ended by describing the benefit brought by this High Priest as "a better hope through which we draw near to God." If you want to understand more about this gracious benefit, read verses 20–25. The pastor urgently desires us to grasp the magnitude of what Christ has done for us so that we will avail ourselves of all that he has provided. Remember, the pastor is interpreting Ps 110:4. He showed us how "according to the order of Melchizedek" substantiated the replacement of the old priesthood in verses 11–19. He now turns to "the Lord has sworn and will not change his mind" in verses 20–22, and to "you are a priest forever" in verses 23–25, in order to explain the extent and ever-present availability of the provision God has provided for us through his Son our High Priest.

Verses 20–22. So, what is the significance, according to verses 20–22, of the fact that "the Lord has sworn and will not change his mind"? You will remember from Heb 6:13–20 that the divine oath is the ultimate assurance. There is no greater way for God to convince us of his faithfulness and the certainty of his promises. Verse 20 reminds us that, although the Aaronic priesthood may have been established by God, the appointment of those priests was not secured by divine oath. On the other hand, the eternal priesthood of the Son is guaranteed by this solemn oath that God swore to the Son himself on the occasion of his session at God's right hand. For that reason he is not simply the "Mediator" of a "better covenant," but its "Guarantor."

As we will discover, the covenant associated with the Aaronic priesthood failed because God's people persisted in sinfulness (Heb 8:7–9; 9:16–22). This covenant is "better" because this High Priest guarantees that those who come to God through him will find entrance into God's presence where they will receive the mercy of forgiveness and the grace necessary to persevere in faithful obedience. He will enable them to exchange "an evil heart of unbelief" (Heb 3:12) for an obedient heart inscribed with the law of God (Heb 10:16). As "the Source of eternal salvation" (Heb 5:9), he himself is the "Guarantor" of this New-Covenant arrangement for approaching God. The Greek text of verse 22 puts emphasis on the word "Jesus." The eternal Son now seated at God's right hand is none other than the "Jesus" who through his incarnate obedience has become our all-sufficient "Guarantor." The one who is our "Guarantor" is able to meet our need because he shares our humanity but overcame its weakness through his obedience.

Verses 23–24. The pastor brings his exposition of Ps 110:4 to a climax in verses 23–25 by focusing on "you are a priest forever." He also draws on the succinct description of Melchizedek as a picture of the Son in verse 3. If "without father, without mother, without genealogy" (v. 3a) was important for verses 11–14, and "without beginning of days or end of life" (v. 3b) for verses 15–19, then "he remains a priest forever" (v. 3d) finds its place here in verses 23–25. The word "remains" plays a key role in the stark contrast between the mortal Aaronic priests in verse 23 and the eternal foundation of the Son's priesthood in verse 24. This contrast substantiates the ultimate sufficiency of the Son's priesthood (v. 25).

In verse 23 the generational succession of the Aaronic priests has become a great crowd. The pastor brings before our eyes an expanding multitude of priests continually bowing and sacrificing. Their ever-increasing multiplicity, based on their mortality, betrays their ineffectiveness and stands in sharp contrast to the Son's eternal singularity and "once-for-all" ministry (Heb 7:27; 9:12; and 10:10). "They are a 'great cloud of witnesses' to the inability of the old to bring people into God's presence."[2]

On the other hand, the Son "'remains' forever" (v. 24). The word translated "remains" is often used to affirm God's eternity (compare Heb 10:34; 12:27; and 13:14). The pastor is saying more than that the Son will be a priest from now on. He is saying that this priest is "without beginning of days or end of life" (Heb 7:3) because he is priest "by the power of an indestructible life" (Heb 7:15). This priesthood, then, is "inviolable," unchangeable, indestructible, irreplaceable because it is not powered by mortal, sinful humanity. It is powered by One who assumed our mortal, sinful humanity, but overcame human weakness by the power of his eternal deity. The pastor understands "you are a priest forever" from Ps 110:4 as "you are a priest who 'remains,'" "you are a priest who is eternal"! This priesthood is not based simply on the longevity, but on the divine nature or quality, of its priest.

"Therefore he is able to save completely those who come to God through him." There is no one English word that captures the breadth and intensity of the Greek phrase that we have translated "completely." Some have translated it "forever" (NASB). This is a completeness that includes forever and a forever that implies completeness. This High Priest is able to supply all the mercy and grace that we need to persevere in faithful obedience until our final entrance into the presence of God (Heb 9:28; 12:22–24). He is able to empower us for perseverance from beginning to end! Although the English may be archaic, it is difficult to do better than the King James' "he is able also to save . . . to the uttermost."

This one "without beginning of days or end of life" "ever lives to intercede for us." The Son's intercession differs from all other intercession because by his once-for-all, fully-effective sacrifice he has made atonement for sin and become "the Source of eternal salvation" (Heb 5:9). His session at the Father's right hand signals the acceptance of his intercession as well as

2. Cockerill, *Hebrews*, 332.

the sufficiency of his sacrifice (Heb 10:11–13). This One who has appeared before God "on our behalf" (Heb 9:24) does not stand before the Father and plead. He sits at the Father's right hand and guarantees that all who "come to God through him" will receive the grace necessary for perseverance. This perpetual intercession of the incarnate, eternal, now-exalted Son of God guarantees timely help for the beleaguered people of God (Heb 4:16). If we draw near to God through him the door of heaven is always open for us to enter and receive cleansing from sin and grace for perseverance in obedience. The pastor fervently desires that those who hear his message take full advantage of this inestimable privilege.

∾ Day Two: A Son Perfected Forever. (Heb 7:26–28)

26 For such a high priest would be precisely fitting for us—covenant keeping, without evil, without blemish, having been separated from sinners and having become higher than the heavens, 27 who does not have daily need, as those high priests, to offer sacrifice first for his own sins, then for the sins of the people. For this he did once-for-all by offering himself. 28 For the law established human beings having weakness as high priests, but the word of the oath, which came after the law, a son having been perfected forever.

It is as if the pastor can restrain himself no longer. He breaks out in this rapturous description of the way in which our High Priest is eminently fitting for the human condition. Each verse adds a new dimension to this picture of an appropriate high priest. Taken together these verses integrate what the pastor is about to say about this High Priest's incarnate obedience in Heb 8:1—10:18, with what he has already said about his session at God's right hand as the eternal Son in Heb 7:1–25. Thus, these verses reinforce what we have already heard and arouse our interest in what is about to be said.

Verse 26. The Greek text of this verse is a beautiful four-line poem. The first line, "For such a high priest would be precisely fitting for us," announces the theme of this passage, which describes the unrivaled appropriateness of the Son's high priesthood. The next line stresses the importance of his incarnate obedience: "covenant keeping, without evil, without blemish." We have already met his obedience in Heb 2:17–18; 4:14–16; and 5:7–8. We will soon see that through his earthly obedience he has offered himself as a sacrifice "without blemish" (Heb 8:3–6; 9:11–15; 9:25—10:14, especially 10:5–10), entered the heavenly sanctuary as a High Priest "untouched by evil" (Heb 8:1–2; 9:1–11; 10:23–24), and established the New Covenant by taking the curse of the broken Old Covenant upon himself (Heb 8:7–13; 9:16–22; 10:15–18). Line three, "Having been separated from sinners," directs our gaze from his obedient life to his session at God's right hand. It introduces his exaltation as the final triumph over sin. Line four, "Having become higher than the heavens," assures us that he has ascended into the very presence of God.

Verse 27. In various ways the pastor has been preparing us for his explanation of the Son's incarnate obedience unto death as a once-for-all sacrifice for sin. The Son took his seat at God's right hand by "having made purification for sin" (Heb 1:3). The Son "tasted death" for everyone (Heb 2:9). It was fitting that God perfect him as our Savior "through suffering" (Heb 2:10). Although he experienced the temptation common to all human beings, he was "without sin" (Heb 4:15). Heb 5:7–8 suggested that the Son's obedience "in the days of his flesh" succeeded where the twofold offering of the Aaronic high priest (Heb 5:3) had failed.

Now we have a clear statement contrasting the Son's once-for-all offering of himself with the oft-repeated double sacrifice of the Aaronic high priest. First, the Son "does not have daily need, as those high priests, to offer sacrifice first for his own sins, then for the sins of the people." There is no doubt that the pastor is thinking about the annual Day of Atonement described in Lev 16. On that Day the Aaronic high priest could offer the annual sacrifice for the sins of the nation only after he had offered a sacrifice for his own sins and the sins of the priestly house. He had to atone for his own sin before he could atone for others.

Why, then, does the pastor use the word "daily" when he knows that these Day-of-Atonement sacrifices were offered but once in the year (Heb 9:25)? First of all, the pastor is not concerned with the Day of Atonement alone. He sees atonement for sin as the ultimate purpose of the entire sacrificial system. Thus, the Son's sacrifice replaces *all* of the old sacrifices (Heb 10:5–10). Moreover, there were other times when the high priest offered a sacrifice for himself. By implying that the old high priests had need of atoning sacrifice "day by day" the pastor underscores the fact that the sinfulness which marred the sufficiency of their sacrifice for the sins of the people was a *daily* reality. The incarnate Son had no such need because he lived a life of *daily* obedience (Heb 5:8).

Thus, the Son had no need to offer for his own sin before offering for the sins of the people. Instead, he offered "himself" for the sins of the people. He offered his own life of human obedience, climaxing in the obedience of the cross, as a "once-for-all" atonement in place of the oft-repeated, ineffective sacrifices of the old, sinful high priesthood.

As we will see, this once-for-all sacrifice of the Son is at the heart of Heb 8:1—10:18. By adequately atoning for sin and satisfying the Old-Covenant curse on disobedience this sacrifice also consecrated Jesus as High Priest in heaven and established him as Guarantor/Mediator of the New Covenant.

Verse 28. The pastor concludes this section appropriately by summarizing what he has said about the eternal Son sitting at God's right hand in chapter seven, before addressing the obedience of the incarnate Son in Heb 8:1—10:18. We have learned that the priests established by the Mosaic "law" could not atone for sin because of the "weakness" inherent in human sinfulness and mortality (Heb 7:11–19, especially 11–14). We know, however, that "the word of the oath" found in Ps 110:4 (Heb 7:20–22), "which came after the law" (Heb 7:11–14), established the eternal "Son" (Heb 7:15–19) as priest "forever" (Heb 7:23–25).

What does the pastor mean, however, when he says that the Son "has been perfected"? In Heb 7:11 and 7:19 we have been told that there was no "perfection" through the Levitical priesthood or the law. Yet chapter 7 does not answer our question. The pastor will not let us avoid this issue. He emphasizes the word "perfected" by reserving it for the end of this verse in the Greek text: "a son forever perfected."

The eternal Son, creator, and judge of the universe (Heb 1:8–12), is, of course, without defect from eternity. However, by his incarnate obedience he has been "perfected" as our Savior and thus become "the Source of eternal salvation" (Heb 5:9). He is able to do what the old priesthood and law could not do, bring God's people into God's presence by cleansing them from sin. Thus, the pastor uses this word to introduce his description of how the eternal Son was "perfected" as our High Priest through his earthly obedience in Heb 8:1—10:18.

In Greek the language of "perfection" suggests that what has been perfected has reached the goal appropriate for its nature. In light of this fact, there are several ways in which "perfection" language is fitting when applied to the Son. First, as we saw when reading Heb 1:1–4, through his incarnate obedience the eternal Son fulfills his Sonship by becoming the "heir of all things." He reaches the goal, enters the "perfection," of his Sonship. Second, by his incarnate obedience the Son reaches the goal of humanity. He becomes the perfect human being. Finally, the language of perfection was used in the Greek Old Testament for the consecration of priests. Thus, it was natural for the pastor, who was very familiar with the Old Testament in Greek, to use this language for the Son's consecration as eternal High Priest. In sum, through his incarnate obedience the Son is "perfected" as our Savior.

By living a completely obedient human life the Son fulfilled his Sonship and was consecrated as the all-sufficient High Priest, the one who is perfectly able to save the people of God. How appropriate that the eternal

Son fulfilled his Sonship and became our all-sufficient Savior through his incarnate obedience. He has done for us what we could not do for ourselves. Re-read verses 26–28 and rejoice in the way God has provided so appropriately for our salvation.

✒ Day Three: A Minister of the Heavenly Sanctuary. (Heb 8:1–6)

¹ *Now this is the main point of the things being said, we have such a High Priest who has sat down at the right hand of the throne of the Majesty in the heavens, ² a minister of the sanctuary and the true Tabernacle that the Lord, and not any human being, has pitched.*

³ For every high priest is established to offer gifts and sacrifices. Therefore it was necessary for this one to have something to offer. ⁴ Now if he were on earth, he would not be a priest at all, because there are those who offer gifts according to the law. ⁵ They minister in a pattern and shadow of the heavenly, as Moses was solemnly commanded when he was about to complete the Tent: For he said, "see that you make all according to the copy shown you on the mountain." ⁶ But now this High Priest has obtained a ministry that is as much superior to theirs as the covenant of which he is Mediator is better, a covenant that has been legitimately established on better promises.

Today we begin listening to the first movement of the pastor's three-movement symphony on the incarnate obedience through which the eternal Son has become our all-sufficient High Priest at God's right hand and the Guarantor of the New Covenant. This first, foundational movement introduces the symphony's three themes—the *sanctuary*, in which our High Priest serves; the *sacrifice*, which he offered; and the *covenant*, which he has established. In today's reading we hear the first two themes, sanctuary (Heb 8:1–2) and sacrifice (Heb 8:3–6). For the third theme, covenant, we will have to wait until tomorrow (Heb 8:7–13).

This first movement rests on God's promises of a new priest who will sit at God's right hand (Ps 110:1, 4) and of a New Covenant (Jer 31:31–34). Since this High Priest will serve in the heavenly sanctuary (Heb 8:1–2) and establish a New Covenant (Heb 8:7–13), his sacrifice must be qualitatively superior to the sacrifices of the priests who serve in the earthly Tabernacle (Heb 8:3–6).

Verses 1–2. Listen carefully to verse one. The author tells us the "main theme" of Heb 7:1—10:18, and, indeed, of his entire sermon: "we have such a high priest who has sat down at the right hand of the throne of the Majesty in the heavens." This is the High Priest "appropriate" for our needs. This is the High Priest who enables our perseverance. This is the High Priest through which we draw near to God in order to find the "mercy" of forgiveness and the "grace" for obedience (Heb 4:16). This is the High Priest who has opened "the new and living way" (Heb 10:20). This High Priest alone is the "Pioneer and Perfecter of the [way of] faith" (Heb 12:1–3), the one who will sustain us until we reach "Mount Zion" (Heb 12:22–24). Keep your eyes on him (Heb 3:1–2, 12:1–3), for he is the eternal Son of God who through his incarnate obedience "has sat down at the right hand of the throne of the Majesty in the heavens." This expanded description, "the right hand of the throne of the Majesty in the heavens," emphasizes the sublime place and ultimate authority of his session at God's right hand.

He and he alone has become "a minister of the sanctuary and the true Tabernacle that the Lord, and not any human being, has pitched." "Sanctuary" and "true Tabernacle" refer to the same reality. "Sanctuary" identifies the place of his present priestly ministry as the true Most Holy Place, the heavenly dwelling place of God. "True Tabernacle that the Lord, and not any human being, has pitched" contrasts this sanctuary with the Tabernacle built by Moses. Since our high priest has opened a "way new and living" (Heb 10:20) into God's presence, this "true Tabernacle" has no outer, "holy place" that separates the worshiper from God (cf. Heb 9:1–10). The angels may have been sent out as "ministers" to assist the faithful (Heb 1:14). He, however, is, even now, a "minister" on our behalf seated in the place of all authority at God's right hand. How does the pastor know that the eternal Son serves as our high priest in this heavenly sanctuary? God, himself, has declared this to be so in Ps 110:1 and 4 as explained in Heb 1:1–14 and 7:1–28. How did the eternal Son enter into this ministry? Through his sacrifice, which the pastor begins to describe in verses 3–5.

Verses 3–5. In these verses the pastor lays a biblical foundation for the superiority of this High Priest's sacrifice. He still has Ps 110:4 in mind. Let's listen carefully to what he has to say.

First, in verse 3 the pastor establishes the *fact of this High Priest's sacrifice*. Here is his major premise: In Ps 110:4 God designated the one sitting at his right hand (Ps 110:1) as a priest. His minor premise is this: "offering gifts and sacrifices" is of the essence of priesthood (see Heb 5:1). The pastor then draws this conclusion: this High Priest sitting at God's right hand must have "something to offer." The singular "something" anticipates the yet-to-be-revealed "once-for-all" character of Christ's sacrifice.

Second, according to verse 4, this sacrifice was *appropriate* for a high priest who, since he has sat down at God's right hand (Ps 110:1), has entered a *heavenly*, rather than an earthly, *sanctuary*. If he were still "on earth he would not be a priest at all" because his sacrifice would have achieved nothing. We already have "those who offer gifts according to the law" on earth.

Third, then, according to verse 5, his sacrifice was both foreshadowed by, and superior to, theirs, because they ministered in what was "a pattern and shadow of the heavenly." The pastor can say this with confidence because in Exod 25:40 God told Moses to construct the Tabernacle and everything in it "according to the copy" that God had shown him on Mount Sinai. In the second movement the pastor will show us how the Tabernacle with its ritual (Heb 9:1–10) suggested and anticipated the effective sacrifice and priestly ministry of Christ (Heb 9:11–15).

This first movement, then, lays a biblical foundation for the pastor's descriptions of the sacrifice of our High Priest in Heb 9:11–15 and 9:24—10:14, especially in 10:5–10. We know, on the basis of the oracles of God (Ps 110:1, 4), that he offered a sacrifice and that this sacrifice was appropriate for one who now ministers in a "heavenly sanctuary." Thus, we know that it was distinct from and superior to those who "offered gifts according to the law" in the earthly sanctuary. And, finally, we know that the earthly sanctuary suggested and foreshadowed the ministry of our High Priest in the presence of God.

Verse 6. A sacrifice appropriate for the heavenly sanctuary must be radically superior to the sacrifices appropriate for its earthly type. This radical superiority is confirmed by the fact that this High Priest's sacrifice has established him as the Mediator of a "covenant" that is "better" because it is based on "better promises." In verses 7–13 below, the covenant section of this first movement, we will discover that these promises are found in Jer 31:31–34. They are "better" both because of *what* they promise and because of the *certainty* of their fulfillment. After all, this covenant is mediated by one who is its "Guarantor" (Heb 7:22).

This first movement is meant to leave us longing for the pastor's full description of our High Priest's ever-available heavenly intercession, his fully sufficient sacrifice, and the benefits of the New-Covenant way of living in fellowship with God. We will begin to explore this New Covenant tomorrow.

∾ **Day Four:** God's Promise of a New Covenant.
(Heb 8:7–13)

> [7] *For if that first [covenant] had been blameless, there would have been no occasion for a second to be sought.* [8] *For finding fault with*

> them he says: "Behold days are coming," says the Lord, "when I
> will complete a New Covenant with the house of Israel and the
> house of Judah. ⁹ It will not be like the covenant that I made with
> their fathers in the day when I took them by the hand to lead
> them out of the land of Egypt; because they did not remain in my
> covenant, and so I showed no concern for them," says the Lord.
> ¹⁰ "For this is the covenant that I will covenant with the house
> of Israel after those days," says the Lord: "I will put my laws in
> their minds and inscribe them upon their hearts; and I will be
> their God and they shall be my people. ¹¹ And they will not teach
> each his neighbor and each his brother saying "Know the Lord,"
> because all shall know me from the least unto the greatest of them.
> ¹² For I will be merciful toward their unrighteous deeds, and their
> sins I will remember no more." ¹³ By saying "new" he makes the
> first obsolete. What is becoming obsolete and growing old is on the
> verge of passing away.

The pastor cites the "New-Covenant" passage from Jer 31:31–34 without comment save for his introductory and concluding remarks in verses 7–8a and 13. The first half of this quotation, Jer 31:31–32 (Heb 8:8b–9), exposes the inadequacy of the Old, now-broken Covenant. In the second half, Jer 31:33–34 (Heb 8:10–12), we find the promises of the New Covenant that describe how it supplies the benefits lacking in the Old.

The pastor quotes this long passage in full because it is a central motif in the symphony he is presenting here. First of all, in Heb 8:10–12 (Jer 32:33–34) we find the "better promises" to which the pastor referred in verse 6 above. The benefits promised through this New Covenant clearly imply the unique character of Christ's sacrifice. Second, this passage from Jeremiah lays the necessary foundation for Heb 9:16–22 and 10:16–18, the covenant sections of the second (Heb 9:1–22) and third (Heb 9:23—10:18) movements of this symphony. According to Heb 9:16–22 Christ has taken upon himself the curse of the broken covenant described in Heb 8:8–9 (Jer 31:31–32). According to Heb 10:16–18, he now sits at God's right hand as the Guarantor of the "better promises" found in Heb 8:10–12 (Jer 31:33–34). It was necessary to remove the curse in order to guarantee the promises. Third, this Jeremiah passage bridges the gap between the disobedient wilderness generation of Heb 3:7—4:13 and the parade of the faithful in Heb 11:1–40. The people of the wilderness generation were the "fathers" (Heb 8:10) with whom God "found fault" (Heb 8:8) because they broke the first covenant. On the other hand, the pastor will urge his hearers to appropriate the blessings of the New Covenant (Heb 8:10–12) in order to join the faithful of chapter 11. This passage harmonizes perfectly with the surrounding themes in the pastor's score.

Verses 7–9. The introductory statement in verse 7 focuses our attention on the inadequacy of the Old Covenant as described in Jer 31:31–32 (Heb 8:8b–9). You will remember that according to Heb 7:11–14 the divine proclamation of a new priest, apart from its fulfillment, exposed the imperfection of the Aaronic priesthood. In the same way, the very fact that God "sought" to establish a New Covenant implied that the Old Covenant was not without blame.

God's declaration in Jer 31:31 (Heb 8:8) that he would establish a New Covenant provided the necessary Scriptural support for that Covenant. The God who announced the Son's deity (Ps 2:7; 2 Sam 7:14; Ps 45:7–8; and Ps 102:25–27, in Heb 1:5–12), invited him to sit at his right hand (Ps 110:1 in Heb 1:13), and proclaimed him priest forever with an oath (Ps 110:4 in Heb 7:1–25), has also declared that he would establish a New Covenant (Jer 31:31–34). This New Covenant "with the house of Israel and the house of Judah" includes the faithful of all time who are part of God's "House" (Heb 3:1–6).

Nevertheless, the pastor's main point here is that by announcing he would "complete" or perfect a New, fully adequate Covenant, God was "finding fault" with the Old Covenant. The pastor's criticism of the Old Covenant is more muted than his insistence that the old priesthood has been abolished because of its "weakness and uselessness" (Heb 7:18). Although the Old Covenant was unable to provide the release from sin and the heart renewal available under the New (Heb 10:15–18), it was possible for people under the Old Covenant to live faithfully, as evidenced by Heb 11:1–40. God's description of his judgment upon the disobedient wilderness generation is all the more alarming for its understatement: "so I showed no concern for them." The inadequacy of the Old Covenant was no excuse for the faithlessness of that generation (Heb 3:7—4:13). God's people today are even more accountable before the abundant adequacy supplied by God through the New.

There can be no doubt that the Old Covenant described in verse 9 was the covenant God made with the wilderness generation (Heb 3:7—4:13). God describes it as "the covenant that I made with their [the people of Jeremiah's time] fathers in the day when I took them by the hand to lead them out of the land of Egypt." Note the tenderness of this expression: in his graciousness God took them by the hand and led them like a child out of Egypt. The problem was that, despite God's tender goodness, "they did not remain in my covenant." The pastor *longs* for his hearers to "remain" in God's New Covenant. It is powered by a High Priest who "remains"

(Heb 7:3, 24) and leads to an eternal destiny that "remains" (Heb 10:34; 12:27; 13:14). The Old Covenant is not like the New because the New furnishes all the resources one could possibly need to "remain," to persevere in faithful obedience until the end.

Verses 10–12. In these verses the pastor quotes Jer 31:33–34, the account of the "better promises" that describe the glorious benefits and privileges available through the New Covenant. These promises support the pastor's contention in verse 6 above that Christ's sacrifice must be something far superior to the sacrifices of the earthly Tabernacle because it establishes Jesus as the Mediator of the effective covenant that fulfills these wonderful promises. Nevertheless, the pastor reserves his explanation of these promises for the conclusion of his symphony in the covenant section (Heb 10:15–18) of the third movement (Heb 9:23—10:18). There are two reasons for this delay. First, we would not be able to adequately understand these promises without the pastor's grand exposition of the Son's sacrifice in the following two movements. Second, the description of these glorious New-Covenant benefits is a most fitting conclusion for this symphony and the perfect point of transition to the pastor's exhortation that follows. The magnitude of these benefits is what makes perseverance possible, and apostasy so tragic.

Verse 13. In this concluding verse of the first movement the pastor completes what he began in verses 7–8 above. According to those verses the *fact* of God's promise that he would "complete" another covenant exposed the fault of the old. According to verse 13, the *fact* that God called it a "New" Covenant showed that the Old was not only flawed, but "obsolete." It was being replaced with a "better" model. When God spoke this promise of a "New" Covenant through the mouth of Jeremiah, the Old Covenant was already "becoming obsolete and growing old" and "on the verge of passing away." It has now been replaced by the One who is "Guarantor" of this "better" New Covenant (Heb 7:22).

At this point the pastor wants us all on the edges of our seats. What are the benefits of this High Priest who is a minister for us in the heavenly sanctuary, sitting at the right hand of God? Please explain the blessings of this New Covenant. Above all, what made Jesus' sacrifice so potent that it consecrated him High Priest of the heavenly sanctuary and established him as the "Guarantor" of this New Covenant? All will be resolved when we have listened to movements two (Heb 9:1–22) and three (Heb 9:23—10:18).

∾ Day Five: An Earthly Sanctuary. (Heb 9:1–10)

[1] *On the other hand, then, the first covenant was having regulations for worship and an earthly sanctuary.* [2] *A Tent had been
prepared, the first, in which were the lampstand and the table and
the presentation of bread. This Tent was called the Holy Place.*
[3] *But after the second curtain was a Tent called the Most Holy
Place,* [4] *having an incense altar covered with gold and the Ark of
the Covenant covered all over with gold, in which was a golden jar
containing manna and Aaron's rod that budded and the tablets of
the covenant.* [5] *Above the Ark were the Cherubim of glory overshadowing the mercy seat. Concerning these things we cannot not
now speak in detail.* [6] *When these things had been prepared, the
priests regularly entered the first Tent in order to fulfill their service,* [7] *but the high priest alone entered into the second once a year,
but not without blood, which he offered for himself and for the
people's sins of ignorance.* [8] *By this the Holy Spirit is showing that
the way into the Sanctuary was not yet revealed while that first
Tent still had validity.* [9] *That Tent was a parable for the time then
present. In relation to that Tent gifts and sacrifices were offered
which were not able to perfect the worshipers in regard to their
conscience.* [10] *Those gifts and sacrifices pertained only to food and
drink and various washings, regulations of the flesh, established
until the time of correction.*

The first movement (Heb 8:1–13) of this symphony on the incarnation of
the Son began with the High Priest in the heavenly *sanctuary* (8:1–2) as
promised in Ps 110:1, 4, and concluded with the New *Covenant* (8:7–13) as
promised in Jer 31:31–34. Jesus' *sacrifice* (8:3–6) must have been superior
to the sacrifices of the earthly Tabernacle because it established him as High
Priest in heaven and Guarantor of the New Covenant.

In this second movement (Heb 9:1–22) the pastor turns his gaze
from the promises of a priest in the heavenly sanctuary and of a New
Covenant to the descriptions of the earthly *sanctuary* (Heb 9:1–10) and
the inauguration of the Old, now broken, *Covenant* (Heb 9:16–22) in the
Pentateuch. These descriptions demonstrate the inadequacy of the sacrifices pertaining to those institutions, and thus underscore the sufficiency
of Christ's *sacrifice* (Heb 9:11–15). He alone can cleanse those who draw
near through him from sin, bring them into God's presence, and deliver
them from the Old-Covenant curse on disobedience.

Verse 1. The *sanctuary* section (Heb 9:1–10) with which this second
movement begins describes the "earthly sanctuary" of the "first covenant"
in verses 2–5, and the "regulations for worship" in that earthly sanctuary

in verses 6–7. Verses 8–10 reveal the "Spirit" intended significance of this "earthly sanctuary" and its worship.

Verses 2–5. The pastor's description of the Tabernacle instituted by Moses in Exodus emphasizes its earthly nature and its division into two parts. The way in which he speaks of the Holy Place and the Most Holy Place as two separate "tents" underscores this division. He reminds his hearers that the two were divided by the "second curtain." The two are also distinguished by their contents. The "lampstand" and the "table" for the "presentation of bread" freshly baked each week were in the "first," preliminary, "Tent." On the other hand, the "incense altar covered with gold," "the Ark of the Covenant covered all over with gold," along with its contents, and "the Cherubim of glory overshadowing the mercy seat" on the top of the Ark pertained to the Most Holy Place. Although the "altar of incense" was technically in the Holy Place, it was sometimes (as here) associated with the Most Holy Place because it was made of gold and stood just before the entrance into that inner sanctuary.

The pastor also distinguishes the Most Holy Place from the Holy Place by pointing out that its furnishings were of gold. This was the dwelling place of God. The "glory" of the Lord dwelt among his people between the "Cherubim" over the Ark that contained "the tablets of the covenant" upon which God himself had inscribed the Ten Commandments. This glowing description of the Most Holy Place makes it a fitting type or picture of the heavenly sanctuary in which God dwells. And yet the wealth of detail in this description reinforces the fact that both "first" and "second" Tents were part of an "earthly" Tabernacle "made with hands" (Heb 9:24).

Verses 6–7. The "regulations for worship" in this "earthly sanctuary" (v. 1) were based on this sharp division between the "first" and "second" Tents, the Holy Place and the Most Holy Place. "[T]he priests regularly entered the first Tent in order to fulfill their service." Day after day and week after week they trimmed the lamps on the lampstand and replaced the "bread" on the table. They offered incense on the altar of incense, but they could not enter the Most Holy Place of God's earthly dwelling. The *only* exception was the "once–a–year" Day of Atonement when the "high priest," and the high priest "*alone*" (italics added) entered that "second Tent." He entered *only* with sacrificial blood which he had to offer first "for himself" and, only then, "for the people's sins of ignorance." In this context "ignorance" does not excuse sin. Sin is characterized by "ignorance" of God and his ways. One exception, on one day in the year, for one person alone. The pastor wants us to see the worship of the "first" covenant going round and round in that first, *preliminary* Tent. The impenetrable barrier is the unresolved "sins of the people."

Verses 8–10. So, what did this perpetual limitation to the "first Tent" mean? By inspiring the Scriptural description of this limitation "the Holy Spirit is showing that the way into the Sanctuary was not yet revealed while that first Tent had validity." The pastor always uses "Sanctuary" for the heavenly Sanctuary unless he qualifies it as "earthly" or "made with hands" (Heb 9:24). It is true, as we will see in verses 11–15, that the high priest entering into the Most Holy Place is a type or picture of Christ. Yet before the coming of God's Son, "while that first Tent had validity," the way into the heavenly Sanctuary was not yet even "revealed." The high priest himself only entered into the *earthly* Most Holy Place. People knew that they did not have direct access to God's presence—they knew all too well! They had no idea how the way would be opened for them to enter God's heavenly presence.

The Holy Place, the first "Tent," says the pastor, "was a parable for the time then present," the time before the eternal Son of God took his seat at God's right hand as High Priest through the sacrifice of his incarnate obedience. Sin was the problem. The "gifts and sacrifices" offered in relation to that "Tent" were "not able to perfect the worshipers in regard to their conscience," they were not able to bring them into God's presence by cleansing them from sin. Those sacrifices "pertained only to food and drink and various washings, regulations of the flesh," which, it is true, were "established" by God, but established to be practiced only "until the time of correction," that is, until the coming of our "Great High Priest."

However now, according to tomorrow's reading, the *sacrifice* section (Heb 9:11–15) of this second movement (Heb 9:1–22), the way into the heavenly Sanctuary has been revealed and made available to the people of God through a sacrifice that "cleanses the conscience from dead works to serve the living God." Thank God for this bountiful, long-anticipated provision that opened the way for his people to enter into his heavenly presence.

∾ Day Six: An Effective Sacrifice. (Heb 9:11–15)

[11] *But Christ has arrived as High Priest of the good things that have come through the greater and more perfect Tent not made with hands, that is, not of this creation.* [12] *He entered once-for-all into the Sanctuary not by means of the blood of goats and calves but by means of his own blood, having obtained eternal redemption.* [13] *For if the blood of goats and bulls and the ashes of a heifer sprinkled on the participants sanctify for the purification of the flesh,* [14] *by how much more will the blood of Christ, who through the eternal Spirit offered himself blameless to God, cleanse our conscience from dead works to serve the living God.* [15] *And on*

account of this he is Mediator of a New Covenant, so that, since a
death has occurred for redemption of the transgressions based on
the First Covenant, those who have been called might receive the
promise of eternal inheritance.

The glorious sufficiency of *Christ's self-offering*, described in this passage, is
illuminated by the preceding description of the *earthly sanctuary* in verses
1–10, and the following description of the old, broken *Covenant* in verses
16–22. Christ serves in the heavenly Sanctuary (Heb 9:11), not the earthly
"Tent" (Heb 9:1–10), because his self-offering has atoned for sin (Heb 9:12–
14). Furthermore, on the basis of that effective self-offering, he has become
Mediator of the New Covenant (Heb 9:15) by taking the sin-curse of the
broken Old Covenant upon himself (Heb 9:16–22).

Verse 11. The ministry of the earthly Tent, as we have seen (Heb 9:1–
10), could never bring people into God's presence. "But Christ," as we saw
in the opening sanctuary section (Heb 8:1–2) of the first movement (Heb
8:1–13), is a "minister in the heavenly sanctuary."

"Has arrived" underscores the continuing, perennial availability of
this High Priest. He has not separated himself from us by entering the
heavenly Sanctuary. His ministry in that sanctuary has opened the way for
the faithful people of God to enter the Divine Presence. The "good things
that have come" include cleansing from sin, access to God's presence, and
heart transformation. The following verses describe these good things as
"eternal redemption" (v. 12), as the cleansing "of our conscience from dead
works to serve the living God" (v. 14), and, ultimately, as "the promise of
eternal inheritance" (v. 16).

"The greater and more perfect Tent" of verse 11 and the "sanctuary"
of verse 12 both describe the heavenly dwelling place of God, the true Most
Holy Place. Viewed from without, "the greater and more perfect Tent" contrasts with the earthly Mosaic Tent through which, according to verses 8–10,
there was no access to God. However, from within, it is the "Sanctuary," the
Most Holy Place of God's dwelling. God's careful instructions for the building
of the old Mosaic Tent (Exod 25:1—31:18), and the detailed account of its
construction (Exod 35:1—40:33), underscore the description of its earthly,
man–made character in verses 2–5 above. The true heavenly Sanctuary, however, was "not made by hands," indeed, it was not "of this creation."

Verse 12. This verse contrasts the self-offering of Christ with the ineffective sacrifices of the earthly Tent described in verses 6–7 above. The
high priests of that Tent could only enter the earthly Most Holy Place,
and only on the annual Day of Atonement (Lev 16:11–19), because they
entered only "by means of the blood of goats and calves." Christ, however,

has made a "once-for-all" eternal and definitive entrance into the true heavenly dwelling place of God "by means of his own blood." This phrase describes his offering of himself in obedience to the Father on the cross (Heb 2:9; 5:7–8; 10:5–10).

It is true, as verse 7 above implies, that the old high priest entered the earthly Sanctuary with the blood of animal sacrifices, which he then sprinkled on the Mercy Seat (the throne of God) above the Ark. Perhaps under the assumption that Jesus did the same, the NRSV and several other versions have mistranslated "by means of his own blood" as "with his own blood." Hebrews, however, never says that Jesus offered his blood in the heavenly Sanctuary. Instead, he entered the true heavenly sanctuary "by means of" his self-offering on the cross in obedience to the Father. By this offering he obtained a "redemption" from sin and death that was "eternal" in both duration and effectiveness. In Heb 10:11–14, the conclusion of the sacrifice section (Heb 9:25—10:14) of the third movement (Heb 9:23—10:18), we will find out what he did do when he entered the Most Holy Place on our behalf. He did not sprinkle blood on a heavenly "Mercy Seat." He sat down at the right hand of the throne of God.

Verses 13–14. The pastor explained why the sacrifices of the earthly Tent were ineffective in verses 8–10 above. Now, by expanding the contrast between the "blood of bulls and goats" (v. 13) and the "blood of Christ" (v. 14), he explains why Christ's self-offering is effective.

The water of purification made with the "ashes of a heifer," which had been slaughtered and burned "without the camp" of Israel (Num 19:1–10), was distinct from the sacrificial "blood of goats and bulls" offered on the Day of Atonement. That water was used for the *ritual* purification of such things as household utensils and clothes, as well as the bodies of human beings defiled by contact with a dead body. The pastor mentions it here because it helps to demonstrate that all of the sacrifices of the Old Covenant pertained only to "the purification of the flesh." Such outward purification allowed people to participate in the worship of the old Tent, but it did not change their lives.

This outward, ritual purification, however, anticipated the inner transformation effected by the "blood of Christ," which is here described as the cleansing "of the conscience from dead works to serve the living God." The word "conscience" refers to our inner, true self, our heart, and emphasizes our moral responsibility before God. By his obedient self-offering Christ cleanses this inner reality from the "works" of sin that lead to death (Heb 2:14–18). This cleansing involves both forgiveness and transformation. By releasing us from "*dead* works" Christ empowers us "to serve the *living* God" (italics added).

The relative clause, "who through the eternal Spirit offered himself blameless to God" (v. 14), reveals the two reasons why Christ's sacrifice brought true, inner cleansing. First, the *eternal* Son of God (Heb 1:1–14, 7:15) offered himself "through the *eternal* Spirit" of God (italics added). His sacrifice was not marred by human frailty (Heb 7:11–19). It was powered by a God who, in contrast to humanity, was *eternal*. Second, by that *eternal* divine power the Son of God offered a genuine, but "blameless," human life to God on the cross. His perfect obedience has provided for our "eternal redemption."

Verse 15. Now we are in a position to see the full significance of Christ's self-offering. By providing the adequate atonement for sin anticipated by the Day of Atonement (vv. 12–14), it consecrated him as high priest of the heavenly sanctuary (v. 11), and established him as "Mediator of a New Covenant" (v. 15).

We will understand how Christ became "Mediator of the New Covenant" if we remember that his fulfillment of the Old Covenant was twofold. That covenant was a covenant of both law and grace. As law, it pronounced judgement on unfaithfulness. The disobedient were under the curse of death. As grace, it offered forgiveness and cleansing through the sacrificial system. On the one hand, Christ demonstrated that the sacrificial system of the Old Covenant, though ineffective as a means of approaching God, was an indispensable type or picture of his all-sufficient sacrifice and eternal priesthood. Without this picture we would be hard-pressed to understand Christ's all-sufficiency as Savior and the "so great salvation" he has provided (Heb 2:3). On the other hand, the very effectiveness of this "so great salvation" only made the Old Covenant's judgement upon disobedience more certain. This enhanced certainty of judgment underlies all the warnings of Hebrews, beginning with Heb 2:1–4. By his atoning "death" Christ has provided "redemption" from the "transgressions" condemned by that "First Covenant."

Verses 16–22 below, the covenant section of this second movement (Heb 9:1–22), show how Christ has freed "those who have been called" from the Old Covenant's death-curse and thus enabled them to "receive the promise of eternal inheritance" that awaits the persevering faithful people of God (Heb 1:14). By taking this curse upon himself, he has become the Mediator, and Guarantor, of the New Covenant, soon to be described in Heb 10:15–18, the covenant section of movement three (Heb 9:23—10:18), as a covenant of genuine forgiveness and heart transformation. All praise to him who has taken our curse upon himself and opened the way for us to enter into our "eternal inheritance."

∾ Day Seven: A Broken Covenant. (Heb 9:16–22)

[16] *For where there is a covenant, of necessity the death of the one making the covenant must be borne.* [17] *For a covenant is confirmed on the basis of deaths, since it never is in force when the one making the covenant is alive.* [18] *Therefore the First Covenant was not inaugurated without blood.* [19] *For when all the ordinances according to the law had been spoken by Moses to the whole people, he took the blood of bulls[3] with water and with scarlet wool and hyssop and sprinkled both the book itself and all the people,* [20] *saying: "This is the blood of the covenant that God has completed for you."* [21] *And the Tent and all the utensils of worship he likewise sprinkled with blood.* [22] *And almost everything is purified with blood according to the law, and without the shedding of blood there is no release.*

It will be helpful to begin with a note about translation. The NASB is the only popular English version that uses the word "covenant" in verses 16 and 17. Other translations use "testament" or "will." In secular writings from New Testament times the underlying Greek word often referred to a "last will" or "testament." However, in the Greek Old Testament, and elsewhere in Hebrews, this word always means "covenant." Has the pastor used this word for "covenant" in verse 15, "will" or "testament" in verses 16 and 17, and then, again, for "covenant" in verses 18 and 20? Such awkwardness is uncharacteristic of his careful style. In a ground-breaking study, Scott Hahn has shown that the word "covenant" is most appropriate in verses 16 and 17 when we realize that throughout this passage the pastor is talking about a *broken* covenant, the *broken* Old Covenant described in Jer 31:31–32/Heb 8:8b–9. Furthermore, when verse 15 above speaks of "transgressions on the basis of the First Covenant," it is referring to the Old Covenant as a *broken* covenant. Our translation above and explanation below are based on this insight from Scott Hahn.[4]

God's promise of a New Covenant (Jer 31:31–34), quoted in the covenant section (Heb 8:7–13) of the first movement (Heb 8:1–13) of this symphony (Heb 8:1—10:18), was a beacon of hope for the people of God. The covenant sections (Heb 9:16–22; 10:15–18) of the second and third movements allow that beacon to shine with clarity and brilliance. Christ overcame the ineffectiveness of the Old Covenant (Heb 9:16–22) so that he could administer

---

3. Some ancient manuscripts read "goats and bulls." A copyist probably inadvertently added the word "goats" from verses 12 and 13 above. Exod 24:3–8 says nothing about "goats."

4. You will find an extended discussion of this issue and the references to Scott Hahn's two articles on this passage in Cockerill, *Hebrews*, 403–19.

the benefits of the New (Heb 10:15–18). The Old Covenant was marred by the disobedience of the people of God (Jer 31:31–32/Heb 8:8b–9). It was a *broken* Covenant. This problem was solved by the New Covenant, under which God's people would find release from the sin of the past and power for obedience in the present (Jer 31:33–34/Heb 8:10–11).

Heb 9:16–22, then, explains how Christ overcame the ineffectiveness of the Old *broken* Covenant described in Jer 31:31–32/Heb 8:8b–9. From yesterday's reading we know that fulfillment in Christ has certified the continuing validity of the Old Covenant's condemnation of disobedience. We also know that "a death has occurred for redemption of the transgressions based on the First Covenant" (v. 15). Such a death was necessary "For where there is a [broken] covenant, of necessity the death of the one making the covenant must be borne" (v. 16).

Verse 16–17. Why doesn't the pastor simply say, "The one who breaks a covenant must die"? Why this impersonal, awkward way of speaking in both verses 15 and 16: "a death has occurred," and especially, "the death of the one making a covenant *must be borne*" (italics added)? The answer is clear. The penalty for breaking a covenant is, indeed, the death of the one who made and then broke the covenant. However, in this case, the death that "has occurred" is not the death of the disobedient. It is the perfectly obedient life of the incarnate Son of God offered up on the cross in obedience to the will of God (Heb 10:5–10) "for redemption of the transgressions based on the First Covenant." "He has *borne* our griefs and carried our sorrows" (Isa 53:4 ESV, italics added).

The pastor adds verse 17 to make sure that we understand why what he has said is true. He is so concerned that we grasp his point that he says it twice—first positively, then, negatively. First, what he has said is true because a broken "covenant is confirmed on the basis of deaths." The validity of this broken covenant is demonstrated when the punishment it pronounced on the covenant breaker comes into effect. The plural "deaths" reminds us of the disobedient wilderness generation described in Heb 3:7—4:11. They are the ones with whom God made the Old Covenant at Sinai. They broke that covenant through their disobedience, which climaxed in the rebellion at Kadesh Barnea. As a result, their "corpses fell in the desert" (Heb 3:17). Second, negatively, a broken covenant is "never in force when the one making [and breaking] the covenant is alive." If the violator goes unpunished, the covenant must not have been valid.

Verses 18–20. The pastor substantiates what he has said by describing the ceremony by which the Old Covenant was established according to Exod 24:3–8. Verse 18 is understatement: "Therefore the First Covenant was not inaugurated without blood." We don't know how many bulls

Moses had the young men sacrifice (Exod 24:5), but there appears to have been gallons of blood!

Moses spoke "all the ordinances" that were in the Book of the Covenant to "all the people" (v. 19). The people promised: "All that the Lord has spoken we will do, and we will be obedient" (Exod 24:7 NASB). Then, according to the Old Testament, Moses "threw" half the blood on the Altar, representing God, and half on the people. Hebrews says that he "sprinkled" the "Book" (containing God's ordinances) and "all the people" (v. 20). The Book had probably been placed on the altar. There must have been blood everywhere. The blood of the sacrifices sprinkled on the people, and on the book/altar representing God, obligated them to keep their vow of obedience on pain of their own blood. Moses made sure that they understood the significance of this blood by declaring: "This is the blood of the covenant that God has completed for you" (v. 20). This ceremony was meant to impress this fact upon the people in the strongest terms: violation of their covenant vow would require their own blood!

Verses 21–22. Everything about the Old Covenant confirmed this truth. After Moses inaugurated the Old Covenant in Exod 24:3–8, he received the instructions for the Old Covenant Tent (Tabernacle, Exod 25:1—31:18) and then oversaw its construction (Exod 35:1—40:33). Although the Old Testament may not be clear at this point, the first-century Jewish historian Josephus and others agreed with Hebrews: Moses sprinkled blood on that "Tent and all the utensils of worship" associated with it (v. 21). In fact, the Old Testament makes it clear that "almost everything is purified with blood according to the law" of the Old Covenant. All of this shows that the life of the covenant breaker is forfeit. "Without the shedding of blood there is no release" from the curse of the Old Covenant upon the disobedient.

In conclusion, let's step back and look at the two scenes the pastor has brought before our eyes in this second movement (Heb 9:1–22). This movement began in Heb 9:1–10 with a description of the Old Covenant Tent and the sacrifices that pertained to it. It concludes in Heb 9:16–22 with a description of the sacrifices by which the Old Covenant was inaugurated and by which its Tent was dedicated. The first scene shows clearly that the "blood of goats and bulls" (vv. 12–13) could not cleanse God's people from sin and bring them into God's presence. The second scene is a vivid reminder of the impending condemnation of the Old Covenant upon the disobedient. "[W]ithout the shedding of blood there is no release" (v. 22) from the curse of death pronounced upon the disobedient by the Old Covenant.

Praise God! The answer to the human dilemma, so vividly conveyed by these two scenes, is "the precious blood of Christ" (v. 14). By offering himself as an obedient human being on the cross the Son of God both cleanses "our conscience from dead works to serve the living God" (v. 14) and redeems us from "the transgressions based on the First Covenant" (v. 15). By thus dealing with the sin that left us accursed and separated from God, he has become the Mediator/Guarantor of the New Covenant, of a new and effective way to enter God's presence and live as God's holy people.

"Behold, I Have Come . . . to Do, O God, Your Will"

Hebrews 9:23—10:31

Introduction

I t will take the first five days of this week to explore movement three (Heb 9:23—10:18) of the grand symphony on the Son's high priesthood and sacrifice (Heb 8:1—10:18). As you will remember, each movement in this symphony progresses through the themes of *sanctuary, sacrifice,* and *covenant.* According to the first movement (Heb 8:1–13), the fact that God had promised a priest in the *heavenly* sanctuary (Heb 8:1–2) and a *New* Covenant (Heb 8:7–13) showed the superiority of the Son's *sacrifice* (Heb 8:3–6). His sacrifice was qualitatively distinct from the sacrifices appropriate for the earthly Tent and Old Covenant. We entitled that movement, "The New Promised." According to the second movement (Heb 9:1–22), the Old Testament descriptions of the earthly *sanctuary* (Heb 9:1–10) and Old *Covenant* (Heb 9:16–22) demonstrated the inability of the old sacrifices to deal with sin. Thus, by his *sacrifice* the Son fulfilled what they in their ineffectiveness only anticipated (Heb 9:11–15). By offering a sacrifice that truly cleansed the faithful from sin he became High Priest in the heavenly sanctuary and the Guarantor of a New Covenant of obedience. We entitled this second movement, "The Old Antiquated: the New Foreshadowed."

Our title for movement three (Heb 9:23—10:18) is "The New Explained." We might, however, have called it, "The New Celebrated." This final movement is a grand celebration of the Son's all-sufficient self-offering. The *sacrifice* section of movement one (Heb 8:1–13) occupied three verses (Heb 8:3–6); and of movement two (Heb 9:1–22), five (Heb 9:11–15). In movement three (Heb 9:23—10:18), the *sacrifice* section runs for eighteen verses (Heb 9:25—10:14). This grand, climactic explanation of the Son's

sacrifice falls naturally into three parts: Heb 9:25—10:4; 10:5–10; and
10:11–14. According to the first and third parts, the "once-for-all" character
of Christ's sacrifice (Heb 9:25—10:4) and his session at God's right hand
(Heb 10:11–14) demonstrate its effectiveness. However, the central section, Heb 10:5–10, gives the *reason* for the effectiveness of his sacrifice—the
incarnate obedience of the Son of God! In this central part, Heb 10:5–10,
the chords of this symphony resolve. This final movement, which begins
with our High Priest's entrance into heaven "on our behalf" (Heb 9:23–24),
concludes with our gaze fixed on the one seated at God's right hand (Heb
10:11–14) as Mediator of the New Covenant (Heb 10:15–18).

When we reach Heb 10:18 we have come to the conclusion of this
symphony (Heb 8:1—10:18). All that remains of the pastor's grand description of Christ's all-sufficient high priesthood (Heb 4:14—10:25) is the concluding summary and exhortation in Heb 10:19–25. The pastor has used
this grand description to press the sufficiency of Christ upon his hearers
as both means and motivation for avoiding the fate of the disobedient wilderness generation (Heb 3:7–19) and for persevering as part of the grand
company of the faithful described in Heb 11:1–40. We can think of Heb
10:19–39 as a three–link chain that joins the life of faith (Heb 10:32—11:40)
with the all-sufficiency of Christ our High Priest who enables us to live
that life (Heb 4:14—10:25). The first link, Heb 10:19–25, is the conclusion
of the pastor's description of our all-sufficient High Priest. The third, Heb
10:32–39, introduces the catalog of the faithful.

The pastor urges his hearers to persevere, first, by encouraging them
with the benefits available through our Great High Priest (Heb 10:19–25,
link one), then, by warning them lest they forfeit those benefits (Heb
10:26–31, link two), and, finally, by expressing confidence, on the basis of
their past conduct, that they are among those who will join the company
of the faithful described in Heb 11:1–40 (Heb 10:32–39, link three). On
days six and seven of this week we will look at links one (Heb 10:19–25)
and two (Heb 10:26–31).

∿ Day One: A Sanctuary that is "Heaven Itself."
(Heb 9:23–24)

²³ *Therefore it was¹ necessary for the pattern of the things in the
heavens to be cleansed with these sacrifices, but the heavenly*

---

1. A literal translation of the Greek text would be, "Necessary therefore on the one
hand the pattern of the things in the heavens to be cleansed by these." Most English
translations supply the verb "was"—"it was necessary" (NRSV, TNIV).

things themselves with better sacrifices than these. [24] *For Christ has not entered into a sanctuary made with hands, a representation of the true Sanctuary, but into heaven itself, now to appear before the face of God on our behalf.*

The sanctuary section (Heb 8:1–2) of movement one announced that, by taking his seat at God' right hand, our High Priest had become "a minister of the Sanctuary and true Tent" pitched by the Lord himself. According to the sanctuary section (Heb 9:1–10) of the second movement, the old high priest, by contrast, could only enter the earthly representation of God's presence in the Tent constructed by Moses, and that only once a year. This sanctuary section (Heb 9:23–24) of the third movement climaxes the pastor's discussion of *sanctuary* by contrasting the two entrances to the two sanctuaries, the "type" or picture with the fulfillment. The pastor explains the means by which Christ has entered, removes any ambiguity as to the place he has entered, and makes it clear why he is there.

Verse 23. The way in which Christ has entered the heavenly sanctuary clears the way for our entrance. It was not sufficient for Christ to cleanse only the "conscience" of believers from sin and empower them to "serve the living God" (Heb 9:14). He had to cleanse the heavenly sanctuary. In Heb 9:21 above we just discovered that the earthly "Tent and all its utensils" were purified with blood. If, then, "it was necessary for the pattern of the things in the heavens to be cleansed with" the blood of animal sacrifices, how much more "the heavenly things themselves with better sacrifices"—with the "once-for-all" (Heb 9:25—10:4) offering of the Son's obedient human life (Heb 10:5–10) by which he took his seat at God's right hand (Heb 10:11–14). The cleansing of the earthly "type" with animal blood foreshadowed the Son's cleansing of the heavenly reality with his self-offering of obedience.

It seems strange to speak of "cleansing" "the heavenly things." How could heavenly things become polluted? By "polluting" the earthly sanctuary the sins of God's people prevented them from coming into God's presence. The pollution of "the heavenly things" represents the barrier that sin erects between us and God. Sin not only binds and corrupts the "conscience," it separates from God. By offering himself in obedience to God, Christ not only set our hearts free from the pollution and power of sin but removed the barrier that separated us from God. By adequately dealing with sin he entered God's presence as our heavenly High Priest and cleared the way for us to enter. By making a sufficient atonement for sin his sacrifice became a sacrifice of priestly consecration.

Verse 24. The pastor removes any ambiguity as to the identity of the Sanctuary that Christ has entered—it is nothing less than "heaven itself." It is no two-part sanctuary located in heaven. The two parts of the earthly, manmade sanctuary were essential for its function as a type. As noted above in the discussion of Heb 9:1–10, the outer part, or Holy Place, showed that there was as yet no entrance into the presence of God typified by the Most Holy Place. "Heaven itself" is the true Most Holy Place, the heavenly dwelling of God.

What, then, is our High Priest doing in this "true Sanctuary"? He has entered "now to appear before the face of God on our behalf." The eternal Son of God has not simply returned to his eternal existence as the Son of God. He is now the incarnate Jesus who through his obedient self-offering has returned to heaven and taken his seat at God's right hand as our all-sufficient High Priest. "Now," even right *now*, he appears "before the face of God on our behalf." There is no stronger way to emphasize that this is no figure or type than the phrase "before the *face* of God" (italics added). He is our representative, ushering those who approach God through him into the divine presence, ministering the mercy of forgiveness and grace for victorious living, guaranteeing the benefits of the New Covenant to the people of God.

Toward the end of the following sacrifice section (Heb 9:25—10:14) the pastor will remind us that this our representative is sitting in the place of all authority at God's right hand (Heb 10:11–14, cf. 8:1–2). In the closing covenant section (Heb 10:15–18), the pastor will conclude with this one seated at God's right hand mediating the forgiveness and heart transformation made available under the New Covenant. This High Priest is available for us "now," "today," if we will draw near through him.

∾ Day Two: A "Once-for All" Sacrifice. (Heb 9:25—10:4)

> [25] Not that he might offer himself often, as the high priest goes into the Most Holy Place year after year with blood other than his own, [26] Because then it would have been necessary for him to have suffered often since the foundation of the world; but now he has appeared once-for-all at the climax of the ages for the abolition of sin through the sacrifice of himself. [27] And just as it is appointed to human beings to die once-for-all, and after this, judgment, [28] so also since Christ has been offered once-for-all in order to bear the sins of many, he will appear a second time without reference to sin for the purpose of bringing salvation to those awaiting him.
> [10:1] For because the Law has a shadow of the good things to come, not the reality itself of those things, it was never able to perfect those drawing near by the same sacrifices which are

offered continuously year after year. [2] Because then would they not have ceased being offered, since those worshiping would no longer have had any consciousness of sin if they had been cleansed once-for-all? [3] But by those sacrifices there was a memorial of sin year after year. [4] For it is impossible for the blood of bulls and goats to take away sin.

We have noted above that there are three distinct but closely intertwined parts to this grand sacrifice section (Heb 9:23—10:14) of movement three. The way in which part one transitions from the *once-for-all* sacrifice of Christ (Heb 9:23–28) to the *repeated* sacrifices of the old priests (Heb 10:1–4) mirrors part three's transition from the old priests *standing* before God (Heb 10:11) to Christ *seated* at God's right hand (Heb 10:12–14). In this way parts one (Heb 9:23–10:4) and three (Heb 10:11–14) showcase the crucial description of Christ's sacrifice as his incarnate obedience in part two (Heb 10:5–10). And yet the pastor ends this sacrifice section with our eyes fixed on the one who can help us, our all-effective High Priest "who has sat down" at God's right hand on our behalf (Heb 10:11–14).

Verse 25. Christ did not enter "heaven itself" (v. 24) "in order that he might offer himself often." The pastor emphasizes the words *himself* and *often*. Christ entered heaven by offering *himself*. The Old Testament high priest entered the earthly Most Holy Place by offering "blood other than his own." Christ entered "once-for-all" time, the Old Testament high priest entered *often*—"year after year" on the Day of Atonement. The pastor will explain Christ's offering *himself* in Heb 10:5–10. In these verses he focuses on the opposite of *often*—*once-for-all*! The fact that Christ offered *once-for-all* demonstrates *that* his sacrifice is fully effective. The fact that he offered *himself* (10:5–10) instead of animal blood shows *why* his sacrifice was effective.

Returning to Heb 9:25—10:4, we see that, if the *once-for-all* character of Christ' offering demonstrated its effectiveness (Heb 9:25–28), the repetitive character of the old sacrifices revealed that they were a "shadow" of the "real" (Heb 10:1–4). They reminded people of the need supplied by Christ.

Verse 26. How do we know that Christ offered himself "once-for-all"? Because he became incarnate and "suffered" only once. If his sacrifice had been multiple, "then it would have been necessary for him to have suffered often since the foundation of the world."

In the second part of verse 26, the pastor states the main point of Heb 9:25–10:4: Christ "has appeared once-for-all at the climax of the ages for the abolition of sin through the sacrifice of himself." Christ's sacrifice was "once-for-all" because it was completely effective, without need of repetition. It solved the age-old problem of sin, thus it was "the climax" toward which God had been directing the "ages." The way in which it solved this problem was so total that it can be expressed as nothing less than the "abolition of sin." Furthermore, this ultimate sacrifice could be accomplished by nothing less than "the sacrifice of himself."

Verses 27–28. How does this abolition of sin fit with the human condition? Verse 27 describes the human condition, and verse 28 the way in which the work of Christ addresses that condition. First, the human condition. It is certain, "once-for-all" that human beings must die and that they must stand before the judgment at Christ's return. We are reminded of the pastor's first description of the human situation in Heb 2:14–16: the devil holds human beings under the fear of death all of their lives because of the threat of judgment following death.

Verse 28's description of the work of Christ makes the answer given in Heb 2:16–18 clear. Christ's "once-or-all" offering of himself "to bear the sins of many" delivers the persevering people of God from the fear of death, their "once-for-all" enemy, because it removes the fear of judgment at Christ's return. This is true because his return will be "for the purpose of bringing *salvation* to those awaiting him" (italics added). The believer lives between the time when Christ made "purification for sins" (Heb 1:3), and the time of his return for "salvation"; between the time when Christ sat down at God's right hand (Heb 1:3a, 13a), and the time when God will put his enemies under his feet (Heb 1:3b, 13b). That is why it is so important to be among the company of those who "await him" with perseverance.

If we must await Christ's return for "salvation," how can we say that he has already "abolished" sin? He has taken our condemnation upon himself (Heb 9:15–22). He has cleansed us from the "works" of sin that lead to death so that we can "serve the living God" (Heb 9:14). He enables us to persevere by providing the "mercy" of forgiveness and the "grace" necessary for faithful obedience (Heb 4:14–16). Verses 19–25 below are the ultimate summary of what Christ has already provided for us. If you want a glimpse of the "salvation" yet to come, have a look at Heb 12:22–24.

Chapter 10, Verses 1–3. When the pastor says, "The Law has a shadow of the good things to come, not the reality itself of those things," he reveals the fundamental principle behind his interpretation of the Old Testament. By "the Law" he is referring to the entire system of approaching God established by Moses at Sinai—covenant, Tabernacle, priesthood, sacrifices, etc. This "Law" is a necessary shadow, picture, type, or pattern of "the good things" that have come in Christ. Without it, we would have no way of understanding Christ or the blessings he provides. Its ineffectiveness as a means of coming into God's presence is essential to its role as "shadow." Thus, the repeated sacrifices of the old system were "never able to perfect those drawing near" to God through them. To "perfect" here is to cleanse the worshipers from sin so that they can come into God's presence. The ineffectiveness of the old sacrifices is demonstrated by their repetitiveness. *If those* sacrifices had truly cleansed the worshipers from sin, *then* the worshipers would have stopped offering them because they would have had no "consciousness" of sin. "Year after year" these sacrifices were a perpetual "memorial of sin," ever reminding worshipers of their need of the "once-for-all" cleansing provided by Christ's sacrifice.

Verse 4. In Heb 9:22 the pastor affirmed that without the "shedding of blood" there was "no release from sin." However, the repetitive character of the old sacrifices proves that "it is *impossible* for the blood of bulls and goats to take away sin" (the word order in Greek emphasizes *impossible*). Nothing will due short of "the precious blood of Christ" (Heb 9:12, 14). In tomorrow's reading, Heb 10:5–10, the pastor will explain what he means by the "blood of Christ." Our release from sin was provided by the Son of God's offering his obedient human life on the cross in accord with the Father's will. He offered *himself.*

∽ Day Three: An Obedient Sacrifice. (Heb 10:5–10)

> [5] *Therefore as he was coming into the world he says: "Sacrifice and offering you did not desire, but a body you have prepared for me.* [6] *With whole burnt offerings and sin offerings you were not pleased.* [7] *Then I said, 'Behold I have come, in the scroll of the book it has been written concerning me, to do, Oh God, your will.'"* [8] *Saying above that "sacrifices and offerings and whole burnt offerings and sin offering you did not desire nor were you pleased with them"— which were offered according to the Law.* [9] *Then he said, "Behold, I have come to do your will." He abolishes the first in order that he might establish the second.* [10] *By which will we are made holy through the offering of the body of Jesus Christ once for all.*

Animal sacrifices provided no release from sin (Heb 10:4). "Therefore" (v. 5) on the eve of the incarnation Christ addresses the Father in the words of Ps 40:6–8, announcing the replacement of those sacrifices with his own incarnate obedience. The pastor quotes Ps 40:6–8 as the words of Christ in verses 5b–7, explains its significance in verses 8–9, and shows the vital importance of Christ's words for the people of God in verse 10.

Ps 40:6–8 and Ps 110:4 are the foundation of the Son's all-sufficient priesthood as described in Heb 4:14—10:25. Just as Ps 110:4 is the heart of Heb 4:14—7:28, so Ps 40:6–8 is the heart of this grand symphony to the

Son's sacrifice (Heb 8:1—10:18). In Ps 110:4 the Father publicly assures the enthroned Son that he is an eternal Priest "by the power of an indestructible life." In Ps 40:6–8 the Son answers by declaring that his incarnate obedience is the all-sufficient sacrifice by which he becomes that all-sufficient High Priest. Only the eternal Son of God could live a perfectly obedient human life and thus become our all-sufficient High Priest at God's right hand—"the Source of eternal salvation" (Heb 5:9). Only he is able "to save completely those who come to God through him, because he is always living to make intercession for them" (Heb 7:25).

Verses 5–7. There are two clauses from these verses that need special comment: "but a body you have prepared for me" in verse 5 (Ps 40:6), and, "in the scroll of the book it has been written concerning me" in verse 7 (Ps 40:7).

If you look up Ps 40:6 in your English Bible, you will find "but you have given me an open ear" (ESV, NRSV), or an equivalent translation, instead of "but a body you have prepared for me." The author of Hebrews follows the Greek translation of the Old Testament (see the TNIV footnote). The Hebrew of this verse is difficult to translate and scholars differ as to how these two interpretations of the verse arose. Suffice it to say, that "you have given me an open ear" means you have enabled me to be obedient. Thus, this alternate translation would fit the pastor's argument since it contrasts the obedience of the one speaking with the "sacrifices and offerings" that God "did not desire." Of course, "a body you have prepared for me" makes it clear that Christ is referring to his obedience as a human being and affirms the incarnation as the will of God. By beginning verse 5 with "therefore as he was coming into the world he says" the pastor identifies the speaker of these words as the Son on the eve of the incarnation.

"Scroll of the book" means a book in the form of a scroll. The psalm does not identify the "scroll of the book" in question. Some have suggested the book of Deuteronomy. It is probably best to take this phrase as a more general reference to Old Testament Scripture. The Old Testament as a whole anticipates the incarnate obedience of the Son of God as the all-sufficient sacrifice. The rest of the sentences in Ps 40:5–7 are repeated in the interpretation that follows.

Verse 8a–b. In verse 8a the pastor collects the words referring to sacrifice in verses 5–6 above (Ps 40:6) and uses them to create one comprehensive description of all Old Testament sacrifices: "sacrifices and offerings and whole burnt offerings and sin offering." He concludes with "sin offering" since he presents the *entire* Old Testament sacrificial system (and not just the Day of Atonement) as an attempt to bring God's people into his presence by removing the pollution of sin.

Then, in verse 8b, the pastor emphasizes God's disapproval of these sacrifices by joining the two expressions of divine displeasure found in verses 5–6 (Ps 40:6): "you did not desire nor were you pleased with them." The purpose of the Old Testament sacrifices was to please God by removing sin. Thus, this very strong expression of divine dissatisfaction with the sacrificial system is its ultimate rejection as a means of removing sin and approaching God.

Verse 8c–9. These sacrifices "were offered according to the" same Law that was the basis of the Levitical priesthood (Heb 7:11). Thus, the priesthood and the sacrifices offered by the priests were all part of the system for approaching God known as "the Law." The Father's declaration, "You are a priest forever according to the order of Melchizedek," signaled the "abolition" of the Levitical priesthood because of its inability to provide access to God (Heb 7:18). The Son's response, "Behold, I have come to do your will," signaled the abolition of the Levitical sacrifices with which God was not pleased because they did not remove sin (Heb 10:4). The Father's declaration established "a better hope through which we draw near to God" in place of the old priesthood (Heb 7:19). The Son's response established a sacrifice based on his incarnate obedience that truly removed sin and thus provided entrance into the divine presence.

Verse 10. The Son's incarnate obedience to the will of God was and is the only sacrifice by which "we are made holy." His obedience removes the curse upon our disobedience and cleanses us from the pollution of sin so that we can live in faithful obedience. This truth sheds light on much that the pastor has already said. We begin to understand why it was "fitting" for God to "bring many sons and daughters into glory" by perfecting the Son as our Savior through suffering (Heb 2:10). We can see the significance of his learning "obedience by the things that he suffered" (Heb 5:8).

Now we can begin to hear the resolution of the music of this grand symphony to the sacrifice of the incarnate Son (Heb 8:1—10:18). In *Movement One (Heb 8:1–13)* we see that his incarnate obedience culminating in the cross was the only possible sacrifice (Heb 8:3–6) appropriate for ministry in a heavenly sanctuary (Heb 8:1–2) and sufficient to establish a "New" Covenant (Heb 8:7–13). In *Movement Two (Heb 9:1–22)* he offered himself by this incarnate obedience, "through the eternal Spirit," as a "blameless" sacrifice (Heb 9:11–15), and thus, both provided the cleansing and access anticipated by the old Tabernacle worship (Heb 9:1–10), and bore the curse of the Old Covenant upon sin (Heb 9:16–22). Finally, in *Movement Three (Heb 9:23—10:18)* it is by this incarnate obedience that he offered himself "once-for-all" (Heb 9:24—10:4) and thus entered God's presence "on our behalf" (Heb 9:23–24), taking his seat at God's right hand as our all-sufficient High Priest (Heb 10:11–14) and Mediator of the New Covenant (Heb 10:15–18).

It is important to note that the pastor who contrasted "the blood of Christ" with the "blood of bulls and goats" in Heb 9:11–15 now contrasts the unrepeatable "offering of the body of Jesus Christ" (v. 10) with the repeated and therefore ineffective "blood of bulls and goats" (Heb 10:4). The pastor is not concerned with the manipulation of the physical substance of Christ's blood on some heavenly altar. However, he will not let us rarify Christ's obedience by separating it from his "blood" and his "body." His was real "flesh and blood" obedience. He offered *his body*, himself, his entire obedient earthly life up on the cross. He offered *his blood,* his obedience was tested by suffering and reached its climax in a violent and shameful death on a cross. Thus, we are saved by the "body and blood" of Christ. He empowers us to live a life of bodily obedience undeterred by the threat of shedding our own blood.

∽ Day Four: A Fully Effective Sacrifice. (Heb 10:11–14)

> [11] *And every priest has stood day after day ministering and fre-quently offering the same sacrifices which are never able to take away sin.* [12] *But this one by offering one sacrifice for sin has sat down forever at the right hand of God,* [13] *for the meantime waiting expectantly until his enemies are put under his feet.* [14] *For by one sacrifice he has perfected forever those who are being made holy.*

As we approach the climax of this grand symphony the pastor directs our gaze back to the main theme with which it began (Heb 8:1–2)—our High Priest who "has sat down forever at the right hand of God" (v. 12). The entire symphony has been the story of how the eternal Son of God became this High Priest "by offering one sacrifice for sin."

The pastor began this sacrifice section (Heb 9:24—10:14) of movement three by establishing the *fact* that Christ's sacrifice was once-for-all and thus effective in removing sin (Heb 9:24—10:4). Then he revealed the *reason* for its effectiveness—the incarnate obedience of the Son of God (Heb 10:5–10). He concludes in Heb 10:11–14 by introducing its *results*: by offering such a sacrifice the Son of God "has sat down forever at the right hand of God" (Ps 110:1) as our all-sufficient High Priest (Ps 110:4) and "the Source of eternal salvation" (Heb 5:9). The following covenant section (Heb 10:15–18) completes this climactic presentation of the benefits provided by the eternal, incarnate Son now seated at God's right hand.

We have noted above how Heb 9:24—10:4 and Heb 10:11–14 mirror each other and frame the description of Christ's sacrifice as incarnate obedience in Heb 10:5–10. This description may be the heart of this third sacrifice section (Heb 9:24—10:14), but Heb 10:11–14 is its goal. The pastor would have us fix our gaze on the "Great High Priest" of Heb 10:11–14 seated definitively at God's right hand for he is the one through whom we receive cleansing from sin, access to God's presence, and grace for perseverance.

Verses 11–12. The contrast in these verses reinforces the truth noted above—by his "once-or-all" sacrifice and resulting high priesthood at God's right hand the Son of God has replaced the entire Old Testament system of priesthood and sacrifice *as a means of approaching God*. Verse 11 contrasts Christ with "every priest," not just with the high priest. And it includes all of the other things the priests do by "ministering" as well as the "offering" of sacrifices. Those priests minister "day by day" continually offering those animal sacrifices which, as we already know from Heb 10:1–4, "are never able to take away sin." We are reminded of the repetitious ministry of the "Holy Place" that was never able to gain access into the inner sanctuary (see Heb 9:1–10). We can see the priests doing over and over again what had proven to be ineffective, like a car spinning its wheels in mud.

Those priests, then, "stood day after day." In the Old Testament it was a great honor to "stand" before God as a priest. Now, however, in light of the fulfillment of Ps 110:1 and 4, standing demonstrates the futility of their ministry as a means of removing sin and approaching God. "But *this one*"—"Jesus Christ" (italics added)—the one who has offered his "body" (Heb 10:10), does not stand as a servant or suppliant. He did not enter heaven and sprinkle his blood on some supposed altar. "By offering one sacrifice for sin" he entered heaven to appear "before the face of God on our behalf" (Heb 9:22–23) and take his seat once-and-for all in the place of ultimate authority at God's right hand.

Verse 13. The pastor prepares us for the exhortations of the following chapters by reminding us that we live in the "meantime" between the session of the Son and the subjugation of his "enemies" at his return. He would have us join our "Great High Priest" in "waiting expectantly" for that occasion by diligently pursuing the life of faithful obedience, remembering that when he comes he will bring salvation for "those awaiting him" (Heb 9:28)

Verse 14. This final verse tells us what this High Priest's taking his seat at God's right hand by offering his "once-for-all" sacrifice means for the people of God: "For by one sacrifice" this High Priest enthroned at God's right hand "has perfected forever those who are being made holy." In verse 10 above, we learned that by his sacrifice "we are made holy." How do these descriptions of what Christ has done for the people of God fit together?

It is important to remember that the pastor thinks of "holiness" and "perfection" as two sides of the same coin. They refer to the same reality from two different points of view. The first refers to being cleansed from sin. The second, to being made fit to enter God's presence. By making an adequate atonement for sin Christ was perfected as our Savior and thus able to bring us into God's presence (Heb 2:10). By being cleansed from sin we are "perfected" in that the pollution of sin has been removed and we are now privileged to enter the presence of God.

Thus, "we are made holy" in verse 10 and "those who are being made holy" in this verse refer to our reception of the cleansing Christ provides. The first is in the perfect tense, denoting a present condition. One could translate it, "we have been made holy." The second is in the present tense, denoting an on-going process. All who belong to Christ "have been made holy." All have received the "release" from sin provided by his sacrifice and have been "cleansed from dead works to serve the living God" (Heb 9:14). By this cleansing they have been "perfected" so that they can enter God's presence.

And yet that cleansing is ongoing. By "those who are being made holy" the pastor is not thinking so much of progress in sanctification as of our continued dependence on the work of Christ for pursuing the holy life of persevering obedience that has been given to us. We are daily dependent on drawing near though Christ to receive the "mercy" of forgiveness and the "grace" for continued obedience. The "perfection" and access to God that we have received by being cleansed from sin is perpetually valid because we are being cleansed from sin.

When the pastor affirms that Christ has been perfected *forever* he affirms the adequacy of Christ to make us holy and bring us into God's presence until the end. Christ has provided all that is necessary to sustain "those who are being made holy" in their obedience. He enables them to receive present grace by "drawing near" to God so they can remain faithful until ultimate entrance into God's presence through that same grace. By our perseverance we join him in "waiting expectantly" for that final entrance (Heb 9:28) when "his enemies are put under his feet" (v. 13).

∽ Day Five: A Covenant that Brings Release. (Heb 10:15–18)

> [15] And the Holy Spirit bears witness to us. For after having said, [16] "This is the covenant which I will covenant with them after those days," the Lord says: "I will put my laws on their hearts and upon their minds I will inscribe them; [17] and their sins and their lawless

deeds I will no longer remember." [18] *And where there is release
from these, there is no longer a sacrifice for sins.*

When God promised the Son with an oath that he would be a "Priest forever" he inaugurated him as the "Guarantor" of a "better covenant" (Heb
7:20–22). According to the previous two sacrifice sections, Christ's sacrifice established him as both heavenly High Priest and Mediator of the New
Covenant (Heb 8:3–6) because it adequately dealt with sin (Heb 9:11–15).
Thus, by taking his seat at God's right hand as High Priest (Heb 10:11–14)
Christ also became Mediator of the New Covenant that is described in the
verses we are now reading.

You will remember that the first covenant section (Heb 8:7–13) quoted Jeremiah's promise of a New Covenant in full—Jer 31:31–34. The first
half of that promise described how the people of God had broken the Old
Covenant through disobedience (Heb 8:8–9; Jer 31:31–32); the second half,
the promised blessings of the New Covenant that would overcome human
faithlessness (Heb 8:10–12; Jer 31:33–34). According to the first covenant
section, the very fact that God issued this New Covenant promise in Jeri-
miah's time meant that the Old Covenant was flawed and on the verge of
its demise. We can feel the anticipation. Something new and better was
coming. In Christ the new has come. The second covenant section (Heb
9:16–22) described how Christ had taken the curse of the broken covenant
described in Jer 31:31–32 upon himself. The third covenant section brings
the covenant theme to a climax by describing Christ's establishment of the
New-Covenant blessings of obedience and fellowship with God described
in Jer 31:33–34. Once more, the *obedience* of Heb 10:5–10 is crucial. By
his *obedience* the Son of God has borne the Old-Covenant curse on our
disobedience and empowered us to live in New-Covenant *obedience*. Thus,
the all-sufficient High Priest at God's right hand is the Mediator of the
New Covenant and the Guarantor of its benefits to all who "draw near to
God through him" because he cleanses from sin and ministers grace for
obedient living. By taking advantage of Christ's provision we can avoid the
fate of the wilderness generation (Heb 3:7—4:13), the preeminent example
of those who break God's covenant through persistent disobedience, and
join the faithful of Heb 11:1–40.

The pastor reintroduces the prophecy from Jeremiah in verse 15, quotes
the relevant parts of this oracle in verses 16–17, and draws a conclusion in
verse 18. There is now no need to dwell on the description of the broken covenant in Jer 31:31–32. We are concerned with the promised benefits of the
New, found in Jer 31:33–34 and now made available by our Mediator seated at

God's right hand. The pastor paraphrases these verses from Jeremiah in order to highlight the issues he considers most important.

Verse 15. The "Holy Spirit," who spoke through Jeremiah, now attests the validity of Jeremiah's prophecy for our situation. By referring to the Holy Spirit as speaker the pastor emphasizes the immediacy and relevance of God's word and the urgency of our response. "For after having said" (v. 15) and "the Lord says" (v. 16) divide this quotation from Jer 31:33–34 into two parts—verse 16a and verses 16b–17.

Verse 16a. God begins by announcing, "*This* is the covenant which I will covenant with them *after those days*" (italics added). These words are filled with anticipation. "This" points to the uniqueness of this New Covenant. "After those days" recalls "at the end of these days" in Heb 1:2. God promised "this" new kind of covenant long ago, but the time has now come for it to be *fulfilled*. The pastor highlights two of the benefits brought by this New Covenant, the first in verse 16b, the second in verse 17. Under the New Covenant, God will change us (v. 16b), and his relationship to us (v. 17).

Verse 16b. God will change us. "I will put my *laws* on their *hearts* and upon their minds I will inscribe them" (italics added). "Laws" and "hearts" are the two key terms in this statement. What are the "laws" to which Jeremiah refers? Jeremiah was not concerned with the "ordinances" that established priesthood and sacrifice. He was not referring to the "Law" understood as the Levitical system. Throughout Jeremiah's life he condemned the hypocrisy of his contemporaries because they thought they could replace the love of God and neighbor with the proper performance of the Levitical rituals. The "laws" that concerned Jeremiah were the great laws, the laws that called for love and loyalty to God and the proper treatment of our neighbors.

The pastor has paraphrased this citation from Jeremiah in order to emphasize the word "hearts." In the Bible "heart," as here, represents the real person, including the person's thoughts, feelings, habits, and choices. The human problem is a heart problem. The pastor warned his hearers against hardening their hearts (Heb 3:8, 15; 4:7) and against the "evil heart of unbelief" that characterized the disobedient wilderness generation (Heb 3:12). That generation always went "astray in heart" (Heb 3:10). Instead, he urges his hearers to "keep drawing near with true hearts in fullness of faith," with "hearts sprinkled from an evil conscience" (Heb 10:22). Under the New Covenant, God remedies this heart problem by "cleansing the conscience from dead works to serve the living God" (Heb 9:14) and by "putting" his "laws" on our "hearts." He transforms unbelieving hearts into obedient hearts. The pastor emphasizes this truth by adding, "and upon their minds I will inscribe them." Those who draw near through Christ will be able to know and do the will of God. By his own incarnate obedience (Heb 10:5–10) Christ offered the all-sufficient sacrifice that both overcame the disobedience so characteristic of many under the Old Covenant and inaugurated a New Covenant that empowered God's people for obedience. Now we are able to see that the blessings of the New Covenant are indeed the blessings that Christ has provided through his all-sufficient sacrifice and subsequent session at God's right hand as eternal High Priest.

Verse 17. By establishing this New Covenant, God will change his relationship to us: "their sins and their lawless deeds I will no longer remember." We might paraphrase, "not only their sins, but even their lawless deeds." Remember how the incarnate Son "loved righteousness but hated lawlessness" (Heb 1:9). The essence of disobedience is "lawlessness," disregard for God's moral law that has now been written on the hearts of the faithful. God's refusal to remember the past wickedness of his people includes forgiveness in the narrow sense, but it implies much more. Under the New Covenant, God "takes away" (Heb 10:4) sin and brings "release" (Heb 9:22). Sin can no longer dominate the believer or separate from God. The "mercy" of forgiveness and the "grace" for faithful obedience available under the New Covenant enable those who draw near through Jesus to live holy lives in fellowship with God (Heb 4:14–16). God's promise that he will no longer "remember" sin is the most thorough affirmation of its demise.

Verse 18. Since the Son's sacrifice truly brings complete "release" from "sins and lawless deeds," there is "no longer" a need for any continuing "sacrifice for sins." The fulfilled promise of the New Covenant is one final reminder that Christ's sacrifice has replaced all other sacrifices because it is the *all*-sufficient sin–remedy. The pastor persistently directs our attention to our High Priest and New-Covenant Mediator at God's right hand. At the same time, he will never let us forget the incarnate obedience and suffering by which that High Priest atoned for sin and assumed his present place as "Source of eternal salvation" (Heb 5:9). That memory is strong motivation for our own perseverance, which is the subject of the following chapters. As Mediator of the New Covenant we can depend on Christ to administer the benefits he has obtained as all-sufficient High Priest to the suffering but persevering people of God.

∽ Day Six: A Great Priest Brings Great Blessings. (Heb 10:19–25)

[19] *Therefore, brothers and sisters, since we have authorization for entrance into the Most Holy Place by means of the blood of*

Jesus, [20] an entrance which he inaugurated for us, a way new and living through the veil, that is, [through] his flesh; [21] and since we have a Great Priest over the House of God, [22] let us keep drawing near with true hearts in fullness of faith, having allowed our hearts to be sprinkled from an evil conscience and our bodies to be washed with pure water. [23] Let us hold the confession of the hope firm, for the One who has promised is faithful; [24] and let us pay attention to each other for the provoking of love and good works. [25] We will accomplish this by not continuing to abandon the assembling of ourselves together, as is the habit of some, but by continually exhorting one another, and all the more as we see the Day approaching.

The pastor urges us to live the life of persevering obedience portrayed in Heb 11:1–40 by appropriating the benefits of our High Priest and Mediator described in Heb 4:14—10:25. Hebrews 4:14–16 introduced this grand description of Christ's all-sufficient high priesthood and sacrifice by urging us to persevere in obedience by drawing near through our "Great High Priest" in order to avoid the fate of the wilderness generation (Heb 3:7–19). Hebrews 10:19–25 urges us to "keep drawing near" so that we can persevere in obedience as members of the faithful people of God, soon to be described in 11:1–40. Hebrews 4:14–16 whetted our appetite by suggesting the greatness of our High Priest. The powerful appeal in Heb 10:19–25 is based on the full disclosure of his superior greatness and the benefits he bestows.

Hebrews 10:19–25 is, then, the first of three links in the chain that joins the life of faith (described in Heb 11:1–40) to the person and work of Christ as described in Heb 4:14—10:25. How do these links interlock? Hebrews 10:19–25 (link one) urges the recipients of Hebrews to persevere by appropriating the high priestly work of Christ just described. Hebrews 10:26–31 (link two), on the other hand, warns them of the dire consequences for failing to persevere by neglecting their all-sufficient High Priest. Hebrews 10:32–39 (link three) assures them that they do not belong to the apostates described in link two but to the company of the faithful soon to be described in Heb 11:1–40. Avoid the apostasy of the wilderness generation (Heb 3:7–19) and join the company of the faithful (Heb 11:1–40) through the all sufficiency or our High Priest seated at God's right hand (Heb 5:1—10:18).

In verses 19–21 the pastor gives us his ultimate, bottom–line description of the grand benefits provided by our High Priest. Those benefits are both compelling motivation and adequate means for obeying the three exhortations in verses 22–24. This section concludes in verse 25 with urgent practical instructions on how to carry out the third exhortation.

Verses 19–21. By addressing his hearers as "brothers and sisters" the pastor reminds them that they are part of the one "House of God" in which Moses was "Steward" (Heb 3: 5) and over which Christ is both "Son" (Heb 3:6) and "Great Priest." As part of this household they have been granted "authorization for entrance into the Most Holy Place," direct *access* to God. This *access* is the bottom line, a privilege both foreshadowed by and unimaginable under the Old Covenant. Ultimate access is the goal of their journey as the people of God (Heb 12:22–29). Penultimate access is their present privilege and means of receiving the grace necessary for perseverance until achieving final entrance (Heb 2:17–18; 4:14–16).

Many believe that "by means of the blood of Jesus" (v. 19) and "through his flesh" (v. 20) are parallel.[2] By his obedience "in the days of his flesh," climaxing in the shedding of his blood, the incarnate Jesus atoned for sin and thus "inaugurated" this entrance into God's presence as our all-sufficient High Priest and Mediator.

The pastor awakens a deep longing within us by portraying this now-opened entrance to the divine presence as "a way new and living through the veil." The word for "new" suggests "fresh," "unspoiled," never antiquated or out of date. It is as "fresh" today as it was when the incarnate, eternal Son of God took his seat at God's right hand, because it is "living." It was established by and leads to the "living" God through his eternal Son, who offered himself "through the eternal spirit" (Heb 9:14) and "by the power of an indestructible life" (Heb 7:16). We need not fear. This undreamt-of entrance into God's presence will not disappear as a mirage in the desert because it is maintained by the one who "remains" forever (Heb 7:24) as our "Source of eternal salvation" (Heb 5:9) at God's right hand.

Finally, this "way new and living" penetrates the "veil," the barrier that separated humanity from God, typified by the curtain before the Most Holy Place of the earthly Tabernacle (Heb 9:3). The unbelief and disobedience that separated us from God has been removed, released, taken away. We have been forgiven, our hearts have been cleansed, and *heaven has been opened.*

When the pastor returned to the subject of priesthood and sacrifice in Heb 6:20 he described Jesus as our "Forerunner" who had gone inside the "veil" for us so that we could follow. The seed sewn in that verse has now reached full fruition with this description of full and free entrance into the divine presence. The pastor, however, will not conclude with our privileges. As always, he points us to their Provider. We receive these

---

2. For a discussion of the way "his flesh" relates to "the veil" see Cockerill, *Hebrews,* 468–71.

privileges only in union with our "Forerunner" whom the pastor now calls "a Great Priest over the House of God."

By condensing "Great High Priest," with which he began (Heb 4:14–16), to "Great Priest," the pastor allows the full force of this expression to fall on the word *Great*. As demonstrated in Heb 4:14—10:25, he is the ultimate "Great Priest over the House of God," "whose House we are if we hold fast our boldness and our boasting in hope" (Heb 3:6).

On the basis of *this* priest and the access he affords, the pastor urges us to draw near (v. 22), to persevere (v. 23), and to encourage the perseverance of our fellow members of the "House of God" (v. 24).

Verse 22. First, then, let us take advantage of this "way new and living" by continuing to draw "near with true hearts in fullness of faith" in order to receive grace for perseverance in holiness. By doubting God's promise of future blessing and his present power to fulfill that promise the wilderness generation revealed an "evil heart of unbelief" (Heb 3:12). We who keep drawing near "with true hearts in the fullness of faith" live in the certainty of God's promised future blessing and the assurance of his present power for perseverance, made available through our "Great Priest." We draw near by allowing God to "sprinkle" our "hearts" and "wash" our "bodies" through the work of Christ. He purifies us within and without so that the obedience of our bodily life springs from a pure heart.

Verse 23. The exhortation in this verse expresses the pastor's ultimate and urgent concern for his hearers—their perseverance until the end. We draw near through our "Great Priest" for grace to "hold the confession of the hope firm." By our persevering obedience we confess that our all-sufficient High Priest, the incarnate, eternal Son at God's right hand, will come "a second time," when his "enemies are made a stool for his feet" (Heb 1:14) with "salvation for those awaiting him" (Heb 9:28). At his coming the faithful will experience the "better resurrection" (Heb 11:35) and enter "once-for-all" into "the City that has foundations, whose architect and builder is God" (Heb 11:10). We live depending on the truthfulness of this promised "hope" because "the One who has promised is faithful."

Verse 24–25. We draw near and persevere as members of the "House of God" and participants in the company of the faithful soon to be described in Heb 11:1–40. Thus, it is vital that we "pay attention to each other." Mutual concern for the perseverance of our "brothers and sisters" is an essential part of who we are as God's people. We leave no room for "a root of bitterness" (Heb 12:15) to spring up among us. We are to be as diligent in "provoking" other members of the believing community to "love and good works" as the faithless are in "provoking" strife.

The pastor is concerned, however, because some of his hearers have been habitually "abandoning the assembling of" themselves "together." You can neither give nor receive this mutual support if you fail, either through neglect or shame, to participate in the community's worship and fellowship. It is there that we encourage one another "by continually exhorting one another." The pastor uses "exhorting" with its full range of meaning—"rebuke," "warn," "encourage," and "comfort."[3] He would have them imitate what he himself is doing in this "word of exhortation" (Heb 13:22) that we call the letter to the Hebrews. The urgency of mutual concern intensifies as the "Day" of reckoning approaches! The coming "Day" transitions smoothly to the warnings against neglecting our "Great Priest" and the access he provides in Heb 10:26–31. We can hear the "clink" as link two (Heb 10:26–31) in our chain joins link one (10:19–25).

∞ Day Seven: A Great Priest Requires Great Accountability. (Heb 10:26–31)

> [26] *For if we persist in willfully sinning after we have received the knowledge of the truth, there no longer remains a sacrifice for sin.* [27] *Instead, there is a certain terrifying prospect of judgment and a fury of fire about to consume the adversaries.* [28] *Anyone who has set aside the Law of Moses dies without mercy on the basis of two or three witnesses.* [29] *Of how much worse punishment do you think any person will be considered worthy who has trampled underfoot the Son of God, and accounted the blood of the covenant by which he was sanctified profane, and insulted the Spirit of grace?* [30] *For we know the one who has said, "Vengeance is mine, I will repay," and again, "God will vindicate his people."* [31] *It is a terrifying thing to fall into the hands of the living God.*

The inestimable privilege of access to God through our Great Priest, described in Heb 4:14—10:25 and summarized in Heb 10:19–25, entails equally great accountability. Verse 26a describes the sin of apostasy; verses 26b–27, that sin's consequences; and verse 28–29, the magnitude of those consequences. Verse 29 also illuminates the magnitude and seriousness of the sin involved. The pastor adds two warnings from Deuteronomy in verse 30, and concludes, in verse 31, with a final fearful warning rich in Old Testament language. The allusions to the Old Testament throughout these verses suggest that abandoning Christ is worse than the idolatry of ancient Israel.

---

3. Cockerill, *Hebrews*, 481.

Verse 26a. What happens if, instead of persevering through drawing near (Heb 10:22–24) "we persist in willfully sinning after we have received the knowledge of the truth"? The sin involved is intentional, willful, persistent, and informed by "the knowledge of the truth." That is, it is informed by the grand description of Christ's all-sufficient high priesthood that the pastor has been laying out before his hearers. The people described have experienced the resources that are theirs through Christ and are well aware of the situation's urgency. The pastor seeks to expose the willful nature of their neglecting the things of God. Laxity cannot be covered with the veil of ignorance. Hesitancy to identify with the assembly of God's people cannot be excused by spiritual burnout or fear of rejection or persecution by the surrounding world.

Verse 26b–27. Through persistence in neglect the believer can drift into apostasy because, when one severs oneself from Christ, "there no longer remains a sacrifice for sins." It is difficult to imagine a more ominous statement. We know that Christ's obedient sacrifice of himself is the *one and only* effective sacrifice for sin (Heb 8:1—10:18). All that follows in these verses is the dire result of being cut off from the benefits of this "once-for-all" sacrifice. Thus, the only "prospect" that remains for the one who has abandoned Christ is ultimate divine "judgment." By using language from Isa 26:11, the pastor describes the utterly "terrifying" nature of this judgment as "a fury of fire about to consume the adversaries." Those who have abandoned Christ have become his "adversaries." They have become the "enemies" who will be subjected to him (Heb 1:13) at his return instead of being those who "will inherit salvation" (Heb 1:14; 9:28).

Verses 28–29. The pastor magnifies the terrifying nature of this judgment by comparing it to Old Testament judgment. According to the Old Testament, certain death, "on the basis of two or three witnesses," was the penalty for "anyone who has set aside the Law of Moses" by committing idolatry (see Deut 13:6–10; 17:2–6). It is as if the pastor says, "Think about it." "Of how much worse punishment do you think any person will be considered worthy who abandons Christ?"

This threefold description of those who abandon Christ in verse 29 makes it clear that the sin involved is repudiation. The pastor is talking about an unchecked course of persistent neglect of the things of God that has led to abandoning Christ. The first two parts of this description are the natural outgrowth of all the pastor has been saying. First, this person "has trampled underfoot the Son of God" who, according to Hebrews chapters 1–7, God has exalted to his right hand! Second, this person has "accounted the blood of the covenant by which he was sanctified profane." Hebrews 8:1—10:18 has described how the "blood of Christ" has established a New Covenant of obedience by removing the curse on sin and cleansing God's people from its pollution. The one who has thus abandoned Christ has tramped on the very Son of God whom God exalted and utterly desecrated the precious "blood" of cleansing by treating it as a common, ordinary thing. The blasphemous nature of this desecration of all that is holy makes one cringe before the horror of impending judgment. The third part of this description brings the whole to a conclusion. The pastor shares the common Christian conviction that the Holy Spirit is God's ultimate gift through the work of Christ to the people of God. He is God present in the hearts and lives of the faithful. As the "Spirit of Grace" he applies the grace of God to the life of the believer and unites us to Christ. How terrible to treat with insolence and prideful distain the one who is God with us and the agent of all God's blessings (see Heb 6:4–8).

The pastor would not be warning his hearers if he believed they had come to this terrible end. He is not writing to torment the consciences of the sensitive. The apostate is beyond the reach of conscience. He is not establishing a standard by which people can be excluded from the people of God. He is putting before his hearers the inevitable end of those who, despite full knowledge of the truth, persist in their neglect of the things of God. Either we persevere in obedience by drawing near to God through our "Great Priest" seated at his right hand, or we drift away through neglecting the things of God. The end of the first course is "salvation"; of the second, "judgment."

Verse 30. The pastor's warning is in full accord with the holiness of the God whom his hearers know from the Old Testament, "the one who has said, 'Vengeance is mine, I will repay,' and again, 'God will vindicate his people.'" The first of these two quotations comes from Deut 32:35a; the second, from both Deut 32:36a and Ps 135:14. Deuteronomy 32:1–43 is the "Song of Moses." Moses warns the people who were about to enter the promised land by singing to them about God's blessings, about his coming judgment on their future sin, and about the assurance that he will vindicate the faithful. The pastor has already described in full our great blessings in Christ. He now underscores his warnings against faithlessness by joining Moses in affirming that God has said, "Vengeance is mine, I will repay." The holy God has the right to judge the unfaithful. The holy God *will* judge the unfaithful. But the pastor joins both Moses and the Psalmist when he reminds his hearers that God's judgment on the unfaithful is his vindication of "his people." God's judgment anticipates the hope soon to be offered in verses 32–39 below.

Verse 31. By ending with "It is a terrifying thing to fall into the hands of the living God" the pastor reminds his hearers of the "terrifying prospect of judgment" with which he began in verse 27. People are completely within the power of the person into whose "hands" they "fall." The pastor wants his faithful hearers to feel "terror" at the prospect of the apostate falling "into the hands of" the true and "*living* God," who *does* "repay." The reader can almost hear them crying out in response, "We are not going to be among those who drift away and suffer that fate." That is what the pastor desires them to say. He answers in verses 32–39, below, "Amen, on the basis of your past faithfulness we have good hope that you are not going to be among those who trample the Son of God and defile his blood, but among those who join the faithful" described in Heb 11:1–40.

Remember, Heb 10:19–25, 10:26–31, and 10:32–39 are three links in the chain that joins the company of the faithful in Heb 11:1–40 to the work of Christ in Heb 4:14—10:25. After urging his hearers to avail themselves of the privileges provided by their "Great Priest" (Heb 10:19–25), and warning them against neglecting these privileges (Heb 10:26–31), the pastor reminds them of their past faithfulness (Heb 10:32–39) as evidence that they are, and encouragement for them to be, members of the company of the faithful (whom he will describe in Heb 11:1–40). The chain is complete. The only way to join the faithful of chapter 11 is through our Great Priest. As we will see, the faithful of all time enter the inheritance God has prepared for them only through him!

A Cloud of Witnesses: a History of the Faithful People of God

Hebrews 10:32—12:3

Introduction

We begin this week with the final link (Heb 10:32–39) of the three–link chain (Heb 10:19–25; 10:26–31; 10:32–39) that joins the history of the faithful people of God with the high priestly work of Christ described in Heb 4:14—10:25. That history, from the creation in Heb 11:1–2 through the glorious consummation of all things in Heb 12:25–29, finds its center in "the Pioneer and Perfecter of the faith, Jesus" (Heb 12:1–3). We will spend days two through six meditating on the history of the faithful before the coming of Christ, as narrated in Heb 11:1–40. Day seven will bring us to Christ (Heb 12:1–3), the centerpiece of this history.

Before looking at chapter 11 in greater detail, let's note the skillful way in which the pastor has brought us from the short—because future-less—history of the unfaithful (Heb 3:7–19) to the glorious history of the faithful that begins in Heb 11:1–40. You will remember that the pastor's grand purpose is to turn us from the unfaithful (Heb 3:7–19) to the perse-vering faithful (Heb 11:1–40) through the sufficiency of our "Great Priest" (Heb 4:14—10:25).

Hebrews 3:1—4:16 is the road by which the pastor brought us from the faithless people of God to the sufficiency of the Son's high priesthood in Heb 4:14—10:25. Hebrews 10:19—12:3 is the route by which he leads us from the Son's high priesthood to the faithful people of God. These two roads are mirror images of each other. The pastor introduces the first (Heb 3:1–6) and concludes the second (Heb 12:1–3) by turning our eyes toward Jesus. The brief history of the faithless wilderness generation in Heb 3:7–19 parallels the grand history of the faithful before Christ in Heb 11:1–40. The pastor's exhortation to enter what the faithless lost in Heb 4:1–11 parallels his encouragement to join the people of faith in Heb 10:32–39. The warning in Heb 4:12–13 prepares for the warning in Heb 10:26–31. Finally, the pastor's initial description of the benefits of Christ's high priesthood in Heb 4:14–16, anticipates his final description of those benefits in Heb 10:19–25. The explanation of Heb 12:1–3 on day seven of this week will reveal the significance of this careful structural arrangement. The high priestly work of Christ is at its heart. The union of the pastor's hearers with those who through Christ (Heb 12:1–3) persevere until the end (Heb 12:25–29) is its goal.

Now, let's have a look at Heb 11:1–40, which we will cover in days two through six. In verses 1–31 the pastor narrates the history of those who lived "by faith" from Abel through Rahab. He continues that history in verses 32–40 by focusing on many deeds done "through faith." As we will see, this change, at the border of Canaan, fits well with the pastor's conviction that the faithful people of God have *always* been—and continue to be—on their way, not to Canaan, but to their heavenly "homeland."

Hebrews 11:1–31 divides naturally into three major sections: verses 1–7, 8–22, and 23–31. The first section (Heb 11:1–7) introduces this history by defining faith and drawing examples from the primeval history in Gen 1–11. The second (Heb 11:8–22) narrates the faith of Abraham and those associated with him. The third (Heb 11:23–31), the faith of Moses and those who followed him. Heb 11:32–40 brings the faith of the ancient people of God to a grand climax. We will dedicate day two to Heb 11:1–7; days three and four to Heb 11:8–22, the long Abraham section; day five to Heb 11:23–31, the Moses section; and day six to the grand finale in Heb 11:32–40.

With each section we grow in our understanding of biblical faith. We will discover that faith is living like God's promise for the future is certain and his power in the present is real. Furthermore, since faith is living in accord with the eternal rather than the temporal, our home is elsewhere. By choosing to live as people whose destiny is "the City that has foundations, whose architect and builder is God" (Heb 11:10), we have chosen to live as strangers in this world. Thus, we must be ready for ostracism and persecution by keeping our gaze on the One who is eternal. His mighty works of deliverance in response to faith prepare us to endure suffering and death without temporal deliverance because they assure us that he has a "better resurrection" in store for the people of God (Heb 10:35). The faith of Heb 11 is faith in a God who "was able to raise from the dead" (Heb 11:19).

We begin, then, with day one. In Heb 10:32–39, the final link of the chain, the pastor encourages his hearers to join the faithful of Heb 11:1–40 by reminding them that their past faithfulness in suffering demonstrates their affinity with the faithful people of God throughout time.

∿ Day One: "My Righteous One Shall Live by Faith." (Heb 10:32–39)

> [32] *Remember the earlier days during which, after your enlightenment, you endured a great contest of sufferings.* [33] *You endured this contest, on the one hand, by being made a public spectacle through insults and also tribulations; on the other, by having become partners of those who lived this way.* [34] *For you showed sympathy to the prisoners and you accepted the seizure of your possessions with joy because you were aware that you yourselves have a better possession and one that endures.* [35] *Do not throw away your boldness, which has great reward.* [36] *For you have need of endurance, so that, when you have done the will of God, you might receive the promise.* [37] *For yet in a very little while the coming one will come and will not delay.* [38] *And my righteous one shall live by faith; but if he should draw back, my soul has no pleasure in him.* [39] *But we are not of those who shrink back and are destroyed, but of those who have faith and preserve their souls.*[1]

This passage is the final link in the chain that shows the dependence of the life of faith (portrayed in Heb 11:1–40) upon the work of Christ (described in Heb 4:14—10:25). First, the pastor encouraged his hearers to pursue this life of faith by assuring them that our Great Priest has provided everything necessary by opening the way into God's presence (Heb 10:19–25). He then warned them that neglecting our Great Priest's provision would lead to eternal loss (Heb 10:26–31). He now recalls their past record of faithful endurance in the face of suffering and persecution (Heb 10:32–39). If they will only continue as they began through their Great Priest they will avoid eternal loss and be members of the grand community of the faithful (described in Heb 11:1–40) who, as aliens in this godless world, often endure persecution because of their faith.

After describing their past faithful endurance of suffering in verses 32–34, the pastor urges his hearers to continue that faithfulness in verses 35–36. In verses 37–38 he appeals to God's warning in Hab 2:3b–4 as support for his exhortation. This word from God clarifies the alternatives and reinforces the urgency of pursuing the life of faith exemplified by the history of the faithful in Heb 11:1–40. The pastor concludes in verse 39 by expressing confidence that those he is so fervently addressing will not be among those who suffer loss but among those who take their place with the company of the faithful whom he is about to describe.

---

1. This translation of verse 39 is taken from the ESV.

Verse 32. The pastor intentionally likens the persecution they endured soon after becoming followers of Jesus to a strenuous athletic "contest." The adjective "great" and the plural "sufferings" describe the intensity of the struggle. Their suffering included, as we will see, the shame, ridicule, and ostracism of the unbelieving world. Nevertheless, those who succeed in this athletic "contest" will receive an eternal "reward" and find a place of honor in the eternal hall of fame.

Verses 33–34. These verses help us understand the nature and magnitude of their sufferings. The pastor begins (v. 33a) and ends (v. 34b) by describing their personal sufferings. In between (vv. 33b–34a) he commends them for readiness to identify with other persecuted believers.

In the first century, recognition of pagan gods was integral to every aspect of social, professional, and political life—from the marketplace to the workshop, to the gymnasium. As a defined community Jews had been granted begrudging exemption. However, as followers of Jesus became a growing body distinct from the Jewish community, they were granted no privileges. Their refusal to participate in idolatrous practices was perceived as unreasonable, subversive, and seditious.

The normal first-century way of dealing with such social deviance was public beating and other forms of public shame, confiscation of property, and execution. Such public dehumanization was a dread fate because it separated victims from the social connections necessary for their livelihood and left them in destitution not unlike the situation soon to be described in Heb 11:37–38. This is the kind of treatment experienced by the pastor's congregation: they were "made a public spectacle through insults and also tribulations" and suffered "the seizure" of their "possessions." Yet their conduct had been exemplary. They maintained an eternal perspective. They "accepted the seizure" of their earthly "possessions" (plural) "with joy" instead of despair, because that "seizure" identified them as belonging to those who "have a better possession" (singular), "one that endures" forever!

The pastor emphasizes their past identification with the suffering people of God because he wants them to continue identifying with the faithful. In the past they had not hesitated to "become partners" with other persecuted believers and to show "sympathy" toward those who had been imprisoned. They supplied the needs of those whose property had been confiscated. They took food and warm clothing to those imprisoned for their faith. By publicly identifying with these "offenders" they exposed themselves to the same punishment. The pastor would urge them: "Continue to take your place with the suffering people of God, soon to be described in chapter 11. After all you have been through, don't abandon the worshiping community out of shame. There is no perseverance apart from the people of God!"

Verses 35–36. "Do not" then "throw away" the "boldness" that you so clearly demonstrated when you took such a public stand for Christ soon after your conversion. That "boldness" dispels the shame unbelieving society would heap upon you. What you need now is to maintain that "boldness" through "endurance."

Verse 36 is a clear, concise description of why the pastor has written to his beloved congregation: "For you have need of endurance, so that, when you have done the will of God, you might receive the promise." "When you have done the will of God" describes the completed life of enduring faith. It describes a life that has been lived in the assurance that God's promise for the future is certain and in the confidence that his power in the present is real. It describes the life of one who has persevered in obedience despite suffering by drawing near through Christ to receive grace for cleansing and victorious living. By doing the "will" of God (Heb 10:5–10) the incarnate, now-exalted, and eternal Son enables the faithful to do God's "will." By referring to the "promise" that the faithful will receive, their "great reward," an enduring "better possession," the pastor awakens longing for God's eternal blessing.

Verses 37–38. These verses are the author's paraphrase of Hab 2:3b–4.[2] This ancient oracle clarifies the issues before the people of God today and adds Scriptural authority to the pastor's appeal. "For yet in a very little while the coming one will come and will not delay" describes God's judgment and the imminent return of Christ. "My righteous one shall live by faith" describes those who will be ready. The "righteous one" lives by the "faith" that the pastor has been advocating and that will be so fully defined, described, and exemplified in Heb 11:1–40. "But if he should draw back" describes the person who lacks "endurance," who throws away "boldness," and does not persevere in faithful obedience. The oracle ends with God's ominous condemnation of such a person: "My soul has no pleasure in him."

Verse 39. The pastor hastens to relieve the fear he has intentionally evoked: "We," that is, you (the hearers) and I (the pastor), "are not of those who shrink back and are destroyed." "Destruction" is a fit description of those in whom God's "soul has no pleasure." We are heirs of the company that I am about to describe "who have faith and preserve their souls." Although the pastor spoke some time ago about a "Sabbath rest" (Heb 9:10), he has been reserved in his references to the ultimate destiny of God's people. As noted above, his use of a "great reward," "better possession," and "promise," arouse curiosity and awaken desire. "Preserve their souls," implies little

---

2. For a discussion of the relationship between the pastor's paraphrase and the Greek and Hebrew texts of this verse see Cockerill, *Hebrews*, 506–12.

more than escape from the destruction of those who "draw back." As they begin listening to the history of the faithful, the pastor's congregation are longing to hear about this "enduring possession," which he will reveal as the goal and end of the history of the faithful people of God.

✑ Day Two: From Creation to Noah: Faith Defined. (Heb 11:1–7)

[1] *Now faith is the reality of things hoped for, the evidence of things not seen.* [2] *For by it the people of old were attested.* [3] *By faith we understand that the worlds were ordered by the word of God, so that what is seen has not come into being from the things that appear.* [4] *By faith Abel offered to God a better sacrifice than Cain, through which he was attested as righteous by God's bearing witness in regard to his gifts. And through this he still speaks, although he has died.* [5] *By faith Enoch was translated so that he did not see death, and he was not found because God translated him. For before his translation he had the attestation that he pleased God.* [6] *But without faith it is impossible to please him. For it is necessary for the one coming to God to believe that he is and that he is a rewarder of those who diligently seek him.* [7] *By faith Noah, having been warned concerning things not yet seen, moved by godly fear, prepared an ark for the salvation of his household, by which he judged the world and became heir of the righteousness that is according to faith*

According to Heb 11:1–7, the history of the faithful begins with creation followed by the examples of Abel, Enoch, and Noah as found in Gen 1–11. These opening chapters of the Bible reveal the fundamental nature of biblical faith. Hebrews 11:1–2 introduces this history by defining faith and by affirming that the faith of the examples that follow was "attested" by God as genuine and pleasing to him. Since this faith, according to verse 3, is founded on trust in the existence of the invisible Creator and his powerful creative "word," it orients the lives of those who practice it toward the unseen world. Thus, we are not shocked when we discover that the examples of Abel (v. 4) and Enoch (v. 5) assure us that this Creator God has a future for his own beyond the grave. Nor are we surprised that Noah's escape from judgment "by faith" points us toward the promise of ultimate salvation that is the final goal of the history of this faithful people of God (v. 7). Verse 6 clarifies the definition of faith given in verse 1. On the basis of these two verses we have defined faith as follows: "Faith is living like God's promises for the future are certain and his power in the present is real." Only those who live by this kind of faith can be called "righteous," because only they "please God."

Verses 1–3. The pastor defines faith. Biblical "faith" is oriented toward the future but rooted in the present; it is both "the reality of things hoped for" and "the evidence of things not seen." By trusting God to fulfill his promises, believers will enter into the "reality" of the future for which they have hoped. By trusting God for daily grace, believers even now experience the power of God as "evidence" of his unseen existence. It was only by this kind of faith that "the people of old," whom we are about to study, were "attested" by God as "righteous," that is, as pleasing in his sight. The way in which God honored their faith is further "evidence" of his unseen power and character.

The pastor accomplishes two important goals with his first example: "By faith *we* understand that the worlds were ordered by the word of God" (italics added). First, he invites *we* his hearers to take our place in this history. Second, he articulates the fundamental foundation of faith: the visible world was made by the invisible word of God. It is *not* the ultimate reality. Throughout this chapter we will see that all who live "by faith" orient their lives toward the invisible Creator, his creative "word," and the eternal world that he has established. Those who live by faith know that the power and promises of God, though invisible, are more reliable than the visible, sensible world in which they live. When we choose to live for the eternal we choose to be "aliens and transients on earth" (Heb 11:13).

Verses 4–5. Those who are "aliens and transients" because they live "by faith" in the Creator are often persecuted by those who live according to the creation without regard for its Maker. The pastor narrates this roll-call of the faithful in order to prepare his hearers to endure the severest persecution without surrendering their faith (see 11:35b–37). It is for this reason, as we will see, that he has chosen Abel (Gen 4:1–16) and Enoch (Gen 5:21–24) as the second and third examples of those who lived "by faith." Let's see what our text says about them.

God "attested" that Abel was "righteous" by accepting his sacrifice. The pastor is convinced that God's acceptance implied that Abel's offering was a true expression of his trust in the promises and power of God. Thus, through the scriptural record, Abel still bears witness that a person who is "righteous" (pleasing to God) will conduct his life "by faith" in the power and promises of God—even though his faith did not save him from death at the hands of his brother. Faithful Abel's death raises a crucial question: "Does faith in the power and promises of God end in the grave?"

On the other hand, "by faith Enoch was translated so that he did not see death." We know that his deliverance from death was "by faith" because

Scripture tells us that, while he was still on earth, he "pleased God."[3] According to verse 6 below, divine pleasure is a sure sign that the person lives by faith in the power and character of God. Abel suffered death although he was faithful. Enoch was delivered from death because of his faithfulness.

Abel and Enoch complement each other. Taken together they are a sketch that will be filled in as this chapter progresses. Like Abel, all who live "by faith," die. Like Enoch, all who live "by faith," will be delivered from death. The faith of the people in this chapter is a faith that awaits "a better resurrection" (v. 35b) because it is faith in a God who is "able to raise from the dead" (v. 19). *Only faith in the unseen God who raises the dead will enable the people of God to endure severe persecution or brave a martyr's death.*

Although the pastor does not mention the injustice of Abel's death, Abel reminds us of those at the end of this chapter who suffered persecution and martyrdom without deliverance in hope of the "better resurrection" (Heb 11:35b–37). The examples of temporal deliverance in Heb 11:32–35a encourage those suffering to await the "better resurrection" by assuring them of the faithfulness of God. However, Enoch's ultimate deliverance is proof positive that God's power transcends the grave. That "better resurrection" (Heb 11:35b) is the only deliverance of ultimate significance.

Verse 6. Now it is obvious that without this kind of "faith" no one could please God. One must believe in his existence and character, in his power and faithfulness. One must believe that God's power is real in the present ("he is"), and his promises for the future are certain ("he is a rewarder of those who diligently seek him"). Thus, this verse in conjunction with verse one above confirms the definition of faith given in the overview of verses one through seven: *Faith is living like God's promises for the future are certain and his power in the present is real.* In him we find the grace that we need in the present to persevere in obedience until we receive his promises of future eternal blessing. This definition applies to those who live before and after Christ: before, the work of Christ was part of God's promises for the future (Heb 1:1, 3:5); after, the work of Christ has become the power of God available for present perseverance—as described in Heb 4:14—10:25. The pastor earnestly wants his hearers to "diligently seek" this God.

Verse 7. God is "a rewarder" of those who pursue him. In the examples that follow, the pastor will describe the destiny promised those who live "by faith" in glowing terms. However, the promise of "things not yet seen" came to Noah as a warning of impending judgment. The pastor's hearers will not

---

3. Your English Old Testament, following the Hebrew text, says that Enoch "walked with God" (Gen 5:22, 24). The pastor, however, used a Greek translation that interpreted "walked with God" as "pleased God." Certainly, Enoch's walking in close fellowship with God was a sign of the divine pleasure.

appreciate the glorious destiny of the faithful unless they stand in awe of the "destruction" (Heb 10:39) from which they have been delivered.

By describing faithful Noah as "moved by godly fear" the pastor reminds us that the life of faith is an awe-filled, obedient response of the entire person to a holy God who is all-powerful and faithful. To live "by faith" is to be "moved" by this acknowledgement so that one lives as if God's promises (and warnings) for the future are certain and his power in the present is real. Living "by faith" is both an orientation of the heart and a course of life.

By recalling the way in which Noah's obedience led to the "salvation of his household" from God's judgment, the pastor reminds his hearers of the impact of their obedience on the "House of God" (Heb 3:1–6, cf. 3:12–13; 10:24–25). By ending with the declaration that Noah's obedience not only "judged the world" but made him an "heir of the righteousness that comes by faith" the pastor turns his hearers' gaze from escaping final judgment to the inheritance (Heb 1:14) prepared for those who live "by faith." The following history of those who are "righteous" before God because they live "by faith" will unveil this inheritance with ever-increasing attractiveness. Keep listening!

The lives of these three foundational examples—Abel, Enoch, and Noah—echo the course of "the Pioneer and Perfecter" (12:3) of the way of faith that they pursued. Like Abel, his offering a sacrifice pleasing to God cost him his life. Like Enoch, he was delivered from death. Like Noah, by his obedience his "household" was delivered from judgment and received the inheritance that God had prepared for those who please him because they live "by faith."

The "righteous," those who please God, live obedient human lives "by faith" (like Abel). They receive eternal life "by faith" (like Enoch). They are delivered from final judgment and enter into the eternal inheritance that God has prepared for those with whom he is pleased (like Noah). This is their story. You are invited, through Christ, to take your place in their company.

❧ Day Three: In the Time of Abraham and Sarah: Faith in an Alien World. (Heb 11:8–16)

> [8] *By faith Abraham obeyed, as soon as he was called, by setting out for a place that he was going to receive as an inheritance. And he set out, although he did not know where he was going.* [9] *By faith he sojourned in the land of promise as in a strange land, dwelling in tents with Isaac and Jacob, who were fellow heirs of the same promise.* [10] *For he was continually looking forward to the City that has foundations whose architect and builder is God.*

> ¹¹ *By faith even Sarah herself, although barren, received power for the disposition of seed, even though she was past the season for childbearing, since she considered that the one who had promised was faithful.* ¹² *Therefore from one man, who was indeed dead, there came into being as many as the stars of heaven in multitude and as the sand along the seashore without number.*
>
> ¹³ *These all died according to faith, although they had not received the promises. However, they had seen them from afar, greeted them, and confessed that they were aliens and transients on earth.* ¹⁴ *For those who say such things show that they are seeking a place where they are citizens.* ¹⁵ *And if they had been mindful of that place from which they had come, they would have had opportunity to return.* ¹⁶ *But now they fervently long for a better, that is, a heavenly place. Therefore, God is not ashamed of them to be called their God, for he has prepared for them a City.*

The faithful people of God begin to emerge as a community in response to God's promises. Although Abel, Enoch, and Noah lived "by faith," it was Abraham (Gen 12:1–6; 13:15; 15:5), Isaac (Gen 26:3–4), and Jacob (Gen 28:13–15) who received God's promises of descendants, land, and blessing for the world. As Abraham's "fellow heirs" (v. 9) Isaac and Jacob represent all those who constitute the people of God because they live "by faith." It is as members of this community of faith that we receive God's promises.

In verses 8–12 the pastor narrates the first three Abrahamic examples. Then, in verses 13–16, he shows how these three foundational examples set the pattern for all that follows. The hope beyond the grave, revealed through the examples of Abel and Enoch (Heb 11:4–5), is more than the escape from judgment experienced by Noah (Heb 11:7, cf. 10:39). The people who live "by faith" are citizens of the promised eternal "City" that God has prepared for them. To live "by faith" in pursuit of that City is to live by choice as an alien and stranger in this present world.

Verse 8–10. These first two examples illustrate the second part of the definition of faith given above: faith is *living* "like God's promises for the future are certain." The story of Abraham begins in Gen 12:1–9 with the most unambiguous example of the intrinsic relationship between faith in God's promise and *obedience*: "by faith Abraham obeyed God." His obedience was immediate. As soon as God "called" him to leave his home, "he set out for a place that he was going to receive as an inheritance"—because he trusted the promise of God. His faith in God's promise was so strong that he obeyed even though God had not yet shown him "where he was going."

Furthermore, this obedience was not only immediate, but continuous. It transcended generations. Abraham, his son Isaac, and his grandson

Jacob all three persevered in obedience by continuing to "sojourn" in the so-called "land of promise as a strange land." They chose to live "in tents" because they were not trying to make this world their permanent home. They were on their way to something truly permanent—"the City that has foundations whose architect and builder is God." As we saw when reading the story of the disobedient wilderness generation (Heb 3:7—4:11), faith and obedience are two sides of the same coin. To live "by faith" is to be faithful. This description fits all the examples that follow. The pastor is burdened that his hearers persevere in unhesitating obedience.

The pastor uses the word "inheritance" in anticipation of the eternal nature of what God has in store for the faithful. The so-called "land of promise" where the patriarchs lived in tents could not be this eternal inheritance. This inheritance is the "salvation" that the faithful will inherit (Heb 1:14) at Christ's return (Heb 9:28) in the "world to come" (Heb 2:5), "the City that has foundations whose architect and builder is God." "City" describes a society, a community. Unlike the "tents" of this world, it "has foundations." As its "architect and builder" God was responsible, from beginning to end, for establishing this eternal City. To live in this City is to enjoy the "Sabbath rest" that "remains" for the faithful people of God (Heb 4:9).

Verses 11–12: On the other hand, Sarah's faith, as described in verses 11–12, illustrates the first half of our definition: faith is *living* "like God's power in the present is real."[4] God will supply what you need in order to persevere until the ultimate promise is fulfilled. An eternal inheritance requires heirs. God had promised Abraham that his descendants would inherit the City that God had prepared. Abraham needed an heir. At the very beginning of the story we are told that Sarah was "barren" (Gen 11:30). She had to wait, however, until after "she was past the season for childbearing" (Gen 18:11, my own translation) so that all would know that God was fulfilling this promise. We can appreciate Sarah's struggles. She tried to solve the problem on her own by giving Abraham her handmaid Hagar as wife (Gen 16:1–4). Old Sarah laughed (Gen 18:9–15) when she heard God affirm that she would bear a son within the next year. But she came to faith on the basis of God's character as "faithful" to his promises. Therefore, she "received power" to accept Abraham's "seed" and bear the son of promise. The fulfillment of her faith is "evidence of things not seen."

Verse 11 ends with the word "faithful." Verse 12 confirms the faithfulness of God. As far as reproduction was concerned, Abraham was as good as "dead." Yet, we can see that, through Sarah, God has fulfilled his promise to

---

4. For Sarah as the subject of verse 11 see Cockerill, *Hebrews*, 542–45. Some translations, such as the NRSV, make Abraham the subject of this verse.

make Abraham's "seed" "as many as the stars [Gen 15:5, 22:17] of heaven in multitude and as the sand [Gen 22:17] along the seashore without number." All the faithful are part of this great company, including the prostitute, Rahab, who is the climax of this list of those who lived "by faith" (v. 31).

Verses 13–16. In these verses the pastor provides the context for the following examples by explaining what it meant for Abraham and his "fellow heirs" to "sojourn" in the so-called "land of promise" anticipating "the City with foundations" (v. 9). This explanation has been carefully crafted to encourage our perseverance during our earthly "sojourn."

Persevere, remembering that, though Abraham and his "fellow heirs" (v. 9) lived "according to faith," they, like Abel, did not receive what God had promised before they died. The promised reward, however, determined the course of their lives in this world.

How did the pursuit of this reward determine the way they lived? With the eyes of faith, they saw the promised eternal home "from afar." By "greeting" it as their own, they "confessed that they were aliens and transients on earth." We might paraphrase Abraham's words in Gen 24:3, "This world is not my home, I'm just passing through." If we pursue God's eternal promise by living in faithful obedience, we too will be strangers in the world of people pursuing earthly goals. Still, we have privileges unknown to Abraham, Isaac, and Jacob while they were on earth. They saw the promise "from afar." We "draw near" (Heb 10:22) through our Great Priest. If they persevered, we have no excuse. In the end, both we and they enter God's "City" through Jesus (Heb 12:22–24).

How do we know that Abraham and his "fellow heirs" were seeking the eternal "City" that God had established? The pastor gives us two pieces of evidence. (1) Since they declared that they were "aliens" in the so-called "land of promise," they must have been "seeking a place where they" would be "citizens." (2) It would have been easy for them to satisfy this desire for citizenship by going back to "the place from which they had come." They paid no heed, however, to their place of origin, because God had promised them an "inheritance." Thus, it is clear, "they fervently long for a better, that is, a heavenly place."

The people of this unbelieving world often repay the choice of God's people to live as aliens in this world with shame and exclusion from society. However, the God who "has prepared for them a City" is not ashamed to be called the God of those who "fervently desire" what he has made ready for them.

∾ Day Four: From Abraham to Joseph: Faith in a God Who Raises the Dead. (Heb 11:17–22)

[17] *By faith Abraham offered Isaac when he was being tested. And he who had received the promises was ready to offer the only begotten,* [18] *he to whom it had been said that "in Isaac will your seed be called."* [19] *He did this because he reckoned that God was able to raise from the dead. Therefore, he received him as a type.*

[20] *By faith Isaac blessed Jacob and Esau concerning things to come.* [21] *By faith Jacob, as he was dying, blessed each of the sons of Joseph and worshiped upon the top of his staff.* [22] *By faith Joseph, as he was coming to an end, remembered the Exodus of the Children of Israel and gave instructions concerning his bones.*

Verses 17–19. The pastor follows the Old Testament by putting great emphasis on Abraham's sacrifice of Isaac (Gen 22:1–19). This act of obedience is the climactic fourth example of faith from the lifetime of faith's premier exemplar. In fact, the pastor makes the offering of Isaac the centerpiece of the "by-faith" saga in verses 1–31. The following examples of Isaac, Jacob, and Joseph in verses 20–22 balance the description of the faith of Sarah and the patriarchs in verses 13–16. The first three examples from the life of Moses in verses 23–27 parallel, as we will see, the first three examples from Abraham's life in verses 8–12. Moses' deliverance of God's people from judgment through the Passover in verse 28 reminds us of Noah's deliverance of God's people from the flood in verse 7. The final three "by faith's" in verses 29–31 offset the first three in verses 1–6. These structural relationships between the examples of faith in verses 1–31 are important for understanding this chapter. Thus, we will make further reference to them as appropriate in days five and six.

At no other time are we told that Abraham's faith was "being tested." The pastor has given the sacrifice of Isaac such a place of prominence because it reveals God as a God who is "able to raise from the dead" (v. 19) and because it shows how this test brought Abraham to a place of ultimate reliance upon God.

"*By faith* Abraham offered Isaac" (italics added). Abraham never hesitated in his obedience from journey's beginning to knife raised above Isaac as he lay bound upon the altar. This sacrifice was complete as far as its effect on Abraham's relationship with God was concerned. He demonstrated that he was fully "ready to offer the only begotten." We will only understand the nature of this test when we remember that (1) Abraham was the "one who had received the promises," especially the promise that "in Isaac shall your seed be called," and (2) Isaac was the "only begotten" son of the promise. God had promised Abraham that he would make him a great nation through none other than Isaac, the miraculous, long-awaited son promised to barren, postmenopausal Sarah. The birth of Isaac confirmed God's faithfulness. Now God asks Abraham to both *sacrifice Isaac* and to continue trusting God to make him a great nation *through Isaac.* Obedience brought Abraham to a place of complete reliance upon God's character and full surrender to his will.

There is only one logical explanation: Abraham reasoned that God was the kind of God who "was able to raise from the dead." The examples of Abel and Enoch showed that God's power transcended death (vv. 4–5). God delivered Noah and his family from judgment (v. 7). He used one as good as "dead" to father a multitude of descendants (v. 12). He is, indeed, a God who is "able to raise from the dead."

While Isaac's resurrection would have been a restoration to mortal life as in verse 35a below, it was a "type" or foreshadowing of the "better resurrection" to eternal life that, according to verse 35b, awaits those who live "by faith." Those who experience this "better resurrection" enter the goal of creation, God's "Sabbath rest" (Heb 4:9) in "the City that has foundations." Nothing less than resurrection faith will sustain God's people during their pilgrim "sojourn" as "aliens" in a world that is estranged from God. Abraham and Isaac remind us of someone else who would offer himself in obedience trusting in "the one who was able to save him out of death" (Heb 5:7).

Verses 20–22. The pastor follows the four examples from Abraham's lifetime with three examples from the lives of Isaac, Jacob, and Joseph. As Abraham's "fellow heirs" (v. 9) they represent the people of God who inherit God's promises. They each illustrate the kind of faith described in verses 13–16 by living their lives in this world with the conviction that "God's promises for the future are certain." Thus, they join Abraham as "aliens and sojourners" in an unbelieving world that has no horizon beyond what is presently visible.

Isaac (Gen 27:1–45) and Jacob (Gen 48:1–22) demonstrate their faith in the fulfillment of God's promises by blessing those who come after them. Two questions arise when we look at verse 20. Why does the pastor say that Isaac blessed *Esau* as well as Jacob? What does he mean by "things to come"? Let us look at the second question first. "Things to come" includes all that God would do to provide for the salvation of his people in fulfillment of his promises to Abraham. Isaac and Jacob demonstrate their faith in God's promises by passing those promises on to their descendants. Of course, God's promises to Abraham include all that he has done in Christ and the City that he has prepared for those who live "by faith." Isaac need not have realized the full extent of the promised "things to come," concerning which he blessed Jacob.

Of course, Esau was present in the pastor's Genesis text and received a kind of "blessing" after Isaac had blessed Jacob (Gen 27:38–40). Unlike Jacob, however, Esau passes on no blessing. The pastor includes him here in anticipation of the way he will use him as a warning in Heb 12:14–17. It is only one who was associated with the people of God who can illustrate the tragedy of falling away in unbelief.

The fact that Jacob, in verse 21, passed on the blessing "as he was dying" reminds us that God's promises transcend death. A careful reading of Genesis reveals why the pastor chose the time when Jacob blessed Joseph's sons (Gen 48:1–22) instead of the time when he blessed his own sons (Gen 49:1–28). Jacob blessed Joseph's sons by passing the promises God had given Abraham on to them. Thus, by this blessing he was "living like God's promises for the future are certain." The description of Jacob worshiping "upon the top of his staff" (Gen 47:31) pictures him as one who lives in awe of God during the pilgrimage of his earthly sojourn.[5]

The mention of Joseph's sons recalls the final actions of Joseph recorded in Gen 50:24–26 and summarized here in verse 22. Joseph persevered "by faith" until the end of his life. By concluding this section with Joseph, the pastor emphasizes the importance of memory and identity. All who live "by faith" truly *remember* God's promises by acting upon them. All who live by faith are careful to maintain their identity with the people of God who are the heirs of the promises. Joseph remembered God's promise of redemption. He did not forget that God had promised "the Children of Israel" an "Exodus" from Egypt. Because he believed that promise, he "gave instructions concerning his bones." This was all the pastor had to say to remind his hearers that Joseph had instructed the Israelites to take his mummified bones with them when God delivered them from Egypt. The one who had been sold into Egypt did not want to be abandoned there. These instructions demonstrated both his faith in God's promise and his determination to be part of the people of God, the recipients of God's promises. The pastor earnestly desires his hearers to persevere, as did Joseph, by remembering the promise of God's eternal "City" and by unashamedly identifying with the faithful people of God who, through Christ, inherit what God has promised. He wants us to keep living in obedience so that we, like Joseph, might come "to an end" with enduring faith.[6]

5. On the translation of Gen 47:31 as "worshiped as he leaned on the top of his staff" (TNIV) see Cockerill, *Hebrews*, 561.

6. "As he was coming to an end" echoes the Greek text of the description of Joseph's death in Gen 50:26.

Joseph's instructions concerning his bones in Gen 50:24–26 prepared for the story of Moses and deliverance from Egypt in the early chapters of Exodus. The pastor's mentioning these instructions provides a smooth transition to the account of Moses and the mighty acts of God in verses 23–31.

∾ Day Five: From Moses to Rahab: Faith under Stress. (Heb 11:23–31)

> [23] *By faith Moses, when he was born, was hidden three months by his parents, because they saw that he was a beautiful child and they did not fear the edict of the king.* [24] *By faith Moses, when he was grown, refused to be called a son of Pharaoh's daughter,* [25] *but chose rather to suffer ill-treatment with the people of God than to have the temporary advantage of sin.* [26] *He did this because he considered the reproach of Christ greater riches than the treasurers of Egypt, for he was continually looking toward the reward.* [27] *By faith he abandoned Egypt having not feared the wrath of the king, for he endured as seeing the Unseen One.* [28] *By faith he established the Passover and the application of blood, in order that the destroying one might not touch their firstborn.* [29] *By faith they passed through the Red Sea on dry ground, which when the Egyptians attempted they were swallowed up.* [30] *By faith the walls of Jericho fell because they had been encircled for seven days.* [31] *By faith Rahab the prostitute was not destroyed with those who disobeyed because she welcomed the spies with peace.*

Just as four examples from the time of Abraham (vv. 8–19) precede three from the family of Abraham (vv. 20–22), so four from the time of Moses (vv. 23–28) precede three from those who followed him (vv. 29–31). This section, however, is no mere repetition of what has gone before. Without neglecting the promises of God for the future, the pastor now underscores God's power for present victory amid suffering. Those who have declared themselves to be aliens in this present unbelieving world should not be surprised when they eperience the anger of that world. Thus, the need for patient waiting in an alien world has become the need for courage in a hostile world. Though it is still important to keep one's eyes on the future "reward," it is just as important to live daily with the eyes of faith focused on the One who is "Unseen" (v. 27). Furthermore, it is vital to identify with the people of God for they are the ones who will receive God's promised inheritance.

The first three examples in this section (all from the time of Moses) call for courage in the face of hostility (vv. 23–27). The last three attest God's power to sustain the courageous amid present persecution (vv.

29–31). The fourth, and central, example joins the power of God to the need for courage (v. 28).

It is important to note that the first three examples from the lifetime of Moses (Heb 11:23–27) parallel the first three examples from the time of Abraham (Heb 11:8–12) *in reverse order*: (1) Moses' departure from Egypt (Heb 11:27) corresponds to Abraham's "setting out" when he was "called" (Heb 11:8). (2) Moses' choosing to suffer with God's people (Heb 11:25–26) corresponds to Abraham's living as a stranger in the land (Heb 11:9–10). (3) The faith of Moses' parents after his birth (v. 23) corresponds to the faith of Sarah that led to Isaac's birth (Heb 11:8). The first three examples from Abraham's life focused on choosing to sojourn as aliens in this world as we wait for the *promise* of life in the City of the world to come. These three examples from Moses' life emphasize the need to courageously depend on the *present power* of God in a world hostile to those who have chosen to pursue the eternal City. (Remember, faith is living as if God's *promises* for the future are certain and his *power* in the present is real!)

Verse 23. Both Isaac, the son of the promise born to "barren" Sarah (Heb 11:11–12), and Moses, a "beautiful child" (Heb 11:23), embodied God's hope for the future. The birth of the first was the reward of parental faith that waited patiently for God to fulfill his promise. The preservation of the second, however, required courageous parental obedience in reliance on God's power (Exod 2:1–8).

Genesis ended with Joseph ruling Egypt. Exodus opens with the descendants of Jacob, now a huge multitude, enslaved by Pharaoh and suffering severe oppression. These were the circumstances that surrounded Moses' birth. When the text says that Moses' parents "saw" that he was a "beautiful child" it implies that they "saw," with the eyes of faith, that God had a special purpose for him. The King of Egypt, however, had ordered that all Israelite boy babies be thrown into the Nile. So, in obedience to God, they "hid him for three months." The courageous nature of their faith is shown by the fact that they were not intimidated "by the king's edict."

Verses 24–26. The people of God choose to live as temporary residents and strangers in this world. In response, the world persecutes those who refuse to make it their home. Thus, the world in which Abraham lived as a stranger because of his faith (Heb 11:9–10) has become the hostile world of Moses' time, oppressing the people of God. Abraham was called upon to "sojourn" awaiting the promised eternal City. Moses, however, was called to courageously identify with the people of God in dependence on God's present power.

"When he was grown" Moses made the courageous faith of his parents his own. By killing the Egyptian who was oppressing an Israelite (Exod

2:11–12), he "refused to be called a son of Pharaoh's daughter" who had adopted him. He "*chose* rather to suffer ill-treatment with the people of God than to have the temporary advantage of sin" (italics added). Any "advantage" that separates us from God is "sin." The word used for "advantage" evokes a sense of luxury and is an apt description of Moses' privileged position in the royal household. Never mind. Moses knew that such "advantage" was very "temporary." The pastor wants his hearers to know that Moses' choice was reasonable and calculated. Not only was the "reward" promised God's people "greater riches" than all "the treasures of Egypt," but the very "reproach of Christ" was greater wealth than Egypt's fabled treasures.

The pastor identifies the sufferings of Moses with "the reproach of Christ" suffered by his hearers in order to strengthen their courage. How could Moses' sufferings be the "reproach of Christ"? Through his own obedient suffering Christ became the "Source of eternal salvation" (Heb 5:9) for the one household of God over which he reigns as "Son" (Heb 3:1–6) and "Great Priest" (Heb 10:19–25), whether its members lived before or after his coming. Thus, Christ accepts all reproach suffered by his people for their obedience as his own. This "reproach" itself was "greater riches" than the "treasures of Egypt" because it identified Moses with the people of God, who would inherit the eternal City. Moses made the only truly logical choice. However, in order to persevere in this choice, we like Moses must "keep looking toward the reward."

Verse 27. Abraham set out for the place he would inherit in dependence on God's promise of future blessing (Heb 11:8). Moses' courage reached its climax when, in dependence upon God's present power for deliverance, he fearlessly "abandoned Egypt" leading God's people to freedom. "By faith" Abraham overcame insecurity and Moses triumphed over hostility. Those who seek the "City with foundations" abandon the city of those who do not believe.

When we read the story we see hesitant Moses become bold before Pharaoh by the power of God (Exod 4:18—14:31). His courage mirrors the courage of his parents. They were not intimidated by "the king's edict" because they saw he was God's special child. He did not fear "the wrath of the King" because by the eyes of faith he kept his vision fixed on the One Unseen by human eyes.

"By faith" Abraham kept his vision on God's promised City. "By faith" Moses' parents could see that he was God's special child. "By faith" Moses kept his focus on the promised "reward." But now, we find that the secret of his persevering courage was that "by faith" he kept his vision on the "Unseen One." The vision of God that was the source of daily victory for Moses has become for us the vision of the mighty "Pioneer and Perfecter of the faith, Jesus" (Heb 12:1–3) seated at the Father's right hand.

Verse 28. We have already suggested that this fourth example of faith from the Moses section joins the power of God in the three following examples (11:29–31) to the courageous faith of the three preceding examples (Heb 11:23–27). God's power is a present reality sufficient to sustain those who exercise courageous faith in the midst of opposition.

It is important, however, to see the relationships between this fourth and central example of faith from the Moses section (Heb 11:28), the fourth and central example of faith from the Abraham section (Heb 11:17–19), and the example of Noah (Heb 11:7). In commenting on Heb 11:17–19 above (day four), we showed that Noah's building the Ark (Heb 11:7) and Moses' establishing the Passover (Heb 11:28) paralleled each other, and that Abraham's sacrificing Isaac (Heb 11:17–19) was the heart of this "by-faith" discourse (Heb 11:1–31) and the mid-point between Noah's "Ark" (11:7) and Moses' "Passover" (Heb 11:28).

Both Noah's building the Ark and Moses' establishing the Passover show that God's people (called Noah's "household," and the "firstborn") are delivered from judgment and death "by faith" (cf. Heb 2:14–15). Abraham's faith in a God who is "able to raise from the dead" suggests that they are delivered from judgment in order to enjoy the "better resurrection" (Heb 11:35) in the "City of the living God" (Heb 12:22).

As the agents through whom God delivered his people from judgment, Noah's "godly fear" and Moses' courageous obedience remind us of the One who "learned obedience through what he suffered" and was heard by God because of his "godly fear" (Heb 5:7–8). He is the one, as your remember, who freed God's people from their lifelong fear of death by delivering them from sin so that, freed from judgment (Heb 2:14–18), they await eternal "salvation" (Heb 9:28) in the Unshakable Kingdom (Heb 12:25–29) at his return.

Moses "established the Passover" in obedience to the command of God and in reliance on God's promise (Exod 12:1–30). God had promised that "the destroying one" would "not touch" the "firstborn" of the faithful upon whose doors was "the application of blood." The only people delivered were those who entered the houses of the people of God to which the "blood" of the Passover sacrifice had been applied. Thus, this event reinforces a theme that has been growing throughout this chapter—only those who participate in the community of God's faithful people experience his power and receive what he has promised.

Verses 29–31. The pastor narrates these last three examples with the crisp brevity of a triumphant march. What could demonstrate the adequacy of God's power for the present better than the deliverance of the firstborn (v. 28), the deliverance of the faithful through, and the destruction of unbelievers in, the Red Sea (v. 29, cf. Exod 14:5–31), and the fall of Jericho's walls (v. 30, cf. Josh 6:1–27). These last two were granted in response to the faith of the entire company of God's people. They obeyed God by "passing through" the opening he had made in the Red Sea and by encircling Jericho "for seven days."

Rahab, in verse 31 (Josh 2:1–21), is the perfect conclusion to this grand parade of those who lived "by faith." There could be no clearer example of one who acted with confidence in the promises and power of God. By welcoming "the spies with peace" she affirmed her faith in God's promise to give his people the land and in his power to fulfill that promise. Unlike "those who disobeyed" by refusing to honor the true God, this "prostitute" escaped God's judgment (Josh 6:25) by unashamedly taking her place with the people of God. Without doubt, she demonstrates that the people of God have always been constituted "by faith" rather than by physical descent.

The pastor has been concerned lest his hearers disassociate themselves from the "assembly" of believers (Heb 10:25) by drifting away and suffer the judgment of "those who disobeyed" (Heb 2:1–4, 3:16–19, 6:4–8, 10:26–31). How ashamed they would be if their faith fell short of the faith of this "prostitute" who boldly identified with the people of God. The grace that was sufficient for "Rahab the prostitute" to live by faith is sufficient for you and me.

∾ Day Six: From Gideon and Barak through the Prophets: Faith in a "Better Resurrection." (Heb 11:32–40)

32 And what more shall I say? For time would fail me if I tried to recount the stories of Gideon, Barak, Samson, Jephthah, David and also Samuel and the prophets, 33 who through faith established kingdoms, worked righteousness, obtained promises; shut the moths of lions, 34 quenched the power of fire, escaped the mouth of the sword; were made strong out of weakness, became powerful in battle, put to flight the armies of aliens. 35 Women received their dead by resurrection. But still others were tortured refusing release in order that they might obtain a better resurrection. 36 And others received trials of mockings and beatings, and even of bonds and prison. 37 They were stoned, they were sawn in two, by murder of sword they died; they went about in sheep skins, in goatskins, destitute, afflicted, mistreated, 38 of whom

the world was not worthy, wandering in deserts and in hills and caves and holes of the earth.
[39] Even though these all were attested through their faith, they did not receive the promise, [40] because God had prepared something better for us, so that they might not be perfected apart from us.

With the history of the faithful from creation to Rahab (vv. 1–31) the pastor has clarified what it means to be part of the community of people who live as if God's promises for the future are certain and his power for perseverance in the present is real. The pastor is burdened, however, lest his hearers fail to enter God's promised City because their faith in the real but invisible power of God might be insufficient to sustain them amid coming adversity. He has urged them to embrace the courage of Moses (vv. 22–28) by a swift and powerful narration of those who "by faith" experienced God's mightiest Old Testament acts of deliverance (vv. 28–31). Is that enough?

In order to reinforce their courage the pastor moves from a documentary of those who lived "by faith" (vv. 1–31) to a fast-moving sequence of mighty triumphs through the power of God (vv. 33–35a) followed by a varied multitude of sufferings endured through trust in God (vv. 35b–38). Verse 32 introduces this new phase of the pastor's appeal.

Verse 32. "And what more shall I say?" suggests that the preceding examples should be more than enough to convince anyone. "For time would fail me if I tried to recount the stories" suggests that the remaining accounts of great triumphs "through faith" in the power of God are beyond number. The evidence is overwhelming. "Gideon, Barak, Samson, Jephthah, David and also Samuel and the prophets" are merely representative of the huge multitude of people who experienced these triumphs throughout the history of the people of God.

Verses 33–35a. We can imagine some of the names that these triumphs suggested to the pastor's congregation who were so steeped in the Old Testament and in the history of God's people. Yet the pastor has refrained from identifying those who experienced these triumphs of faith because he intends for each category to be suggestive of many people.

It is even more evident in Greek than in English that the pastor divides these triumphs "through faith" into three sets of three, followed by the grand triumph of resurrection in verse 35a. Each set surpasses the last in grandeur as they march before us three by three in a victory parade. The first three approach us in verse 33abc: "who through faith established kingdoms, worked righteousness, obtained promises." This triad describes those who experienced political success and instituted a godly social order "through faith." "Worked righteousness" means that they established justice.

"Obtained promises" encourages the pastor's congregation to persevere un-til they obtain all that God has promised.

As they march past us the second triad, verses 33d–34ab, presents us with those who "through faith" were delivered from death by execution: "shut the mouths of lions, quenched the power of fire, escaped the mouth of the sword." The first two evoke vivid memories of Daniel in the lions' den (Dan 6:1–28) and his three friends in the fiery furnace (Dan 3:1–29). The third pic-tures a multitude of the faithful escaping the "mouth" of a devouring sword. There should be no surprise when the God who is "able to raise from the dead" (v. 19) delivers the faithful from execution by the ungodly.

The final triad, verse 34cde, brings great military victories before us. Note the building crescendo in this progression: "through faith" many "were made strong out of weakness" so that they could become "powerful in battle" and thus "put to flight the armies of aliens." What could be greater than rout-ing "armies of aliens" who oppressed God's people? Read verse 35a: "women received their dead by resurrection." "Resurrection," in the sense of resto-ration to mortal life, is the hero of this parade, marching behind the three ranks of honor guards. Even so, it pales before the "better resurrection" of verse 35b. This grand parade of the mighty acts of God on behalf of his own reassures the suffering people of God that they can depend upon him for the ultimate deliverance—a "better resurrection."

Verse 35b. With that assurance, the pastor recounts the story of "still others" who "were tortured refusing release in order that they might obtain a better resurrection." We can see how the pastor has been preparing us for this "better resurrection." The translation of Enoch showed us that Abel's death was not the end (vv. 4–5). Through both Noah (v. 7) and Moses (v. 28) God delivered the faithful from the death experienced by the disobedi-ent. Abraham's offering Isaac (v. 17–19) in the confidence that "God was able to raise from the dead" was at the heart and center of verses 1–31. In the same way, the "better resurrection" in this verse is the heart of verses 32–40. It is the ultimate deliverance from the fear of death that plagues all humanity (Heb 2:14–15). The pastor introduces this "better resurrection" in order to prepare his hearers for the life of the suffering described in verses 36–38. He is preparing his hearers for such a life because he believes it is the normal experience of people who live as "aliens" in this unbelieving world (vv. 13–16 above). The "better resurrection" assures us that maintaining our faith under torture is infinitely worthwhile.

Verses 36–38. As we will see, this threefold description (v. 36, verse 37abc, verses 37d–38) of the suffering people of God parallels in reverse order the threefold account of God's mighty acts in verses 32–34 above. This story of suffering, however, is no march of triumph. By the time we reach the third part of this description in verses 37d–38, the disarrayed structure of the pastor's Greek sentence reflects the flight of refugees rather than a disciplined military parade.

The pastor begins in verse 36 with the kinds of things his hearers have already suffered for their faith (see Heb 10:32–35): "trials of mockings and beatings, and even of bonds and prison." The purpose of public beatings accompanied by public ridicule was to bring the kind of shame on the sufferers so dreaded in the ancient world. Such public humiliation was the antithesis of the glorious military victories described in verse 34cde, the third triad of the triumphant.

Worse, however, may await them. The ancient church distinguished between "martyrs" and "confessors." The first died rather than deny their faith. The second endured torture rather than abandon Christ. The pastor describes the first in verse 37abc; the second, in verses 37d–38.

The second triad of triumph above (vv. 33d–34ab) attests that the God who is "able to raise from the dead" (11:19) has delivered many of his own from unjust execution. The faithful, however, have often been called upon to die a martyr's violent death in order to enter into the "better resurrection": "they were stoned, they were sawn in two, by *murder* of sword they died" (v. 37abc, italics added).

Martyrdom, however, is not the pastor's chief concern. He is preparing us to persevere confessing our faith amid the circumstances described in verses 37d–38. This exclusion from society is the antithesis of the just political order of the first triumphant triad above (v. 32abc). Those who live as "aliens and sojourners" in this world may well experience the banishment from society and loss of the means of livelihood described in these verses. The faithful "went about in sheep skins, in goatskins" because they were bereft of clothing. They were "destitute" of food, "afflicted" and "mistreated" in every way. They wandered "in deserts . . . and in hills and caves and holes of the earth" because they were homeless, deprived of shelter and excluded from civic life. The "mockings and beatings" (v. 32) that the pastor's hearers had experienced were a step toward such exclusion from the security and resources of society. For many ancient people banishment was a great shame that made life hardly worth living. Thus, the pastor reminds us that "the earth was not worthy" of these "confessors." After all, God's eternal City was their true home. They were fully convinced "that what is seen has not come into being from the things that appear" (Heb 11:3). If the pastor knew the increasing hostility of the modern world against Christians, he would urge us to follow the example of these confessors.

Verses 39–40. God's faithful people today are one with the faithful of this chapter who "were attested" by God as "righteous" (v. 2 above) "through their faith." We serve the same God and we have trust in the same promise. However, the work of Christ that was still part of God's promise for their future has become his power for us in the present. Thus, in Christ we enjoy "something better." They could only see God's eternal City "from afar" (v. 13 above). We, however, are able to "draw near" with confidence during our present sojourn (Heb 10:22), enter preliminarily at our death (Heb 12:22–24), and finally at Christ's return (Heb 9:28, 12:25–29). We might say that "in order to attain the promised eternal city, "we" need their persevering faith; "they" needed the benefits that are "ours" through Christ."[7]

Since Christ has come, however, they too have been "perfected" by being cleansed from sin so that they can enter the divine presence. Thus, in Heb 12:22–24 we meet them, along with those who have died in Christ, as "the spirits of righteous people made perfect." Their lack of our privileges during their earthly pilgrimage makes their witness all the more compelling. We are left without excuse.

⚘ Day Seven: Jesus: "the Pioneer and Perfecter of the Faith." (Heb 12:1–3)

> [1] *Therefore, because we ourselves have such a great cloud of witnesses surrounding us, let us lay aside every hindrance and sin that so easily clings to us, and let us run with endurance the race set before us.* [2] *Let us run looking unto the Pioneer and Perfecter of the faith, Jesus, who for the joy set before him endured a cross despising the shame and has taken his seat at the right hand of the throne of God.* [3] *For consider the One who endured such opposition from sinners against himself, in order that you might not become weary, giving up in your souls.*

As noted in this week's introduction, the discourse begun in Heb 3:1–6 comes to fruition here in Heb 12:1–3. In Heb 3:1–6 the pastor directed our attention to "the Apostle and High Priest of our confession, *Jesus*," before warning us against associating with the faithless wilderness generation (Heb 3:7–19). Now, after urging us to join the faithful of all time (Heb 11:1–40), he fixes our gaze on "the Pioneer and Perfecter of the faith, *Jesus*" (italics added). Now we know what the pastor meant when he announced the *faithfulness* of the Son in Heb 3:1–6. Through his *faithful obedience* as the incarnate *Jesus* he became a "merciful and faithful High Priest" (Heb 2:17). He fulfilled the old sacrificial system that had been *faithfully established* by Moses as a "witness" to the "things that would be spoken." By his *faithfulness* he became

---

7. Adapted from Cockerill, *Hebrews*, 598.

"the Pioneer and Perfecter of the faith." He alone empowers God's people to live faithfully from the beginning of their pilgrimage to the end of their journey. He alone brings the faithful into God's eternal presence when they have completed their course. Only by keeping our eyes fixed on him will we be able to run this race with endurance until the end.

Verse 1. The pastor is emphatic, "*we ourselves* have such a great cloud of witnesses surrounding us" (italics added). The faithful of old are "witnesses" to us of God's faithfulness during their earthly pilgrimage. Their lives attest the "reality" of God's "hoped for" promises and provide undeniable "evidence" of God's unseen power (see on Heb 11:1–3, 6). The pilgrimage of faith, however, has become a race of endurance. They are also "witnesses" of our performance. The victors of old sit in the stands urging us to persevere in faithful obedience until we win the eternal prize. The unbelieving world may hiss and boo and do all in its power to deter us from the race. However, we never face opposition or persecution alone. The unbelieving world cannot compare with the "great cloud" of the faithful cheering us on. It is as if we can reach out and feel this multitude urging us forward. We exchange the shame heaped upon us by an unbelieving world for the approval and honor bestowed by the faithful people of God on those who persevere. How can we reach the finish line? Success requires *preparation, endurance,* and *focus*.

First—*preparation*: "let us lay aside every hindrance and sin that so easily clings to us." A successful runner strips down. A successful runner loses excess weight and removes clothes or gear that would hinder the race. *Anything* that causes the runner in this race of faith to stumble is "sin." "Sin" is like a rope, excess clothes, or a trap in the path that easily entangles the feet and causes the runner to fall. Get rid of any distraction.

Second—*endurance*: "run with endurance the race set before us." This "endurance," this perseverance in faithful obedience, has been the pastor's concern from the beginning (see Heb 10:39). This race has not been "set before us" by human authorities, but by God himself and its reward makes it the only race truly worth winning.

Verse 2. Most important of all—*focus*. Every victorious runner looks steadily toward the goal. When we focus on the finish line of this race we see "the Pioneer and Perfecter" of the way of faith who is none other than the incarnate "Jesus" now seated at the Father's right hand. With this description of Christ the pastor brings the entire weight of his argument to bear on his hearers' need for perseverance. "Pioneer and Perfecter of the faith" encompasses everything that the pastor has said about the full sufficiency of Christ as "the Source of eternal salvation" (Heb 5:9) in Heb 1:1—2:18 and 4:14—10:25. It includes all that he is saying about Christ as the premier example of those who, like the faithful of Heb 11:1–40, but in contrast to the disobedient of Heb 3:7—4:13, endure to the end of the race. Thus, it describes Christ as both the perfect example of persevering faithfulness (Heb 11:1–40) and the source of grace for faithful endurance (Heb 4:14—10:25).

It was natural for the pastor to conclude with this union of the saving sufficiency and perfect example of the Son of God because both realities have the same source. Both are the result of the faithful obedience of the incarnate "Jesus" in the face of suffering. By that obedience he atoned for human disobedience (Heb 9:11–15; 10:5–10) and thus was "perfected" as (1) the all-sufficient High Priest able to bring God's people into his presence by cleansing them from sin (Heb 5:9, 7:28), (2) the Guarantor of the New Covenant able to empower them for obedience (Heb 7:22, 10:15–18), and (3) the Pioneer of their salvation able to bring them into their ultimate inheritance as the people of God (Heb 2:10). As the "Pioneer and Perfecter of the faith" he has provided everything necessary for the people of God to walk the way of faithful obedience from beginning to end. At the same time, the "Pioneer and Perfecter of the faith" is the premier example of perseverance in faithful obedience from beginning to end. By keeping our eyes fixed on him we receive both the inspiration and power to persevere until we reach the goal!

It was quite appropriate for the pastor to support this climactic description of Christ as "the Pioneer and Perfecter of the faith" with his most graphic description of Christ's motivation and incarnate suffering. The "joy that was set before him" was the joy of bringing "many sons and daughters into glory" (Heb 2:10). It was the joy that came to expression when the exalted Son of God declared, "I will announce your name to my brothers and sisters, in the midst of the congregation I will praise you" (Heb 2:12), when he could say to the Father, "Behold I, and the children God has given me" (Heb 2:13). He obtained this joy only by *enduring* "a cross, despising the shame."

We modern readers cannot appreciate the impact of this brief statement: "who endured a cross, despising the shame." There is nothing in our world that compares to the shame of a Roman cross. The whole point of crucifixion was to rob victims of personhood and deprive them of all human dignity by exposing them helpless, naked, suffering, and dying before the eyes of the public. Passing crowds were expected to taunt the sufferers and gloat over their condition. The pastor's hearers turned away in horror from the scene evoked by this brief phrase. Jesus, however, "despised the shame." He counted it as nothing "for the joy" of our salvation that was "set before him" as the reward of his suffering. Thus the pastor fortifies us for endurance by reminding us of Jesus and of the fact that the "joy" of our own salvation "set before" us by him far outweighs all the shame and suffering the unbelieving world could heap upon us.

Verse 3. "Endured the cross, despising the shame" at the end of verse two brought the horrible disgrace and suffering of Christ vividly before our eyes. The pastor, however, does not want us to focus our attention on the suffering itself, but on "*the One* who endured such opposition from sinners against himself" (italics added). Obsession with suffering leads to despair. Concentration on "the One who endured" brings encouragement resulting in perseverance.

By describing the suffering of Christ as "such opposition from sinners against himself" the pastor invites his hearers to identify their suffering with his. "Such opposition" underscores the intensity of Christ's suffering; "from sinners," its source and cause; and "against himself," the intentionality of its perpetrators and its personal impact. We as God's people often suffer the intentional harassment of the unbelieving world because of our faithful obedience.

We, however, need not "become weary, giving up in [our] souls." Most of us can readily identify with this word picture. We know the weariness of body that comes, not simply from physical exhaustion, but from emotional stress and discouragement. We have experienced the temptation to "give up" in our inmost being because we feel empty and all appears hopeless. From the beginning the pastor has been concerned about such laxity, drifting, weariness, and inner discouragement (Heb 2:1–4). He knows that the battle is lost or won in "the soul." However, if we will "consider the one who endured such opposition," we need not give in to despair. Inspired by his example, and empowered by his grace, we too can *endure*.

You Have Come to Mount Zion

Hebrews 12:4—13:25

Introduction

Hebrews 12:4–29 concludes the History of the Faithful People of God that began at the Creation in Heb 11:1–2. As we have seen, Heb 11:1–40 recounted the history of God's people before the coming of Christ, and 12:1–3 depicted his coming as the crucial turning point of history. Heb 12:4–24 describes our situation as the people of God between the coming of Christ and the final Judgment, as described in Heb 12:25–29. With this description of the Last Judgment, the pastor brings this history of the faithful to its grand finale and reaches the climax of his sermon proper.

As was the custom of his time, the pastor adds a section of concluding exhortations in chapter 13 (Heb 13:1–17). These exhortations give him the opportunity to reemphasize his main concerns and apply them to daily life. Since he is sending this sermon as a letter to a congregation of believers whom he holds dear, he ends with an intimate letter conclusion (Heb 13:18–25).

During days one through three, we will explore the ever-increasing urgency of the present situation of the faithful people of God. Hebrews 12:4–13, the Scripture for day one, describes the importance of present suffering for spiritual formation. Hebrews 12:14–17, the passage for day two, warns us lest we surrender our birthright. Hebrews 12:18–24, the reading for day three, brings before our eyes as incentive for perseverance a graphic contrast between our glorious privileges and destiny on the one hand and the fate of those who have turned away in apostasy on the other. On day four the pastor's appeal for endurance reaches full intensity in his description of the final Judgment (Heb 12:25–29). On day five (Heb 13:1–6) and day six (Heb 13:7–17) we will heed the concrete, practical exhortations with which the pastor ends his urgent appeal. Finally, on day seven (Heb 13:18–25) we will examine the significance of his final greetings and bid him farewell.

Just as Heb 10:19—12:3 was the mirror image of 3:1—4:16 (see the introductions to weeks five and six), so Heb 12:4–29 mirrors 1:1—2:18. The formative suffering of the faithful in Heb 12:4–13 recalls the suffering of the Son through which he was "perfected" as our Savior in 2:5–18. The warning against apostasy in Heb 12:14–17 is the counterpart of the warning against laxity in 2:1–4. The contrast between Zion and Sinai in Heb 12:18–24 recalls the contrast between the Son and the angels in 1:5–14. Last of all, the final word of God which he will speak at the Judgment in Heb 12:25–29 brings the word of redemption described in 1:1–4 to final fulfillment. Thus Heb 10:19—12:29 is the mirror image of 1:1—4:16.

Observing this arrangement yields three important insights. (1) The pastor has made the all-sufficient sacrifice, high priesthood, and New Covenant mediatorship of the Son (Heb 4:14—10:25) the heart and center of his sermon. There is no doubt about his main point: "we have such a high priest who has sat down at the right hand of the throne of the Majesty in the heavens" (Heb 8:1). (2) The pastor urgently desires his hearers to abandon the disobedient wilderness generation (Heb 3:1—4:13) and join the faithful of old (Heb 10:26—11:40) by appropriating the sufficiency of their "Great High Priest" (Heb 12:1–3, 4:14—10:25). (3) The present life of the faithful and the final Judgment, as described in Heb 12:4–29, bring closure to the fundamental teaching about Christ with which Hebrews began in Heb 1:1—2:18. The pastor has carefully constructed every part of his sermon and arranged the whole in order to encourage perseverance in faithful obedience until his hearers cross the finish line. From beginning to end he focuses their—and *our*—attention on the incarnate, eternal Son of God seated at God's right hand (Heb 1:13) as "the Pioneer" of our "salvation" (Heb 2:10), "the Apostle and High Priest of our confession" (Heb 3:1), our "Great High Priest" (Heb 4:14), "High Priest according to the order of Melchizedek" (Heb 5:10), our "Forerunner" (Heb 6:20), the "Guarantor of a better covenant" (Heb 7:22), our "Great Priest over the House of God" (Heb 10:21), and the "Pioneer and Perfecter of the faith, *Jesus*" (Heb 12:2, italics added).

∽ Day One: Legitimate Children Disciplined by Suffering. (Heb 12:4–13)

⁴ *You have not yet resisted unto blood in your struggling against sin.* ⁵ *And have you completely forgotten the exhortation that addresses you as sons and daughters? "My son, my daughter, do not*

> belittle the discipline of the Lord nor loose heart at his reproof. [6]
> For whom the Lord loves, he disciplines; and chastises every son
> or daughter whom he accepts." [7] Endure these sufferings as dis-
> cipline, since God is treating you as sons and daughters. [8] For if
> you are without the discipline of which all have become partak-
> ers, then you are illegitimate children and not sons or daughters.
> [9] Furthermore, we have had our fathers according to the flesh as
> disciplinarians and we respected them. How much more rather
> should we submit completely to the Father of our Spirits,[1] and live.
> [10] For on the one hand they disciplined us for a few days as seemed
> best to them; but he for benefit in order that we might come to
> share his holiness. [11] And all discipline for the time being does not
> seem to be of joy but of grief; but afterward it yields the peace-
> ful fruit of righteousness to those who have been trained by it. [12]
> Therefore straighten the drooping hands and the enfeebled knees.
> [13] And make straight paths with your feet so that what is lame may
> not turn aside but rather be healed.

This description of how the "sons and daughters" of God are established in
the life of faith through the opposition they suffer is deeply indebted to the
description of the Son's perfection as our Savior through suffering in Heb
2:5–18. According to that passage, the faithful people of God have always
been God's "sons and daughters." Thus, it was appropriate for the eternal
Son of God to assume their humanity in order that, by atoning for sin, he
might bring them into their inheritance as the "sons and daughters" of God
(Heb 2:14). The suffering that he endured established the genuineness of the
obedience by which he was perfected as the "Pioneer of their salvation" (Heb
2:10). God also uses the suffering endured by his "sons and daughters" to
perfect in them the salvation the Son has provided and to mature them for
the enjoyment of their inheritance. Thus the pastor moves naturally from the
suffering by which the Son became "the Pioneer and Perfecter of the faith" in
Heb 12:1–3 to the suffering by which the "sons and daughters" are perfected
(matured) in the faith according to Heb 12:4–11.

The pastor is doing everything in his power to encourage his hearers
to persevere in faithful obedience despite the resistance from an unbelieving world that has always characterized the pilgrimage of the sons and
daughters of God. First, he reminds them that God's people of old bore
witness to the faithfulness of God and the insignificance of this suffering when compared with the eternal reward that awaits the faithful (Heb

---

1. Literally, "the Father of the spirits." The Greek article, here translated as "the,"
can be used for the possessive pronoun, "our." The pastor is referring to God not as the
universal "Father" but as the "Father" of the faithful. See Cockerill, Hebrews, 624–25.

11:1—40). Then, he described how the incarnate Son of God, by his own obedient suffering, confirmed their testimony and became "the Pioneer and Perfecter of the faith" for all who draw near to God through him (Heb 12:1–3). Now, in Heb 12:4–13, he reveals the indispensable role that this suffering plays in identifying the faithful as the "sons and daughters" of God and fitting them for their inheritance.

The pastor uses verse 4 to transition from the suffering of "the Pioneer and Perfecter of the faith" in Heb 12:1–3 to the suffering of the "sons and daughters" of God in Heb 12:4–13. He then quotes Prov 3:11–12 in verses 5–6, interprets this passage from Proverbs in verses 7–11, and applies it in verses 12–13.

Verse 4. The pastor begins by putting the sufferings of his hearers in perspective. His language recalls the violence suffered by the bloodied and broken loser of a boxing match. "You have not yet resisted" until you were beaten to a bloody pulp. "You have not yet resisted" until you shed your life's blood. "You have not yet resisted" until you "endured a cross" (Heb 12:2). Yes, his hearers face a formidable foe. They are continually "struggling against sin." They face "the opposition of sinners against" themselves (Heb 12:3). But they have not yet shed their blood. The pastor chides them for their hesitancy before introducing the Scripture that documents the great value of their suffering.

Verses 5–6. The pastor introduces Prov 3:11–12 with an unusual rhetorical question: "And have you completely forgotten the exhortation that addresses you as sons and daughters?" It is as if he expected his hearers to remember this passage of Scripture as the important place where God addresses his people as "sons and daughters." Perhaps he had discussed these verses with them before. These verses from Proverbs may have been his authority for believing that God's people have always been his "sons and daughters" (see Heb 2:5–18).

In the interpretation that follows the pastor does not repeat the words "reproof" or "chastises." He identifies "the discipline of the Lord" with the sufferings endured by the people of God because of their faithfulness. These sufferings are the mark of "every son or daughter whom [God] accepts." In verses 7–8 the pastor explores the significance of this "discipline" for our identity as God's "sons and daughters." Then, in verses 9–10 he examines its significance for our formation by a God who is our "Father."

Verses 7–8. The sufferings that we incur because of persistence in faithful obedience are crucial to our identity. We should be ready to "endure these sufferings" because they are God's "discipline" administered to all his legitimate "sons and daughters." In fact, the only way to avoid these sufferings would be to cease persevering in obedience. Thus, if we avoid this discipline, we become "illegitimate children," no longer faithful to the God who has prepared a "City" for his own (Heb 11:16).

Verses 9–10. Because these sufferings are our heavenly Father's discipline, they are crucial for our spiritual formation. The pastor argues from the lesser to the greater, from our earthly fathers to our heavenly Father, first in verse 9, and then again in verse 10. The first less-to-greater comparison underscores the supreme loyalty we owe our heavenly Father; the second, the eternal benefit we receive from complete submission to his discipline.

"Our fathers according to the flesh" are mortal, frail, and limited by ignorance and prejudice. The "Father of our Spirits," however, is the utterly transcendent "living God," the Creator, the source of all life, temporal and eternal, without limitation in wisdom, knowledge, and power. So, if we respected our earthly fathers, limited though they were, because it was their responsibility to discipline us for a brief part of our mortal lives, "how much more rather should we *submit completely* to the Father of our Spirits, and *live*" (italics added). Submission to our earthly fathers' discipline was intended to prepare us for life. Submission to our heavenly Father's discipline prepares us for eternal life.

Our earthly fathers disciplined us during the short period of our childhood according to their limited knowledge and for their own convenience. Our heavenly Father, however, disciplines us without fail for our maximum "benefit in order that we might come to share his holiness."

What does "share his holiness" mean? Our "Great Priest over the House of God" (Heb 10:21) has already made us holy by cleansing us from sin and empowering us for faithful obedience (Heb 9:14, 10:10). Nevertheless, as we persevere in obedience by drawing near through him for cleansing and empowerment we develop an ever-stronger character of obedience that prepares us to share ever more fully in the holiness of God. Sharing in God's holiness includes, but is much more than, moral transformation. It is intimate fellowship with him as part of the people of God. It is entering into his own "Sabbath rest" (Heb 4:9), joining him in the "City" that he has built (Heb 11:10, 16), and receiving from him the unshakeable kingdom that he has prepared for his own (Heb 12:28). The pastor's finite descriptions of this reality could never satisfy our curiosity, but they awaken deep longing for the ultimate destiny of the people of God.

Verse 11. The pastor concludes his interpretation of Prov 3:11–12 with a succinct statement of the main point. This is the bottom line. Yes, God's fatherly discipline, like "all discipline," is a matter "of grief," not "joy," when we are going through it, "*but afterward* it yields the peaceful fruit of righteousness to those who have been trained by it" (italics added). Long ago at the beginning of this history of the people of God the pastor told us that the "righteous" are those who live "by faith" (Heb 10:38). Thus "righteousness" is living obediently in reliance on the promises and power of God. The faithful sons and daughters of God are both "righteous" and being "trained" in "righteousness." By living the life of faith in the face of opposition they are confirmed and strengthened in the life of faith. Opposition overcome by faith is God's "training" that results in a fixed disposition of trust and obedience. It results in a holiness of reliance upon God in fellowship with the community of God's people that the pastor describes as the "peaceful fruit of righteousness." The cultivation of this "peaceful fruit" prepares God's people to "partake of his holiness."

Verses 12–13. So, in light of this truth, how should we live? First, "straighten the drooping hands and the enfeebled knees." The boxer's guard begins to fall. His knees begin to buckle. The pastor shouts "No." Take courage: "straighten" those drooping hands and buckling knees. Second, "make straight paths with your feet," do not hesitate, do not turn aside, run straight for the goal. Your brother or sister may have become "lame" from the rigors of the race. Open the way for them by setting them an example so that they might "not turn aside but rather be healed."

❧ Day Two: Do Not Forfeit Your Birthright! (Heb 12:14–17)

> [14] *Let us together[2] pursue peace and holiness, without which no one will see the Lord.* [15] *Pursue these goals by watching out lest anyone fall short of the grace of God; lest any root of bitterness springing up cause trouble and through it many be defiled;* [16] *lest there be anyone immoral or godless like Esau who sold his own birthright for a single meal.* [17] *For you know that even afterwards when he was seeking to inherit the blessing he was rejected, for he did not find a place of repentance, although he sought it [the blessing] with tears.*

This climactic warning against apostasy is the counterpart of the pastor's initial warning in Heb 2:1–4. The intervening chapters have made it very clear. If left unchecked, the drifting and lack of concern for "such

---

2. The TNIV reads "Make every effort to live in peace with everyone," and the ESV, "Strive for peace with everyone." However, the Greek words translated "with everyone" should go with the verb translated "make every effort," "strive," or "pursue," rather than with the word "peace." The pastor is not asking us to try to live at peace with everybody else. He is urging us to work together to preserve the peace and holiness of the Christian community. Thus, I have translated "with everyone" as "together." "Let us together pursue peace and holiness."

a great salvation" against which the pastor cautioned his hearers in Heb 2:1–4 will become the tragic godlessness and apostasy against which he now warns them. Heb 12:14–17 is also strategically located between the pastor's descriptions of the sufferings (Heb 12:1–13) and the privileges (Heb 12:18–24) of the contemporary people of God. It provides additional impetus to persevere in the face of the former and is a proper prelude to the latter, for warning followed by encouragement is the most powerful motivation for perseverance.

The pastor begins in verse 14 by urging his hearers to "pursue peace and holiness" so that they will not suffer eternal loss. The three-fold warning found in verses 15–17 ("lest anyone fall short . . . lest any root of bitterness . . . lest there be anyone immoral . . .") shows them how to carry out this pursuit. This three-fold warning recalls the warning against apostasy in Deut 29:15–20. The "immoral" and "godless" apostate Esau with whom this passage concludes is the equivalent (fulfillment) of the covenant breaker described in that Old Testament passage as cut off from the people of God.[3] The pastor would have his hearers, ancient and modern, heed this final, climactic warning with all diligence.

Verse 14. From the beginning the pastor has demonstrated his awareness that we enjoy our salvation as members of the community of the` faithful in union with the one who is "the Source of eternal salvation" (Heb 5:9). Perseverance, then, is not simply an individual, but a communal concern (Heb 3:12–14; 10:24–25). We are each to be concerned with the wellbeing and perseverance of the church. We persevere together. Thus, the pastor exhorts us, let all God's people "together pursue peace and holiness."

As noted above, we have been given the gift of holiness through the work of Christ. He has cleansed us from sin and empowered us to live in obedience (Heb 10:10, 14, 16). He has "cleansed our conscience from dead works to serve the living God" (Heb 9:14). Through him we regularly draw near to receive the "mercy" of cleansing from sin and the "grace" for perseverance in obedience (Heb 4:14–16). The peace of the community is the result of that holiness. It is the wholeness and wellbeing of community life that comes from mutual love and concern. If both peace and holiness are gifts that Christ has given to us, in what way are we then to "pursue" them? We must give all diligence to maintain the holiness and harmony of the community of the faithful that God has given us, since without this holiness, and the peace that it brings, "no one will see the Lord."

---

3. For a careful analysis of the relationship between this passage and Deut 29:15–20 see Cockerill, *Hebrews*, 635–37.

Verses 15–16. The three warnings in verses 15–16 tell us how to maintain the holiness given us by Christ and the resulting harmony and wellbeing of the people of God. These warnings build on each other reaching a climax in warning three. First, then, pursue peace and holiness "by watching out lest anyone fall short of the grace of God." Nothing could be more fundamental. The "grace of God" is nothing less than "the great salvation" (Heb 2:3) that Christ has provided and that the pastor has described in the heart of his sermon (Heb 4:14—10:25). The pastor spent the first two-thirds of Hebrews urging his hearers to appropriate all that Christ has done for them as their all-sufficient High Priest and "Source of eternal salvation" (Heb 5:9). Without Christ there is no holiness, no peace, and no perseverance. The people of God watch "out lest anyone fall short" of this grace by teaching, exhorting, warning, and encouraging one another, just as the pastor has been doing in this sermon. They hold one another up in prayer and mutual accountability.

Second, pursue peace and holiness by watching out "lest any root of bitterness springing up cause trouble and through it many be defiled." When God's grace is lacking a "root of bitterness" will certainly spring up in its place. This "root of bitterness" is a refusal to trust God and an insistence on going one's own way. One embittered person can cause such disruption in the community of God's people that many are "defiled." The pastor may be thinking of the ten spies who led the entire wilderness generation astray (Num 13:26—14:10).

Finally, pursue peace and holiness by watching out "lest there be anyone immoral or godless like Esau who sold his own birthright for a single meal." An uncorrected "root of bitterness" will produce an "immoral or godless" person like Esau. After we determine why Esau was called "godless," it will be easier to understand why he is described as "immoral."

The "godless" person refuses to give God his rightful place. Such a "godless person" does not acknowledge God as God, honor God, obey God, or trust God. The "godless" disregard both God's promises of blessing and threats of judgment. In sum, the "godless" person acts as if God were not there. Thus, this godlessness is the opposite of the "godly fear" that characterized the perfect obedience of the incarnate Son of God (Heb 5:7). Noah (Heb 11:7), and by implication, the rest of the faithful in chapter eleven, were people of "godly fear." Esau demonstrated his godlessness when he "sold his birthright for a single meal." His birthright was God's promise to Abraham that would result in the salvation of the world. Esau acted as if God's promise was nothing by cavalierly selling it to his brother for one "single" measly "meal."

The word translated "immoral" usually refers to sexual immorality. The Scripture, however, does not picture Esau as sexually promiscuous. It does, however, describe him as one controlled by his bodily desires. One might even say that he sold himself cheaply to satisfy his stomach. The pastor has been concerned that his hearers would be turned from the way of faith by suffering. The wilderness generation succumbed to intimidation. However, one can also be lured from the way of faith by the pleasures of the unbelieving world. No matter how great those pleasures might appear, they are less than a "single meal" when compared with the glorious promises of God. Whether from intimidation or attraction, the eternal loss is the same. The pastor would have been happy for his hearers to pray this prayer, "May thy dear Son preserve me from this present evil world, so that its smiles never allure, nor its frowns terrify."[4]

Verse 17. Esau's utter disregard of God was indeed apostasy. The pastor's hearers were familiar with Esau's story in Gen 25:29–34 and 27:1–40. The first passage records his godless selling of his birthright to his brother Jacob. The second, his subsequent attempt "to inherit the blessing" and his rejection. Despite Isaac's desire to bless Esau, it was God's will that he be rejected. Because of his godlessness he had forfeited his right "to inherit the blessing" that God had given Abraham and that would be passed down to Jacob and his descendants (Heb 11:20–22). Gen 27:34–35 describes how Esau was grieved at his loss and sought the *blessing* "with tears," but it says nothing about him repenting of his godlessness. Like the apostate wilderness generation, he regretted the loss of God's blessing but did not repent of his refusal to honor God as God by trusting in his promises and power. The pastor leaves the tragic words "though he sought it with tears" ringing in his hearers' ears.

✎ Day Three: The Tragic Destiny of the Disobedient and the Privileges of God's "Firstborn." (Heb 12:18–24)

> [18] *For you have not come to something that can be touched and to something that has been burning, to a fire, and to darkness, and to gloom, and to storm,* [19] *and to a sound of a trumpet, and to a voice of words, which those who heard begged that no word be added to them.* [20] *For they were not able to bear what was commanded: "If even an animal touches the mountain, it shall be stoned."* [21] *And so terrifying was the appearance that Moses said, "I am full of fear and trembling."*

---

4. Bennett, *Valley of Vision*, 79.

> [22] *But you have come to Mount Zion, and to the City of the Living God, a heavenly Jerusalem, and to myriads of angels, a festal gathering,* [23] *and to the assembly of the firstborn enrolled in heaven, and to a Judge who is God of all, and to spirits of the righteous made perfect,* [24] *and to the Mediator of a New Covenant, Jesus, and to blood of sprinkling that speaks better than Abel.*

The pastor is quick to assure his hearers that, unlike Esau, "they have not come" (v. 18) into a state of judgment (vv. 18–21). Through the mediation of Christ "they have come" (v. 22) into a state of blessed fellowship with God (vv. 22–24) that anticipates the eternal destiny he has prepared for them as described in Heb 12:25–29.

They have not come to this mountain "that can be touched" (Sinai) as described in verses 18–21. The vision of this mountain brings all of the pastor's warnings into sharp focus. The vision of Zion in verses 22–24 encompasses all that he has said about the present privileges and promised destiny of the faithful people of God. Mount Zion is both the heavenly Most Holy Place to which they have had access during their journey and the "Sabbath rest" that is the goal of their pilgrimage. The two are one and the same. Thus, by describing this glorious reality to which they "have come" the pastor whets their appetite for final entrance into "the City of the living God."

The pastor contrasted the Son with the angels in Heb 1:4–14 in order to show that God's ultimate revelation in "one who was Son" fulfills all that he spoke at Sinai through the angels (Heb 2:1–4). Heb 12:18–24 envisions the people of God as "having come to" God's Sinai revelation as it has now been fulfilled in the Son. By providing an effective atonement for sin and becoming "the Source of eternal salvation" the Son has fulfilled the Sinai revelation in several ways. First, the Son showed that the Sinai sacrificial system was obsolete as a means of approaching God because it was only a type or picture of the access to God now available through him (Heb 4:14—10:25). Second, however, since he has abundantly provided for cleansing from sin and obedient living, the consequences pronounced upon disobedience by the Sinai revelation, far from being removed, have become exponentially more certain (Heb 2:1–4).

Thus, the first vision (vv. 18–21) depicts what Sinai has become for the disobedient. It is Sinai for those who have rejected the grace of God made available in his Son. The second vision (vv. 22–24), however, describes what Sinai has become for the faithful people of God. The first is a place of exclusion and terror at the presence of God. The second, a place of intimate community and joyful fellowship with God.

Verses 18–19. Every feature of this sevenfold description emphasizes isolation, terror, and separation from God and from fellowship with his people.[5] Although we would expect the pastor to call this place "Sinai," he has left it nameless to underscore its fearsome character. His narration is devoid of persons. He wants his hearers to experience what he is describing, so he appeals concretely to the senses. He begins with that most intimate of senses, touch: "to something that can be touched and to something that has been burning, to a fire." Next comes sight: "and to darkness, and to gloom, and to storm." Finally, he mentions hearing: "and to a sound of a trumpet, and to a voice of words." It is as if one is awakening to a nightmare. First one touches, discovering that this is truly a concrete reality. It "has been burning." It is, indeed, "a fire." Then one opens one's eyes, but there is no light, only "darkness." Worse than darkness, foreboding "gloom." Worse than gloom, the confusion and destruction of "storm." Then there is the awesome "sound of a trumpet" announcing the foreboding presence. Finally, at the climax, the speech of God has become an impersonal, hair-raising "voice of words." God's proclaiming the Ten Commandments from the mountain, called in Hebrew the "ten words," is the climax of this fearsome event. According to Exod 20:19, after God spoke the Ten Commandments, the people "begged that no word be added to them." They could not stand the voice of this holy God.

Verses 20–21. The responses of the people and of Moses make it clear that this separation from God is based on the awesome holiness of God and the unrepentant disobedience of the people. According to verse 20, the people "were not able to bear what was commanded: 'If even an animal touches the mountain, it shall be stoned.'" This command emphasized the unapproachable holiness of God. The penalty applied not only to human beings, but even to unwitting animals. The death penalty was to be executed by stoning so that no one would even have to touch the person or animal that had touched the mountain of God. Furthermore, "so terrifying was the appearance that Moses said, 'I am full of fear and trembling'" (v. 21). According to Deut 9:19, Moses made this declaration of fear *after* the people, while still at Sinai, had fallen into gross disobedience and broken God's covenant at its most basic level by flagrantly creating and then worshiping the golden calf. Thus, the fear of Moses, the mediator of the Sinai covenant, underscores the terrible condemnation and separation from God that is the destiny of those

---

5. The description is sevenfold if we take "to something that has been burning, to a fire" as one aspect of this description. The way in which the pastor separates each of these seven aspects of his description with "and" gives them a powerful, cumulative impact.

who in imitation of Esau and the disobedient wilderness generation turn from God in utter disregard for his commands.

Verses 22–24. In stark contrast to verses 18–21, every feature of this sevenfold description emphasizes joyful life in the presence of God and in fellowship with the people of God.[6] This is not a picture of condemnation and separation, but of redemption and communion. The pastor has no hesitation in naming this place. No Old Testament image could invoke the place of blissful fellowship with God and his people as powerfully as "Mount Zion." This, however, is no earthly Mount Zion. It is "the City of the Living God," the "City with foundations whose architect and builder is God," the true eternal "heavenly Jerusalem" that has been the goal of the faithful since the beginning. This is the place of God's "Sabbath rest." The pastor's description elicits joy at the present privilege of access to this blessed place and longing for ultimate entrance.

There is nothing impersonal about this description. When we the faithful enter here we join "myriads of angels" surrounding the presence of God. Their worship of him is "a festal gathering," a joyful, exuberant celebration, a grand and glorious party. We join "the assembly of the first-born enrolled in heaven." The word "firstborn" is plural. We enter with the faithful of all time, living and dead, the "assembly of the firstborn" children of God whose citizenship is in this place.

At the center and heart of this vision is "a Judge who is God of all." This is "the City of the living God." The worship led by the "myriads of angels" centers around him. This is his "Sabbath rest." His presence is what makes this place what it is. The pastor will not let us forget, however, that the sovereign God is a "Judge." We enter here because by the grace of God we have become a holy people who live lives of faithful obedience. Even now, the pastor is still cautioning us against cheap grace.

"The spirits of the righteous" are the faithful of chapter 11 and all those who have died in the faith. Since they have now been "made perfect" through the blood of Christ they live here awaiting the return of Christ (Heb 9:28), the resurrection of the dead (Heb 11:35), and the final Judgment (Heb 12:25–29).

The climax of this vision could be no one other than "the Mediator of a New Covenant" who, in these heavenly surroundings, is still the incarnate "Jesus." Moses trembled before God at the disobedience of the generation that stood before Sinai. Jesus, however, is the one who, though his earthly obedience, has provided for our redemption. He is the founder

---

6. This description is sevenfold if we take "Mount Zion, and the City of the living God, a heavenly Jerusalem" and "myriads of angels, a festal gathering" each as one item.

of the feast, the life of the party, the one who has made all this possible. We are a City of New-Covenant people who live in intimate fellowship with God because our sins have been forgiven and God's laws have been written on our hearts (Heb 10:15–18). All of this is due to the "blood of sprinkling," the blood of Jesus by which we have been cleansed from our sin. Abel's blood cried out for judgment upon the guilty (Gen 4:9–11). Jesus' blood "speaks" a much "better word," a word of pardon, cleansing, and transformation. Once again, the pastor leaves us with our eyes fixed on "the Apostle and High Priest of our confession" (Heb 3:1), "the Pioneer and Perfecter of the faith" (Heb 12:2), the "Mediator of a New Covenant" who enables us to persevere in faithful obedience until we enter finally into this exuberantly joyful "City of the living God."

∾ Day Four: "The One Who is Speaking." (Heb 12:25–29)

> 25 See to it that you do not refuse the one who is speaking. For if those people did not escape when they refused the One who warns on earth; how much less shall we escape who turn away from the One who warns from heaven? 26 Then his voice shook the earth. But now he has promised saying, "Once more I will shake not only the earth but also the heavens." 27 Now the "once more" shows the removal of the things that can be shaken as things that have been made, in order that the things that cannot be shaken might remain. 28 Therefore, since we are receiving a kingdom that is unshakable, let us be thankful. Through which let us serve God appropriately with godly fear and awe. 29 For indeed our "God is a consuming fire."

The pastor who began by affirming that God has spoken (Heb 1:1–4) concludes appropriately with this pressing exhortation: "See to it that you do not refuse the one who is speaking." These final verses of the main body of Hebrews summarize the pastor's teaching on God's speaking in order to impress upon his hearers the dire urgency of responding with faithful obedience. The proper response to God's self-revelation is not speculation, but wholehearted submission! Above all else, we "must not refuse the One who is [even now] speaking."

This passage provides an appropriate occasion for us to summarize Hebrews' vital teaching about the God who speaks. First, God has not been, is not, and will not be silent. God's speech is threefold. He can be described as "the One who warns on earth" (v. 25), "the One who warns from heaven" (v. 25), and as the One who "'Once more . . . will shake not only the earth but also the heavens" with his voice (v. 26). The first of these descriptions refers to God's speaking at Sinai; the second, to God's speaking in the incarnate, eternal Son Jesus now seated at God's right hand; the third, to God's speaking at the final Judgment.

Second, God's threefold speech is contemporary. God's speaking at Sinai and in "one who is Son" are both historical events and present realities. The Old Testament envisions all subsequent generations as standing before God's Sinai revelation (Deut 5:3; 29:14–15). God continues to address his people in the "today" (Heb 3:7, etc.) of their pilgrimage through the eternal, incarnate Son seated at God's right hand. One could even say that God's self-disclosure at Sinai, as fulfilled in the Son, continues to address the people of God with renewed power. God's final speaking at the Judgment is a future event that already touches the present as both promise of ultimate blessing and threat of final loss. Thus, all three phases of God's self-revelation address the contemporary world.

Finally, God's threefold revelation finds its unity in "one who is Son." He is the fulfillment of God's Sinai revelation. What God has said in his Son will reach its climax when his Son returns at the Judgment. At that time those who await him will receive "salvation" (Heb 9:28), but his "enemies" (Heb 1:13) will be put under his feet.

A brief overview will help us understand the explanation that follows. The pastor focuses on God's revelation as warning. Thus, he begins by urging his hearers not to "refuse the one who is speaking" because the consequences of disobedience are dire. He supports this exhortation with two less-to-greater arguments. In verse 25 he compares God's speaking at Sinai and in the Son. Fulfillment in Christ has made the consequences of disobedience all the more certain. In verse 26 he compares God's speaking at Sinai and at the final Judgment. According to verse 27, the trembling of Sinai pales into insignificance when compared with the world-shaking Last Judgment. Verse 28 describes the proper conduct of those who do not "refuse" God's revelation. Verse 29 reinforces this conduct with a concluding warning.

Verse 25. In Heb 4:14—10:25, the heart of this sermon, the pastor has given us a grand description of the "great salvation" announced in Heb 2:3. Thus, he can now conclude by restating his initial exhortation from Heb 2:2–3 in a much more powerful way. He argued from less to greater in Heb 2:2–3: if everyone who violated God's angel-mediated Sinai revelation was sure to receive punishment, how could those who neglected the as yet undescribed "great salvation" expect to "escape" judgment? The Sinai revelation has now become "the One [God] who warns on earth," and "such a great salvation" has been replaced by "the One [God in the Son] who warns from heaven."

We have already seen how fulfillment in Christ (Heb 12:22–24) exposes the full terror of Sinai (Heb 12:18–21) for the disobedient.

Verses 26–27. In the second less-to-greater argument the pastor compares the time when God's "voice shook the earth" at Sinai with the time "promised" in Hag 2:6 when God's voice would "shake not only the earth but also the heavens" at the final Judgment.[7] There is no more graphic Old Testament image of God's judgment than Sinai quaking at the voice of God (Ps 67:9). Yet the time is coming at the final Judgment when there will be a much more fearsome shaking. God's voice will "shake not only the earth but also the heavens" once and for all and bring this temporal order to an end.

The description of "Mount Zion" in 12:22–24 gave us a glimpse of "the things that cannot be shaken." What do we know about this unshakable reality that is the ultimate destiny of the people of God? It is God's "Sabbath rest" that he established as the climax of creation (Heb 4:9). It is that permanent "City that has foundations" (Heb 11:10), prepared by God as the place of eternal joy and fellowship. It is the place where the faithful are "citizens" (Heb 11:14). It is their true home. It is the infinitely valuable "reward" upon which Moses fixed his gaze (Heb 11:26). The Son of God took on the humanity of the sons and daughters of God so that he might bring them into this their inheritance (Heb 1:2, 6, 14) and thus enable them to join God in his own "Sabbath rest."

These "things that cannot be shaken," are far more concrete and real that the temporal world in which we live, here described as "the things that can be shaken." At the final Judgment the temporal will give way to the eternal, the sons and daughters of God will enter his "glory" (Heb 2:10), and the creation will reach its intended goal. The Son of God will indeed have borne "all to its intended end by the word of his power" (Heb 1:3). The pastor, however, wants his hearers to feel the terror of this "shaking." This "earthquake" will make Sinai seem like a mere tremor. All that is familiar will crumble, and only the faithful will have a place to stand. "The things which cannot be shaken will *remain*" (italics added).

---

7. The Greek text of Hag 2:6 reads, "Once more I will shake the heavens, and the earth, and the sea, and the dry land." Haggai is describing God's judgement on the nations by which the world order with which he was familiar would be overturned and Jerusalem would be exalted as never before. This prophecy anticipates the ultimate Judgement that will bring this entire temporal order to an end and reveal the "heavenly Jerusalem" as that which "cannot be shaken." Thus, the pastor paraphrases Haggai. The final Judgment will be so thorough and powerful that it will "shake" not only the "earth," but also God's dwelling in the eternal "heavens." "The heavens," however, will survive the "shaking" without being removed. For more on Hebrews' use of Hag 2:6, see Cockerill, *Hebrews*, 664–66.

Verse 28–29. As the pastor approaches the conclusion of his sermon he once again fortifies his appeal by joining encouragement with warning. He embraces his hearers by using the first person "we" ("you and I"). "We," however, "are *receiving* a kingdom that is unshakable" (italics added). How should we live as those who are in the process of receiving such a treasure? How should we live as those for whom God has prepared "such a great salvation" through his exalted Son, "the Source of eternal salvation"?

The pastor begins to answer this question with "Let us be thankful," and concludes by reminding us that "our 'God is a consuming fire'" (from Deut 4:15). He wants us to live with profound gratitude for the "great salvation" God has provided for us in his son and with a deep sense of God's holiness first clearly revealed at Sinai. When we live in this way, we "serve him with godly fear and awe" (see on Heb 5:7–8 and 11:7) by giving him his rightful place in our lives, we internalize the life of faithful obedience. Gratitude and a sense of God's holiness complement one another like two sides of the same coin. Those who live with such gratitude and reverence live in joyful "awe" of God.

The pastor, then, brings the main body of his sermon to a conclusion with this powerful appeal for pursuit of the life of "godly fear," exemplified by Noah (Heb 11:7) and the faithful of chapter 11, but perfectly executed by "the one who learned obedience through what he suffered" (Heb 5:7–8). He will give particular instructions for the life of gratitude and "godly fear" in chapter thirteen.

∾ Day Five: A Common Life of "Gratitude and Godly Fear." (Heb 13:1–6)

> [1] *Let brotherly love continue.* [2] *Do not forget hospitality, for through this some did not notice it when they entertained angels.* [3] *Remember those imprisoned as if you were imprisoned with them; those persecuted as yourselves also being in a body.* [4] *Let marriage be honored in everything, and let the marriage bed be undefiled, for the sexually immoral and adulterers God will judge.* [5] *Let your conduct be free from the love of money; be content in your present circumstances, for he himself has said, "I will never leave you nor will I ever forsake you."* [6] *So let us confidently say: "The Lord is my Helper, I will not fear. What can a human being do to me?"*

The pastor has just described the life of the faithful people of God as a life of gratitude and "godly fear" (Heb 12:28–29). The four pairs of exhortations/warnings with which chapter 13 begins (vv. 1–5) paint a clear, crisp picture of that life in practice. The pastor concludes these exhortations by inviting us to join in a scriptural affirmation of commitment to life lived in dependence upon God (v. 6). With this response of faith we together, as the people of God, embrace all that God has now spoken to us "in one who is Son" (Heb 1:1).

Two pairs of exhortations to love (vv. 1–2) and care for the persecuted (vv. 3), are followed by two pairs of warnings against sexual immorality (v. 4) and greed (v. 5). It is impossible to fully express the brevity, balance, and wordplay that make this passage so beautiful in the original language.

Verses 1–2. The first pair of exhortations ("Let brotherly love continue. Do not forget hospitality") set the tone for all that follows. All subsequent exhortations and warnings are the outworking of "brotherly love."

Listen to the pastor's play on the words translated "brotherly love" and "hospitality." The Greek word for "brotherly love" is *philadelphia*, and for "hospitality" is *philoxenia*. The *phil* in both words is Greek for "love"; *adelphia* means "brotherhood" and *xenia* is "stranger." Thus "hospitality" (*philoxenia*) involves love for strangers. In Greek this sentence has an elegance born of brevity: "Love-of-brother, continue; love-of-stranger (hospitality), don't forget."

The pastor urges them to "continue" the "brotherly love" that they have been showing one another. This "brotherly love" comes out of their rich heritage as the "sons and daughters" of God (Heb 2:10), the "brothers and sisters" of God's eternal Son (Heb 2:12), and members of God's household (Heb 3:6) over which Christ is both firstborn Son (Heb 3:6) and Great Priest (Heb 10:21). They are indeed the "firstborn" heirs (Heb 12:23) of "the City of the Living God" through the one who is the "Firstborn" (Heb 1:6, 14). The pastor has repeatedly urged them to watch over each other as members of the same family so that they might all enter their inheritance through faith and obedience (Heb 3:12–14; 10:24–25; 12:14–15).

Brotherly love extends to "hospitality," to "love-of-stranger." Such hospitality was both a necessary and enriching aspect of the common life of the faithful. The pastor may have been thinking especially, but certainly not exclusively, of evangelists, teachers, or other believers who needed accommodations as they traveled. Yet this exhortation reminds us that the service of love extends to the needy stranger "within your gates." "For through this some did not notice it when they entertained angels" recalls the experiences of Abraham (Gen 18:1–15) and Lot (Gen 19:1–29). One never knows the benefits that might rebound from the "brotherly love" of generous hospitality.

Verse 3. "Brotherly love" can be costly. "Remember" means much more than think about, feel sorry for, or pray for. "Remember" those imprisoned and persecuted for their faith by identifying with them and meeting their needs. Roman jails supplied little if any food, clothes, or provision for warmth. If fellow believers did not expose themselves to arrest by meeting these needs, imprisoned believers would have no relief. Be as diligent to supply these needs as if you were already "imprisoned with them." Remember, the Son of God assumed a human body and suffered for you. You are already in a human "body" subject to the same vicissitudes as your persecuted brothers and sisters. Do all you can to meet their needs and ease their suffering.

Verse 4. In verses 4–5 the pastor deals with two sins that readily destroy "brotherly love" and evoke the wrath of God—sexual sin (v. 4) and greed (v. 5). "Let marriage be honored in everything" is comprehensive and definitive. "Let the marriage bed be undefiled" is specific and pointed. In Greek the first of these exhortations begins emphatically with the word "honored" and concludes with "in everything," which could also be translated "by everyone." Our teaching, conduct, and every aspect of our common life should reinforce respect for marriage as an honorable, life-long, unbroken bond of loyalty between a *man* and a *woman*. The heart of such respect, however, is a "marriage bed . . . undefiled." "Marriage bed" is a polite way of referring to sexual intercourse as permissible only between a married man and woman. Indulging in sexual intercourse either before marriage or outside the marriage bond is a defilement of the "marriage bed." There is cleansing from this "defilement" for the truly repentant. However, we who live in an indulgent time when sexuality outside of marriage is approved on every side need to hear the pastor's severe warning: "the sexually immoral and adulterers God will judge." In Hebrews such judgment can be nothing less than exclusion from God's "Sabbath rest" (Heb 4:9).

Verse 5. If there is any warning more needful in our time than the warning against sexual sin, it is this warning against greed. How can I tell if my "conduct" is "free from the love of money"? Am I constantly thinking about money? Is amassing wealth the goal of my life? Am I ready to give to the needy and to the work of God until it hurts? Am I tempted to dishonesty by the hope of gain?

Everything in our society works against "be content in your present circumstances." The pastor is not condoning poverty or discouraging the making of an honest living. He is reminding us that happiness is not the result of accumulation and that the desire for more engenders perpetual discontent.

Furthermore, our source of peace and security is elsewhere. We need not grasp for material goods because we serve the God who has said, "'I will never leave you nor will I ever forsake you.'" This quotation, paraphrasing Moses' reassurance to Joshua (Deut 31:6), is all the more powerful because it echoes several other Old Testament passages (Deut 31:8; Josh 1:5). Everything that the pastor has said in this sermon about the "great salvation" (Heb 2:3) that God has supplied through his Son, "the Source of eternal salvation" (Heb 5:9), underscores the faithfulness of God. He wants us to keep our eyes on the "reward" so that we will remain undistracted by the "treasures of Egypt" (Heb 11:26).

Verse 6. We may face strong resistance and severe hardship from an unbelieving world. Nevertheless, in response to God's affirmation that he is ever with us, and to all that our faithful God has provided for us in his Son, let us "confidently" affirm the way of faithful obedience by joining in this affirmation from Ps 118:6: "The Lord is my Helper, I will not fear. What can a human being do to me?"

∾ Day Six: The Life of "Gratitude and Godly Fear" in an Unbelieving World. (Heb 13:7–17)

> [7] *Remember your leaders who spoke the word of God to you. Considering the outcome of their conduct, imitate their faith.* [8] *Jesus Christ, yesterday and today the same, and forever.* [9] *Do not be carried about by various and strange teachings. For it is good to confirm the heart with grace, not with foods, in which those who walk have not been profited.* [10] *We have an altar from which those who worship in the Tent do not have authority to eat.* [11] *For the blood of those animals is brought for sin into the Most Holy Place by the high priest. Their bodies are burned outside the camp.* [12] *Thus Jesus also, in order that he might sanctify the people through his own blood, suffered outside the gate.* [13] *Therefore let us go out to him outside the camp bearing his reproach.* [14] *For we do not have here an enduring city, but we are earnestly seeking one to come.* [15] *Through him therefore we continually offer a sacrifice of praise to God, that is, the fruit of lips confessing his name.* [16] *Do not forget doing good and sharing, for with such sacrifices God is well pleased.* [17] *Obey your leaders and submit to them, for they themselves watch carefully over your souls as those who will give account, in order that they might do it with joy and not with groaning. For this would be without profit for you.*

With this evocative summary of his sermon the pastor issues a final, powerful appeal for perseverance in the life of "gratitude and godly fear."

Verse 7. He has warned his hearers against joining the disobedient wilderness generation (Heb 3:7—4:13) and urged them to identify with the faithful of all time (Heb 11:1–40). He concludes with an appeal to the exemplary lives of the faithful leaders "who spoke the word of God to" them in the past. The authority of these "leaders" was based on the divine origin of their saving message substantiated by the faithfulness of their conduct. The pastor is not calling for sentimentality, but calculation: consider "the outcome of their conduct." You know these people. You know how they lived. You know how God sustained them. You know how they died. So, "imitate their faith."

Verse 8. The pastor supports this appeal to imitate the faithful with a capstone description of the one who provides all that is necessary for our perseverance (Heb 4:14—10:25): "Jesus Christ, yesterday and today the same, and forever." Notice the emphatic reference to the historical person, "Jesus Christ" (cf. 10:10). *He* is "yesterday and today the same, and forever." *He* is the eternal Son of God who, in contrast to the temporal universe that he has created, remains forever "the same" (Heb 1:12). Because *he* is a Priest "according to the power of" the "indestructible life" of God (Heb 7:16), *he* "remains forever" (Heb 7:24) and is thus able "to save completely those who come to God through *him*, because *he* is always living to make intercession for them" (Heb 7:25, italics added). The "leaders" of "yesterday" could depend on him. We, the people of God "today," can rely upon him. We can be sure that he will see us to the end of our journey because he remains the all-sufficient Savior "forever."

Verses 9–10. Throughout this sermon the pastor has expressed concern lest his hearers be deterred from the way of faith through inattention, fatigue, persecution, or by the attraction of the temporal rewards of compromise (Heb 2:1–4; 5:11–14; 11:1—12:13; 12:14–17). Through his incarnate obedience, the eternal Son of God has fulfilled the Mosaic covenant and provided all that is needed for the faithful to persevere in the face of these temptations.

As he brings his sermon to a conclusion, however, the pastor mentions certain false teachings because they made it easier for his hearers to succumb to these other pressures. Notice how he brands these erroneous doctrines as "various and strange teachings." They were practiced by "those who worship in the Tent" and pertained to "foods," but brought their practitioners no benefit. "Those who worship in the Tent" describes people who attempted to live as if the Old Covenant had not been fulfilled in "Jesus Christ." "Foods" suggests that these teachings concerned the saving value of ritual meals that were part of synagogue worship. They "have not been profited" recalls the inability of the old priesthood and sacrifice to cleanse from sin (Heb 9:25—10:4).

It is easy to understand the attraction of such teachings. Like other first–century followers of Jesus, most of the recipients of Hebrews were probably Jews or godfearing gentiles who had been closely associated with the synagogue before their conversion. Others who joined them would have been shaped by this Jewish environment. Thus it would not have been surprising if, suffering from fatigue and persecution, they were tempted to relinquish the commitment to Christ that distinguished them from other Jews or godfearers, and indeed from Roman society in general. By so doing they could escape the ire of the larger Jewish community and perhaps gain the protection from Rome afforded by the legal status of Judaism. In like manner, our contemporary world is happy for us to talk about "God" or "spirituality," but deeply offended when we bear witness to the unique claims of "Jesus Christ, yesterday and today the same, and forever" (v. 8).

So, "do not" through neglect or fear "be carried about" by these useless teachings. No, let your "heart" be confirmed in steadfast faithfulness through the "grace" you receive (Heb 2:17–18) by drawing near through our "Great High Priest" (Heb 4:14–16). For "We have an altar," the cross of Christ, "from which those who" reject our exclusive, all-sufficient Savior have no "authority to eat."

Verses 11–12. The stunning comparison in these verses between "the blood of animals" and "his own blood" focuses our attention on the suffering Jesus. Scene one: the Day of Atonement sacrifice reached its climax when the high priest brought the ineffective "blood" of witless "animals" into the earthly Most Holy Place, after which the bodies of those "animals" were burned in an unclean place outside "the camp" of God's people (Lev 16:27). Scene two: Jesus' sacrifice reached its climax when in obedience to the Father (Heb 10:5–10) he "suffered" in the midst of the world's uncleanness, ostracized from society "outside the gate" of Jerusalem "in order that he might" cleanse his "people" from sin and empower them for holy living "through his own blood."

Verses 13–14. At every crucial point the pastor has focused our attention on the eternal, incarnate Son at God's right hand (Heb 1:3, 13; 4:14–16; 81–2; 10:19–25; 12:1–3) who enables us to persevere. In Heb 12:1–3 he reminded us that this One seated at God's right hand had "endured a cross, despising the shame." Now he boldly fastens our attention on the "Jesus" who "suffered outside the gate" and urges us to "go out to him outside the camp bearing his reproach." We, too, live in a world that rejects the exclusive claims of Christ and ridicules his moral standards. The first-century world called followers of Jesus "haters of mankind." Should we be surprised if they malign us?

Thus, it is crucial to "bear his reproach" even when it means ostracism from society because "we do not have here an enduring city." You can disown Christ and receive unbelieving society's approving embrace—but it will soon be over. By joining him "outside the gate" of society's approval and embracing his "reproach" "we are earnestly seeking" the coming eternal "City of the living God" (Heb 12:24). Only those who join him "outside the gate" and publicly embrace his shame will take their place with him in that eternal City, which we glimpsed so tantalizingly in Heb 12:22–24.

Verses 15–16. "Within the context of the unbelieving world, the life of faith is best described as going out to Christ and bearing 'his reproach' (vv. 11–13). When considered, however, in relation to God and the Christian community, this same life is most appropriately represented as the offering of praise and good works to God through Christ (vv. 15–16)."[8] The pastor describes "praise" as "the fruit of lips confessing his name." The people of old offered the "first fruits" of their harvest to God in thanksgiving. We offer "the fruit of lips" by "confessing" Christ's name and declaring what he has done in the company of the faithful and before an unbelieving world. "Doing good and sharing" is a holistic description of the kindness and mutual concern that should characterize our common life (Heb 10:24–25, see verses 1–6).

The perpetual offering of the Levitical sacrifices demonstrated their inability to remove sin. We, on the other hand, continue to offer praise and good works out of gratitude for Christ's once-for-all atoning sacrifice. Praise and good works replace the worship of the "Tabernacle." Together they are the sacrifice with which "God is well pleased." Such praise and mutual concern are fulfilled in the joyful worship of the "City of the living God" (Heb 12:22).

Verse 17. The pastor is confident that the leaders of his congregation share his concern for the people of God. Thus, he concludes by urging his hearers to wholeheartedly accept their oversight. These leaders are worthy of this obedience because of the task they have been given and the conscientious way in which they carry out that task. They have been charged with watching over the eternal welfare of God's people. They carry out these responsibilities as faithful ministers of Christ. They do not work for personal gain but as those who "will give account" to God. They have great "joy" when their people prosper, but deep "groaning" when they turn away from God. The pastor brings his appeal to an end with a most effective use of understatement: to disregard your leaders and neglect the things of God "would be without profit for you."

---

8. Cockerill, *Hebrews*, 705.

❧ Day Seven: A Sermon Sent by Mail. (Heb 13:18–25)

> ¹⁸ *Pray for us, for we are persuaded that we have a good conscience, determining to conduct ourselves well in everything.* ¹⁹ *And I urge you to do this all the more in order that I might be restored to you soon.*
>
> ²⁰ *And may the God of peace, the one who brought again from the dead the Great Shepherd of the sheep, by the blood of the eternal covenant, our Lord Jesus,* ²¹ *empower you in every good thing to do his will, doing in us what is well pleasing before him through Jesus Christ, to whom be glory forever. Amen.*
>
> ²² *And I urge you, brothers and sisters, give attention to this word of exhortation, for I have instructed you very briefly.* ²³ *Know that our brother Timothy has been released, with whom if he comes soon I will see you.*
>
> ²⁴ *Greet all your leaders and all the saints. Those from Italy greet you.* ²⁵ *Grace be with you all.*

These final verses include the normal elements of a letter ending: (1) a request for prayer (vv. 18–19), (2) a blessing (vv. 20–21), (3) a concluding exhortation (v. 22), (4) travel news (v. 23), (5) greetings (v. 24), and (6) a final benediction (v. 25). It is probable that the "Timothy" whom the pastor mentions in verse 23 was co-author of six Pauline letters and the recipient of 1 and 2 Timothy.[9] If so, then both the pastor and his congregation were among those who knew Paul. Thus, this traditional letter ending with its Pauline associations reinforced the pastor's authority and facilitated Hebrews' taking its place with the other letters of the New Testament.

Since the pastor was prevented from visiting this beloved congregation, he sent this sermon as a letter to be read to them during their service of worship. A traditional letter introduction would only have detracted from the powerful way he began his message. However, by ending his sermon as a letter he undergirds his authority, reinforces his appeal for perseverance, and strengthens the bonds of fellowship that unify the people of God. Perhaps most important of all, he prays that God will empower those who hear this sermon to do what he has been exhorting them to do. As we come to the end of Hebrews, let us acknowledge the authority of the pastor's message, renew the bonds of Christian fellowship, and accept the pastor's blessing, concluding exhortation, and final benediction as our own.

Verses 18–19. This request for prayer strengthens the bonds of love between pastor and congregation. "We are persuaded that we have a good conscience, determining to conduct ourselves well in everything" was a

9. See 2 Cor 1:1; Phil 1:1; Col 1:1–2; 1 Thess 1:1; 2 Thess 1:1; and Phlm 1.

tactful but firm way for the pastor to support his message by affirming the integrity of his character. A "good conscience" is the antithesis of the "evil conscience" of Heb 10:22 and of the "heart" of the wilderness generation that had been hardened by sin's deceitfulness (Heb 3:12–14). It is a conscience that has been "cleansed from dead works to serve the living God" (Heb 9:14). Since God's laws have been written on the pastor's heart (Heb 10:15–18), he determines—he intentionally wills—to "conduct" himself in a manner that pleases God in everything. We can add him, along with the past leaders of the congregation, to the roll-call of the faithful in Heb 11:1–40. We have confidence in the pastor's message because we have felt his integrity in every line of his sermon. The one who urges us to persevere through the all-sufficiency of the Son of God is one who himself perseveres. His request that his hearers pray for his restoration is a reminder that he will call them to account at his return.

Verses 20–21. With this beautiful and profound blessing the pastor calls on God to empower his beloved hearers to live the life of faithful obedience that he has been urging upon them. Verse 20 describes the God upon whom the pastor is calling; verse 21, the blessing that he asks God to bestow upon his hearers. Jesus is at the center of both verses. This God has revealed himself in the salvation that he has accomplished through "the Lord Jesus" (v. 20). It is "through Jesus Christ" (v. 21) that he blesses us by applying this salvation to our lives.

The God whom the pastor evokes is, indeed, "the God of peace." By removing sin he has reconciled the faithful to himself and established a community of peace, wholeness, and well-being (Heb 12:14) that is destined for "the City of the living God" (Heb 12:22). He has accomplished this by raising "again from the dead the Great Shepherd of the sheep, by the blood of the eternal covenant, our Lord Jesus."

This description enriches all that the pastor has said about our "Great Priest over the House of God" (Heb 10:22, cf 4:14) who "through his own blood" (Heb 9:14) has made atonement for sin and become the "Guarantor of a better covenant" (Heb 7:22). It also recalls the Greek translation of Isa 63:11 that describes Moses as "the shepherd of the sheep" whom God "brought up from the land" of Egypt. The "Lord Jesus," however, is "the *Great* Shepherd of the sheep" whom God "brought again [up] *from the dead*" (italics added). Through Moses God delivered his people from Egypt. Through "our Lord Jesus" he delivered them from death. Through Moses he led them toward the earthly promised land. Through "our Lord Jesus" he shepherds us on our journey to the "heavenly City" foreshadowed by that earthly type. Moses had only the animal blood of the Old Covenant (Heb 9:16–22). Jesus conquered death "by the blood of the eternal covenant."

That "eternal covenant" is ever-effective because it has been established by one who offered his earthly obedience (Heb 10:5–10) "through the eternal Spirit" (Heb 9:14) and by "the power of an indestructible life" (Heb 7:16), and who thus "remains" (Heb 7:24) forever as our High Priest. "Jesus Christ, yesterday and today the same, and forever" (Heb 13:8).

Perhaps the pastor has reserved this description of "our Lord Jesus" as "the Great Shepherd of the Sheep" for his conclusion in order to effectively apply his teaching to our daily lives. As "Forerunner" (Heb 6:20) and "Pioneer and Perfecter of the faith" (Heb 12:1–3) the incarnate Son of God has provided all that we need to persevere in the life of faith until we enter "the City of the living God." It is reassuring, however, to know that as "the Great Shepherd of the sheep" he is with us every day "shepherding" us along the way of faith. The term "*Great* Shepherd" is appropriate only for "the *Lord* Jesus" (italics added). God, himself, has become the "shepherd" of his people (Ezek 34:15). The *Lord* is indeed our Shepherd (Ps 23:1).

It is this God upon whom the pastor calls to "empower you in every good thing to do his will." "Every good thing" encompasses the full provision that Christ has made for our perseverance—forgiveness (Heb 10:15), cleansing from sin (Heb 9:14), an obedient heart (Heb 10:16), continual access to God for needed grace (Heb 4:14–16), strength for endurance in the face of suffering (Heb 12:1–4), and final entrance into "the City of the living God" (Heb 12:22). "To do his will" is to live as if God's promises for the future are certain and his power for perseverance in the present is real. When we live "by faith" we do his will.

By fulfilling the will of God (Heb 10:5–10), Christ has provided an atonement that enables his people "to do [God's] will." This life of obedience is possible only through the inner transformation that comes from God's *continually* "doing in us what is well pleasing before him." By *constantly* "drawing near" to receive the grace he provides (Heb 4:16), we are enabled to have a "good conscience" (Heb 13:18) and to maintain a "true heart" (Heb 10:22) upon which God's laws have been inscribed (Heb 10:16). Both to God, who does this great work, and to "Jesus Christ," through whom it is done, "be glory forever."

Verses 22. By now we should not be surprised that the pastor follows this great prayer for our empowerment with a final plea for our obedience. The term "exhortation" includes both encouragement and warning. As we have seen, the pastor has skillfully balanced the encouragement that comes from "such a great salvation" with warning against the dire consequences of neglecting it. By thus interweaving encouragement and warning the pastor has urged us forward in the life of faithful obedience. Hebrews is indeed a "word of exhortation." This final exhortation in verse 22 is, then, a last reminder of all that he has said. By claiming that he "instructed them very briefly" the pastor suggests that much more could have been added to his argument. The prayer for God's empowerment becomes effective when we heed the pastor's exhortation to live "by faith" and thus to persevere in obedience through our Lord Jesus Christ.

Verses 23–24. When the pastor gives news of "brother" Timothy's "release" and sends the greetings of "those from Italy" he provides a tantalizing glimpse into the interconnection and fellowship of believers throughout the Roman world. He encourages us by reminding us that we are not alone. We are part of the worldwide people of God, past and present. "Greet all your leaders" reinforces the pastor's earlier injunction to respect and imitate those who faithfully watch over the people of God (Heb 13:7). The use of the term "saints" or "holy ones" to describe believers reminds us of "the cleansing from sin provided by Christ (2:11; 9:11–14; 10:10, 14, 29; 13:12) and of the resulting holiness that we are to pursue (12:14)."[10]

Now that we have concluded our meditation on Hebrews we come to the pastor's final benediction: "Grace be with you all." This prayer may have been traditional, but it is a fitting blessing for the ending of this letter/sermon about the One through whom we "find grace to help us in time of need" (Heb 4:16). Through that grace we can fulfill the pastor's urgent desire for his hearers that they not fall in with "those who shrink back and are destroyed," but take their place among "those who have faith and preserve their souls" (Heb 10:39). We have journeyed together through this meditation on the letter to the Hebrews. We have listened obediently to the pastor's sermon. Let us receive his concluding benediction: "Grace be with you all."

---

10. Cockerill, *Hebrews*, 721.

The Beauty of Hebrews

Art in Service to Truth and
Spiritual Well-being

S tudents of Hebrews have long acknowledged the quality of the author's
Greek and the elegance of his language. Two developments in contemporary research have helped to reveal the overall literary beauty of this
letter/sermon: first, renewed interest in the value attributed to persuasive
speech by the ancient Greeks and Romans and the attention they gave to
its cultivation have enabled us to look at Hebrews with new eyes. Hebrews
was written to be *heard* and to *persuade.* That is one of the reasons we call
it a sermon. Second, careful attention to Hebrews' structure from this oral
perspective has revealed how each part fits appropriately into the whole
and contributes to the writer's purpose. The beauty of Hebrews is a beauty
in service to the truth and to the pastoral concern of the writer for his
hearers' eternal wellbeing.

The pastor who wrote Hebrews wants his hearers to "see" what he is
describing. First, then, we are going to give attention to the pastor's pre-
ferred biblical imagery. Next, we will get the "big picture" by examining the
careful way in which he has arranged his material to impact his hearers.
Finally, some observations about the pastor's use of Scripture will provide
the proper vantage point from which to view the pastor's masterpiece and
enter into its message.

The Biblical Imagery of Hebrews: God Has Spoken

The Pastor's Three Favorite Biblical Scenes from the Old Testament

The pastor uses three interrelated biblical scenes to communicate the nature
of the present existence of the people of God. The first scene is God's people

assembled at Sinai; the second, God's people in the wilderness on the way to the Promised Land; and the third, the Tabernacle and sacrificial ritual of the Sinai covenant. A moment's reflection reveals the relationship between these pictures. Sinai was the place where God *spoke*. He revealed himself by establishing a covenant with his people so that they could approach him. In *obedience* to that revelation his covenant people journeyed through the wilderness toward the Promised Land. While on this journey they *approached God* through the priesthood and Tabernacle given them at Sinai. It was faithful obedience to God's word spoken at Sinai that constituted and preserved that ancient people as the People of God.

The Pastor's Three Favorite Biblical Scenes as Used in Hebrews

God, however, has now fulfilled all that Sinai anticipated by *speaking* in "one who is Son." The people of God are, and always have been, on their way through the "wilderness" of this unbelieving world to God's eternal "Sabbath rest" (Heb 4:10) the "City of the living God" (Heb 12:22). Now, however, they do not *approach God* through an earthly sacrificial system, but through the all-sufficient sacrifice of their "Great High Priest" (Heb 4:14) they enter into the true, heavenly Most Holy Place anticipated by the Sinai arrangement. It is still faithful *obedience* to God's word that constitutes and preserves them as the People of God.

Thus, when the pastor is describing our present access to God he uses the language of priesthood. Just as God's people of old approached him during their wilderness journey through the priesthood and Tabernacle, so we enter the heavenly Most Holy Place during our earthly pilgrimage through our "Great High Priest" (Heb 4:14). When, however, the pastor speaks about our final entrance he uses "Promised-Land" language, such as "rest" (Heb 3:7—4:13). However, just as in the Old Testament "Mount Zion" became the embodiment of the earthly Promised Land, so in Hebrews the eternal destiny of the people of God has become "Mount Zion, the City of the living God, a Heavenly Jerusalem" (Heb 12:22). Thus, although used in different contexts, the heavenly Most Holy Place which we now enter and the Mount Zion which is our destiny both describe the same ultimate reality.

Further Reflections on the Importance of Sinai in Hebrews.

God's *speaking* at Sinai and his *speaking* in "one who is Son" are both historical events and perennial present realities. God's people of old continued to stand before Sinai, especially when they approached the presence of God in the Tabernacle. God's people since the incarnation continue to approach God through the Son who *remains* seated at God's right hand! What God *has spoken* in his Son he continues to *speak*. As the content of the Sinai revelation was the Tabernacle and its sacrificial system through which the people could approach God, so the content of God's final revelation is the "great salvation" provided by our "Great High Priest" (Heb 4:14) through whom we enter God's presence.

Furthermore, the God who shook the earth by *speaking* at Sinai, and who now *speaks* through the incarnate Son seated at his right hand, will shake and remove all that is temporal by *speaking once more* at the final judgment (Heb 12:25–29). There are, then, three "Sinai's" or "Mountains" of God's *speaking*. God *spoke* at Sinai. God now *speaks* in the incarnate Son seated at his right hand. God *will speak* at the Judgment. Sinai was a type of the way God would provide for our salvation by speaking "in one who is Son" and a picture of the final judgment spoken over those who reject the Son. Hebrews begins with the former (Heb 1:1 – 4) and concludes with the latter (Heb 12:25–29). Our existence as the people of God is conditioned by these two realities. We wait until the "enemies" of the One seated at God's right hand are made a "footstool" for his feet (Heb 1:13) at the Judgment.

The Effective Structure of Hebrews: Arranged to Persuade

The Three Main Sections of Hebrews

An appreciation of the pastor's biblical imagery is helpful for understanding the structure of Hebrews and the pastor's persuasive strategy. The main body of Hebrews, Heb 1:1—12:29, divides naturally into three sections, Heb 1:1—4:13, 4:14—10:25, and 10:26—12:29. In the first section (Heb 1:1—4:13) the pastor moves from Sinai (Heb 1:1—2:18) to the wilderness (Heb 3:1—4:13). The central section (Heb 4:14—10:25) focuses on priesthood. The third section (Heb 10:26—12:29) mirrors the first by moving from the wilderness (Heb 10:26—12:3) to Sinai (Heb 12:4–29). Table 1 below shows these relationships:

Table 1.

Section One:	
SINAI (Heb 1:1–2:18)	WILDERNESS (Heb 3:1—4:13)

Section Two:	
PRIESTHOOD	
(Heb 4:14—10:25)	

Section Three:	
WILDERNESS	SINAI
(Heb 10:26—12:3)	(Heb 12:4–29)

It was not unusual for ancient speakers to reinforce their message by adding instructions and exhortations after they had finished the main body of their address. The pastor adds such instructions in Heb 13:1–17, followed by a prayer request and a blessing in Heb 13:18–21, and a letter ending in Heb 13:22–25. Since the purpose of this appendix is to give a big-picture overview of the pastor's message, we have reserved comments on chapter thirteen for the daily readings.

Section Three a Mirror Image of Section One.

We have already suggested that the first (Heb 1:1—4:13) and third (Heb 10:26—12:29) sections of Hebrews mirror each other. The first half of the first section affirms that the God who spoke at Sinai has now spoken through the eternal, incarnate Son seated at his right hand (Heb 1:1—2:18, "Sinai" scene). The second half of the first section warns those who have heard God speak in his Son to avoid the terrible fate of the disobedient wilderness generation who once stood before Sinai (Heb 3:1—4:13, "wilderness" scene). The first half of the third section urges us to join the faithful people of old in their pilgrimage through the "wilderness" of this unbelieving world to the heavenly City (Heb 10:26—12:3, "wilderness" scene). The second half of the third section urges God's people to persevere amid suffering in order that they might enter their inheritance when God speaks "once more" at the Judgment (Heb 12:4–29, "Sinai" scene). We might redo Table 1 above as follows:

Table 2.

Section One:	
God *has Spoken* in the Son (SINAI) (Heb 1:1–2:18)	Avoid the Disobedient (WILDERNESS) (Heb 3:1—4:13)

Section Two:
The All-Sufficient Priesthood of the Son (PRIESTHOOD) (Heb 4:14—10:25);

Section Three:	
Join the Faithful (WILDERNESS) (Heb 10:26—12:3)	God *will Speak* at the Judgment (SINAI) (Heb 12:4–29)

From this diagram it is clear that both the second half of section three (Heb 12:4–29) and the first half of section one (Heb 1:1—2:18) focus on God's speaking. The introduction to week seven explores the way in which the individual passages in these sections mirror each other: the formative suffering of the "sons and daughters" in Heb 12:4–13 corresponds to the suffering by which the Son was perfected as their "Pioneer" in 2:5–18. The final warning against apostasy in Heb 12:14–17 completes the warning against neglect in 2:1–4. The comparison between the two "mountains" in Heb 12:18–24 corresponds to the contrast between the Son and the angels in 1:5–14. Finally, God's universe-shaking speaking at the Judgment in Heb 12:25–29 brings God's speaking in the Son in 1:1–4 to its intended end. Table 3 shows the relationships between the passages in these sections:

Table 3.

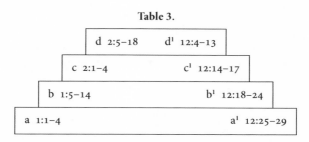

From diagram 2 it is also easy to see that the roll-call of the ancient faithful in the first half of section three (Heb 10:26—12:3) counters the

disobedient wilderness generation in the last half of section one (Heb 3:1—
4:13). We have shown in the introduction to week six how the individual
passages of this section mirror each other: the faithful Son of Heb 3:1–6 has
become the "Pioneer and Perfecter of the faith" in 12:1–3. The disobedient
wilderness generation of Heb 3:7–19 has been replaced by the faithful of
11:1–40. The exhortation to enter the rest forfeited by the wilderness generation in Heb 4:1–11 corresponds to the urgency of identifying with the
faithful in 10:32–39. Accountability before the word of God in Heb 4:12–13
corresponds to the warning of 10:26–31. One could go a step further and
point out that Heb 4:14–16, the introduction to the grand description of the
Son's priesthood and sacrifice, corresponds to its conclusion in 10:19–25.
We can now enlarge Table 3 as follows:

Table 4.

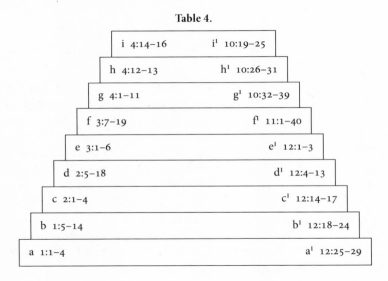

i 4:14–16	i¹ 10:19–25
h 4:12–13	h¹ 10:26–31
g 4:1–11	g¹ 10:32–39
f 3:7–19	f¹ 11:1–40
e 3:1–6	e¹ 12:1–3
d 2:5–18	d¹ 12:4–13
c 2:1–4	c¹ 12:14–17
b 1:5–14	b¹ 12:18–24
a 1:1–4	a¹ 12:25–29

The daily readings substantiate this mirror image relationship between
sections three and one by showing how the individual passages in section
three correspond to the passages of section one. This correspondence finds
further verification through the insight it brings to the interpretation of the
passages in section three.

The History of the Disobedient vs. the History of the Faithful.

Before leaving sections one and three, it might be helpful to give them names.
The first section (Heb 1:1—4:13), especially 3:1—4:13, is "A Short History of
the Disobedient People of God." Their history was cut short by the tragedy of

their disobedience. The third section (Heb 10:26—12:29) is "The History of the Faithful People of God from Creation to Consummation." Heb 10:26–39 joins this history to Heb 4:14—10:25. Then the history proper begins with creation (Heb 11:2), finds its turning point in Jesus (Heb 12:1–3), and its consummation at the Judgment (Heb 12:25–29). Thus, Heb 11:1–40 describes the history of God's faithful people before Christ (Heb 12:1–3), and Heb 12:4–24, our life as the people of God between the coming of Christ and the Judgment yet to come. We live between the time God began *speaking* in "one who is Son" (Heb 1:1–4) and his final *speaking* at the Judgment (Heb 12:25–29). The pastor gives more attention to the history of the faithful (whose example he wants his hearers to follow) than to the story of the disobedient (whose catastrophic errors he wants them to avoid).

"Our Great High Priest" The Heart of Hebrews.

The explanation of the Son's all-sufficient high priesthood in the central section (Heb 4:14—10:25, "priesthood" scene) reveals the relationship between the first (Heb 1:1—4:13) and third (Heb 10:26—12:29) sections of Hebrews. The pastor proclaimed the incarnation, exaltation, and session of the eternal Son in Heb 1:1—2:18. In this central section he explains the full significance of this reality in terms of priesthood and sacrifice in order to motivate and empower his hearers to turn away from the disobedient wilderness generation (Heb 3:1—4:13), join the faithful of old (Heb 10:26—12:3), and persevere as the people of God in light of the coming Judgment (Heb 12:4–29). This section answers the desperate question raised by the unbelief of the wilderness generation (Heb 3:1—4:13): "How can we escape that generation's fate and enter the 'rest' they forfeited?" The pastor answers, "By approaching God through our Great High Priest who is our one and only all-sufficient Savior."

Let us examine this central section of Hebrews, Heb 4:14—10:25, in greater detail. The pastor's opening exhortation (Heb 4:14–16) arouses hope and whets the hearers' appetite for the full description of Christ's all-sufficient high priesthood to come. He follows this exhortation in Heb 5:1–10 with a comparison/contrast between the priesthood of Aaron and the priesthood of the Son. This comparison/contrast lays the foundation for the description of the Son's fulfillment of the Aaronic priesthood in Heb 7:1—10:18. Before going further, however, the pastor would arouse his hearers from lethargy and awaken them to the vital importance of this subject for their eternal destiny with the passionate appeal of Heb 5:11—6:20.

Only after thus alerting them does he resume his teaching on the high priesthood of the Son. In Heb 7:1–28 he shows that the one seated at God's right hand as High Priest and Guarantor of the New Covenant in fulfillment of Ps 110:4 is none other than the eternal Son of God. Then in Heb 8:1—10:18 he demonstrates that the Son obtained this ministry by atoning for sin through the "once-for-all" sacrifice of his incarnate obedience.

In the introductions to weeks four and five we have shown how Heb 8:1—10:18 is a delicately crafted "symphony" in three movements (Heb 8:1–16, 9:1–22, 9:23—10:18). According to the first movement (Heb 8:1–16), the Old Testament promised a better sanctuary, sacrifice, and covenant. According to the second (Heb 9:1–22), the insufficiency of the old sanctuary, sacrifice, and covenant anticipated the new. The third (Heb 9:23—10:18) is the climactic exposition of the long–anticipated full sufficiency of the new: by offering a "once-for-all" sacrifice for sin (Heb 9:25—10:15), the Son has become an all-sufficient High Priest in the "true" sanctuary which is "heaven itself" (Heb 9:23–24), and the Mediator of a New Covenant that provides forgiveness and grace for obedience (Heb 10:15–18). Thus, the pastor's description of the Son as the "Source of eternal salvation" (Heb 5:9) reaches a powerful climax in this third movement, designed to motivate his hearers to join the people of old who lived "by faith" as described in Heb 11:1–40. The pastor concludes this presentation of Christ's high priesthood in Heb 10:19–25 with a summary of the wonderful benefits provided by our "Great Priest" and with an exhortation to make use of those benefits. Just as Heb 4:14–16 introduced this presentation of Christ's high priesthood and related it to section one, so Heb 10:19–25 concludes this section and begins to relate it to the history of the faithful that follows. The introduction to week five shows how Heb 10:19–25, 26–31, and 32–39 are a three-link "chain" that joins the history of the faithful in Heb 11:1–40 to the all-sufficient High Priest in Heb 4:14—10:25. We join the faithful in the life of faith by drawing near to God through our "Great High Priest."

Arranged to Persuade—A Summary

Let us summarize what we have said so far about the way the pastor has arranged his material to persuade his hearers. The God who spoke at Sinai has now given his final revelation by providing "such a great salvation" in "one who is Son" (Heb 1:1—2:18). Therefore, at all costs avoid the tragic loss of the disobedient wilderness generation that stood before Sinai (Heb 3:1—4:13). Instead, through the all-sufficient High Priest and "Source of eternal salvation" described in Heb 4:14—10:25, embrace the faithful of old (Heb

10:26—12:3) and, aware of your perils and privileges, endure present suffering (Heb 12:4–24) in anticipation of the future when God will speak the final word of Judgment (Heb 12:25–29). The description of the Son's high priesthood in the central section (Heb 4:14—10:25) of this sermon may be the sermon's heart. However, the third section (Heb 10:26—12:29) is the sermon's goal. The pastor would turn his hearers *from* the disobedience of the wilderness generation (Heb 1:1—4:13), *through* the sufficiency of their "Great High Priest" (Heb 4:14—10:25), *to join* the faithful of old in a life of persevering faithfulness until the final Judgment (Heb 10:26—12:29).

The Divine Conversation in Hebrews: An Opportunity to Respond

Overhearing the Conversation between the Father and the Son

Finally, one often gains perspective by finding the appropriate place from which to view a painting. Hebrews' conversational use of Scripture gives us the proper vantage point. When we read Hebrews, we listen in on the Scriptural conversation between the Father and the Son that forms the backbone of this sermon. This conversation celebrates the Son's taking his seat at God's right hand as all-sufficient Savior. In chapter one God confirms the Son's eternal deity and invites him to sit at his right hand by addressing him with Ps 2:7; 2 Sam 7:14; Ps 45:6–7; Ps 102:25–26; and Ps 110:1. God proclaims him Son, God, and enthroned Lord. In chapter two the Son answers with Ps 22:22; Isa 8:17–18; and 2 Sam 22:3, humbly acknowledging his incarnate obedience as the means of his exaltation as Savior. This conversation continues in Heb 4:14—10:25. The Father confirms the priestly nature of the Son's assuming his position at the right hand by addressing him with Ps 110:4. The Son confirms the corresponding sacrificial nature of his incarnate obedience by which he entered this priesthood by responding with Ps 40:6–8. Thus, we "overhear" this sermon's teaching on the sufficiency of the Son our High Priest when we listen in on this ever-present divine conversation in celebration of the Son's taking his seat at God's right hand.

Responding in Faith to the Divine Address

As we are drawn into the dialog and the reality that it establishes, God the Holy Spirit addresses *us*, urging our obedience ("Today, if his voice you hear, do not harden your hearts," Heb 3:7) and assuring us of his sufficient provision ("I will put my laws upon their hearts, and upon their minds I will inscribe them; and their sins and their lawless deeds I will no longer remember," Heb 10:16b–17). *Even while we are in the wilderness of this world* we are invited to draw near to God (Heb 7:19, 10:22) and to take our vantage point within the Most Holy Place where God dwells as we persevere until final entrance. "You have come to Mount Zion" (Heb 12:22).

Finally, in the closing reprise of this sermon we who enter the divine presence through the Son are invited to participate in this Scriptural conversation by affirming our faith. We know the God who has said: "Never will I leave you; nor will I ever forsake you" (Heb 13:5, cf. Deut 31:6) and proven his faithfulness by speaking in his Son. Thus, we can join the writer of Ps 118:6–7 and say with confidence, "The Lord is my Helper; I will not fear: What can a human being do to me?" (Heb 13:6). Through the Lord Jesus Christ our "Great High Priest" we experience the reality that Hebrews describes from the inside. By joining those who live "by faith" we become part of the big picture that Hebrews paints of the people of God throughout history.

A Sentence Outline of Hebrews

A. Avoid the fate of the disobedient Sinai/Wilderness Generation. (Heb 1:1—4:13)

    1. By obtaining "such a great salvation" through his suffering and death the Son has taken his Seat at God's right hand as the ultimate revelation of God. (1:1—2:18)

    2. Therefore, avoid the fate of the disobedient wilderness generation and pursue the "Sabbath rest" that they forfeited. (3:1—4:13)

B. By drawing near through the eternal exalted Son our All-sufficient High Priest. (Heb 4:14—10:25)

    1. Embrace His full sufficiency. (4:14–16)

    2. He fulfills what Aaron only anticipated. (5:1–10)

    3. Pay close heed to what I am saying! (5:11—6:20)

    4. The Eternal Exalted Son *is* the *only* All-sufficient High Priest. (7:1–28)

    5. He attained this position through the Once-for-All Sacrifice of His Obedient Human Life. (8:1—10:18)

    6. Therefore, draw near to God through our "Great Priest" and take full advantage of the benefits he has provided. (10:19–25)

C. So that you can join the faithful in persevering obedience. (Heb 10:26—12:29)

    1. Through the resources that the Son has provided join the company of those who have lived "by faith." (10:26—12:3)

2. Persevere in obedience enduring God's discipline and drawing on the resources available to God's children as you await the unshakable kingdom that is yours at the Judgment. 12:4–29

D. Reprise: May God empower you through Jesus Christ to do his will so that you can follow my instructions and heed this letter that I have sent you. 13:1–25

Select Books on Hebrews for the College Student and Serious Lay Reader[1]

Bateman IV, Herbert W. *Four Views on the Warning Passages in Hebrews.* Grand Rapids: Kregel, 2007.

Cockerill, Gareth Lee. *The Epistle to the Hebrews.* The New International Commentary on the New Testament. Grand Rapids: Eerdmans, 2012.

Gutherie, George H. *Hebrews.* The NIV Application Commentary. Grand Rapids: Zondervan, 1998.

Kistemaker, Simon J. *Exposition of the Epistle to the Hebrews.* New Testament Commentary. Grand Rapids: Baker, 1984.

Laansma, Jon C. *The Letter to the Hebrews: A Commentary for Preaching, Teaching, and Bible Study.* Eugene, OR: Cascade, 2017.

Peterson, David G. *Hebrews: An Introduction and Commentary.* Tyndale New Testament Commentaries. Downers Grove, IL: IVP Academic, 2020.

Schreiner, Thomas R. *Commentary on Hebrews.* Biblical Theology for Christian Proclamation. Nashville: Holman, 2015.

---

1. For an extensive list of commentaries on Hebrews see Cockerill, *Hebrews,* xxiv–xxvi.

Bibliography

Bartholomew, Craig G. *Introducing Biblical Hermeneutics: A Comprehensive Framework for Hearing God in Scripture.* Grand Rapids: Baker Academic, 2015.

Bennett, Arthur. *The Valley of Vision: A Collection of Puritan Prayers and Devotions.* London: Banner of Truth Trust, 2007.

Bruce, F. F. *The Epistle to the Hebrews.* New International Commentary on the New Testament. Grand Rapids: Eerdmans, 1988.

Cockerill, Gareth Lee. *The Epistle to the Hebrews.* New International Commentary on the New Testament. Grand Rapids: Eerdmans, 2012.

Tuckman, Barbara W. *A Distant Mirror: The Calamitous 14th Century.* New York: Ballantine, 1987.